The Vineyard Years

A Memoir with Recipes

Susan Sokol Blosser

Foreword by Alison Sokol Blosser

WESTWINDS
PRESS®

Portions of this book were previously published in *At Home in the Vineyard*
published by the University of California Press, Berkeley in 2008 and
in *Letting Go* published by susansokolblosser.com in 2015.

Library of Congress Cataloging-in-Publication Data
Names: Sokol Blosser, Susan, author. | Sokol Blosser, Susan. At home in the
vineyard.
Title: The vineyard years : a memoir with recipes / by Susan Sokol Blosser.
Description: Portland, Oregon : WestWinds Press, 2017. | "Portions of this book
were previously published in At Home in the Vineyard"—Title page verso.
Identifiers: LCCN 2017005980 | ISBN 9781513260716 (paperback) |
ISBN 9781513260723 (e-book) | ISBN 9781513260730 (hardbound)
Subjects: LCSH: Sokol Blosser, Susan. | Women vintners—Oregon—Biography.
| Vintners—Oregon—Biography. | Wineries—Oregon—Dundee. |
Wine and wine making—Oregon—Dundee. | Cooking—Oregon.
Classification: LCC TP547.B56 A3 2017 | DDC 663/.20092 [B] —dc23
LC record available at https://lccn.loc.gov/2017005980

Edited by Jennifer Newens
Designed by Vicki Knapton
Cover Photo by Andréa Johnson

Published by WestWinds Press®
An imprint of

GRAPHIC ARTS
BOOKS®
www.graphicartsbooks.com

Printed in the U.S.A. on FSC Certified Paper.

CONTENTS

Dedication

To those fortunate few who, like me, have been lucky enough to experience the profound joys, and blistering challenges, of being part of a family business.

Foreword

My mother could have had an easy and grand life, following in her mother's footsteps, with a French poodle by her side and a Mercedes in the garage. Instead, she chose to marry a boy from the West— my father—and become a farmer in Oregon. This is the story of that life.

My mother's life did not follow a conventional path. Admittedly, I am biased, yet I think you'll find her story a fascinating one, touching on themes many women—myself included—have struggled with for decades. Her frank retelling of the joys and heartaches of a life lived among the vines echoes that of the vines themselves—growing from a young cutting to a fruit-bearing plant, giving generously of one's life force like the grapes at harvesttime, pulling back during cold, hard times, like the grapes in dormancy, only to resurge again, full of life, in the new season.

My mother grew up surrounded by opportunity. From a well-to-do family in the Midwest, my mother attended private schools and went to Stanford University. She went on to earn a master's degree, not a common occurrence for women of her generation. While she was privileged by most definitions, my mother never took anything for granted. In fact, I'll never forget the story my mother told me when she and my father got married. My grandfather, her father, offered to give the young married couple his Mercedes convertible. They politely declined the offer, preferring to piece together the money to buy a VW camper instead.

She grew up in a time and place where, by society's definition, she needed only to marry well and her life would have been relatively stress-free. Instead, my mother and father sank everything they had into creating a business dependent on convincing people to drink wine from an undiscovered region made by people with no winemaking pedigree.

In 1991, when my mother took over running the winery in addition to her vineyard duties, she had no financial acumen, no sales or marketing training, nor any prior management experience. Undeterred, she was determined to convince people that Oregon could produce world-class wines. Selling each vintage was a struggle, yet my mother never gave up. Her endless stamina to work years of seven-day weeks eventually paid off. Sure, there were small victories along the way that kept her inspired to keep going, but those victories were spread out amongst enormous challenges. She's told me she relished them. Today, in little more than a generation, Oregon has a multibillion-dollar, world-renowned wine industry. And my mother played a huge part in creating that industry and helping it flourish.

Like the grapevines that grow, then die back as part of their life cycle, my mother's life did not always go in an upward direction. Sometimes it was all she could do to just keep moving forward. For example, my mother ran for elective office three times. Each race was harder than the previous with all the normal election-induced drudgery and personal attacks. Our family and business were often pulled into the uglier parts of it. Yet she kept her head high, even when she lost each time. This alone speaks volumes about the woman my mother is. Never letting defeat thwart the causes for which she fought, she continued to serve on the local school board and then started her own nonprofit organization to provide much-needed community support.

My mother approached her retirement from the winery with grace, wit, strength, and an unending love for our family. It was not an easy road for her, and you'll learn just how hard that struggle was in these pages, in her own words. I will just say that I only hope I can transition out of the business as graciously and gracefully as she did when it's my turn.

When I read the manuscript for *The Vineyard Years*, I suddenly realized that there are a lot of parallels between my life and my mother's. We both married young, divorced our first husbands, and remarried. We both had three kids: two boys and a girl, and our first babies were four weeks early. We both ran (or run) a winery, an uncommon role for women in our industry. We are both introverts, an obstacle when operating a business often in the public eye whose salon success is dependent on being outgoing and engaging. We're both impatient, ready to dive in, wanting to see results.

And we both love to eat. Not in the closet-eating kind of way, but in the belief that from time to time, a culinary experience can be a spiritual affair. We both relish that occasional meal that makes the stars shine brighter in our eyes and delights our taste buds and stomachs. We've been lucky to share a few such occasions together. You'll soon understand how important food is to our family from the recipes my mother includes in the book, each reflecting different times of her life and evoking unique memories.

In reading her story, I couldn't help but reflect on my mother's life and, honestly, I just don't know how she did it. She raised three kids (who, for all intents and purposes, aren't terribly screwed up), started and helped grow not just a business but a multibillion-dollar industry, transitioned said business to the next generation, and then began a new phase of her life characterized by continued self-discovery and giving back to the local community. She has an impressive resume and an even more impressive heart.

My mother and I have clashed at times, but with the wisdom that comes with age, I can now see much more clearly who my mother is; she is the woman the little girl inside of me aspires to be. My mother learned early on to turn failure into opportunity. She always tells me it's okay to make mistakes. Actually, she encourages me to make them. But the key, she says, is to make interesting mistakes. The more interesting the mistake, the better the opportunity to learn. I hope you enjoy reading about both the amazing successes and the interesting mistakes of her life.

ALISON SOKOL BLOSSER
Copresident/CEO, Sokol Blosser Winery
December 2016

Acknowledgments

The Vineyard Years retells my story from the perspective of age, adding a culinary theme and updating the thirteen years that have passed since *At Home in the Vineyard* ended. While *The Vineyard Years* includes selected parts from both *At Home in the Vineyard*, the story of the early days of Sokol Blosser Winery, and *Letting Go*, the story of my transition of control of the winery to my children, there is also much that wasn't included in either.

Emphasizing the culinary side of my winery experience gave me the chance to address an aspect of my life that has been so basic that I took it for granted. In previous books, I wrote about farming, family, and business challenges, ignoring the sensuality that wine and food provide. No more. Food and wine have taken their rightful place, front and center, in *The Vineyard Years*. The recipes included represent food memories and experiences I savor in many ways.

Credit for the new emphasis on food and wine goes to my editor,

Jennifer Newens, for making helpful suggestions and giving me critical guidance. Special thanks to Kerry Tymchuk, executive director of the Oregon Historical Society, for encouraging me to continue my story and introducing me to Jen.

My husband, Russ Rosner, is the best copyeditor I know and made sure the final draft was grammatically correct before it was submitted. During the many months I spent writing in our home office, he gave me the gift of space and time so I could work, uninterrupted by dogs, cats, or chickens.

Ultimately, of course, I alone am responsible for what I have chosen to include and what I have left out, for the writing, and the interpretation of events, but my whole family played a part. Russ, my former husband Bill Blosser, and our children Nik, Alex, and Alison read drafts, gave helpful suggestions, and wrote sidebars giving their perspective. Kudos to Alison, my amazing daughter who, between running the winery, traveling for business, having a baby, and raising a family, took time to write the foreword.

The winery staff was uniformly supportive, especially Caitlin Sessa and Michael Kelly Brown, who helped source the best photos to include. Michael also wrote a sidebar for me and helped with recipes. Rachael Woody, head of Linfield College's Oregon Wine History Archive, and her students found material I needed from the Sokol Blosser papers whenever I asked.

I am grateful to friends Brad Cloepfil, Eugenia Keegan, Michaela Rodeno, Marie Simmons, and Heidi Yorkshire, who took the time to write sidebars for me, giving their perspective on events.

Thanks to the chefs who worked with me to provide recipes to recapture those memories, crafting them to be reproduced at home. In addition to my former and current husbands, Bill and Russ, both accomplished cooks, I am grateful to chef friends Jack Czarnecki, Nick Peirano and Joan Drabkin, Henry Kibit, Jody Kropf, and Marie Simmons. It was a special pleasure to include a recipe from Sokol Blosser's chef, Henry Kibit, who has become a critical part of the winery team. Marie Simmons, whose cookbooks I have used for years, not only provided me with recipes, but tested others. Anne Nisbet also performed valuable help as a recipe tester.

I hope *The Vineyard Years* gives readers insight into the sense of place and closeness to nature that having a vineyard entails; the joy as well as the angst of a family developing a vineyard, a winery, and an industry; and the flavor of a profession so dedicated to the enjoyment of drinking and eating well.

L'Chaim and Bon Appétit!

SUSAN SOKOL BLOSSER
Dayton, Oregon
December 2016

CHAPTER ONE

Mac & Cheese Days

In the last two weeks of 1970, my husband, Bill Blosser, and I each gave birth. I had our first child, Nik, and Bill closed the deal on our first piece of vineyard land. We were together in our excitement about both, but since the vineyard began as Bill's passion and I was utterly alone having Nik (fathers at that time weren't allowed in the delivery room), I think of them as one birth for each of us.

Baby Nik actually had a longer gestation period than our land purchase. The idea of a vineyard seemed to arrive out of nowhere, a bit of whimsy that took on a life of its own. We were driving our Volkswagen camper bus from Chapel Hill back to Oregon, where Bill was to teach urban planning at Portland State University. Near Lancaster, Pennsylvania, we stopped to browse at a flea market. It was Pennsylvania Dutch country, and we thought we might find an antique treasure hidden in the junk. We meandered through with the other bargain hunters and, somewhere in the midst of tables laden with wooden clocks, rusty fruit bins, and old kitchen utensils, Bill started talking about starting a vineyard. He later confessed he had been thinking about it for some time and finally had enough nerve to bring it up.

"What do you think about growing grapes?" he asked, as we bent over a particularly handsome mantel clock.

"Grow grapes?" I asked. I turned to look at him. "You mean to make wine?" His question—unexpected and unconventional—startled me.

"Why not? I think it would be a neat thing to do." He sounded a bit defensive and I understood why. It was a wild, improbable idea.

We lost interest in the mantel clock and headed back to our camper. All the way back to Oregon, this outlandish idea kept coming up. We'd drive along in silence, listening to whatever local radio station we could get, and suddenly Bill would bring up the subject, again. I listened, wanting to be a supportive wife, and the more we talked about it, the more interesting it became.

We both liked wine. Bill had spent a year in France during college, taking classes in Paris and then working as a dishwasher at a mountain resort near Grenoble. He had emerged from that experience a wine-drinking, French-speaking Francophile, with a worldliness that had attracted me to him in college. I had spent the summer after high school studying in France, and I had grown up drinking wine from my father's wonderful wine cellar.

The idea of going back to the land and growing something that made life more enjoyable appealed to us. We would never have been attracted to soybeans or corn, but growing wine grapes had both aesthetic and emotional appeal. Wine symbolized culture and sophistication. People had been making wine for centuries—how hard could it be?

Really hard, as it turned out. The arrival of our two new babies determined the direction of our lives from then on. In our mid-twenties, we had been married four years, and had spent most of that time in graduate school, first in Oregon for my Master of Arts in Teaching from Reed College and then in North Carolina for Bill's Master of City and Regional Planning from the University of North Carolina, Chapel Hill. We had studied hard and played hard.

Our 1968 Volkswagen camper bus, a miniature house on wheels, had carried us all over the continent. We hiked and picked wild huckleberries in the Mount Adams Wilderness in Washington State. We camped near Old Faithful at Yellowstone National Park and fled, early the next morning, singing loudly to scare off a nosy grizzly bear that had appeared during the night. We drove to Lake Louise and across the wheat-colored plains of Saskatchewan, fighting headwinds that held our boxy vehicle under forty miles per hour. We explored the entire Blue Ridge Parkway of Virginia and North Carolina, sleeping in the bus and cooking over campfires, stopping only for supplies and a new block of ice for our tiny refrigerator. With no kids, no pets, no house to worry about, we never hesitated when another trip beckoned.

Summers in Chapel Hill, we played tennis every evening, waiting for the muggy heat to retreat before we went out. Winters, we tried out complicated recipes from Julia Child's new cookbooks. We judged the recipes by how long and involved preparation was against how much we enjoyed eating the finished product. Over elaborate dinners with the other student couples, mostly Northerners like us who were fascinated with Southern culture, we discussed politics, civil rights, and feminism. We protested the Vietnam War and drove to Washington, DC with friends to join the candlelight vigils and marches.

When the baby and the vineyard arrived, life abruptly changed course. Road trips, camping and hiking, tennis after dinner, spontaneous parties—all these became memories. After a few years, I started to think of them as a past life.

Back in Portland, we found a house to rent and began researching the geography, soils, and climate that wine grapes required. We had celebrated our engagement at a picnic on the grounds at Beringer Winery in 1966, but locating in Napa didn't interest us. Other parts of northern California might be possible. On a visit to Bill's folks in Oakland, we scouted for possible vineyard sites around Ukiah and Mendocino, where Bill's family had homesteaded in the 1850s. Northern California could be the place for us, but we continued looking.

Driving through Oregon's Willamette Valley countryside one Saturday, we stopped at a one-room real estate office in Newberg to inquire about land. It was useless to ask directly about vineyard land back then, because real estate agents had no idea what that meant. Bill was describing the kind of land he was looking for, in terms of slope and exposure and soils, when the agent said, "See that guy over there, looking at the book of listings? He just asked me the same question." That guy, Gary Fuqua, was soon to plant one of the earliest vineyards in the Dundee Hills and become one of Bill's best friends.

The real estate agent, shaking his head at what crazy things people wanted to do, tried to help. "Have you talked to the guy up on Kings Grade Road?" he asked. "A big friendly guy. He has just planted a vineyard and seems to know what he's talking about." Following the agent's directions, we found the ramshackle house where Dick Erath, his wife, Kina, and their two toddler sons were living. Dick had bought the property and planted vines in 1968.

But Dick and Kina had not been the first, either. Two other couples, the Courys and the Letts, had bought land in the Willamette Valley a few years earlier. Dick and Nancy Ponzi had also just bought land. These four couples were working regular jobs, living as cheaply as possible, and putting all their extra time and money into their vineyards. Finding them inspired us to keep going; we were not alone.

These founders of the Willamette Valley's wine industry, plus those who, like us, came shortly after—Myron Redford, David and Ginny Adelsheim, Joe and Pat Campbell—stood out with their quirky individuality. Scruffy sideburns, beards, and mustaches aside, they were smart and enterprising, finding various paths to wine, discovering it as a passion and changing course to pursue it against all odds. With diverse backgrounds in engineering, music, philosophy, history, and the humanities, coupled with a fierce spirit of independence, we were united in a passion for Pinot Noir. We were trying something that hadn't been done before and we eagerly shared information. The collaborative nature of the Oregon wine industry became one of its most notable features. Did any of us anticipate that our youthful adventure would create an industry that would, in one generation, add over two billion dollars to the Oregon economy? I surely didn't.

In the early 1970s, it was a boys club. And an interesting group of boys it was. Dick Erath brought his engineering mentality and love of science to the table, spending long hours researching grape clones, trellis systems, cultivation methods, propagation systems, and the like. He always had a hearty laugh and welcomed everyone into the industry, just as he had Susan and me. Dave Lett was something of a hermit, not really liking committee work or lobbying, but he was deadly effective in marketing and was an early supporter of tough labeling standards and land use laws. Dave Adelsheim was one of the easiest possible people to work with and had a keen perception of what was needed to develop a lasting industry, from labeling laws, to the grape tax, to marketing programs, to being a key player in the establishment of the International Pinot Noir Celebration. When we needed an effective diplomat to solve a knotty problem, Adelsheim was the man.

Bill Blosser
Cofounder, Sokol Blosser Winery

Like most of the other couples, neither Bill nor I had any business experience. We hadn't even taken a business class in college.

That didn't stop us; we could learn. No tradition of fine winemaking in Oregon? We would create one. We knew we could lose everything, but none of us had much, so that was no deal killer. Our college professors had touted a liberal-arts education as training for life—we could do anything with it. Planting wine grapes in Oregon represented a risk most easily made by people in their twenties, an age when optimism has not yet been tempered by experience.

To prove we were not entirely crazy, we would point to the master's thesis Chuck Coury had written at the University of California, Davis, in which he showed that the climate of the Willamette Valley was virtually identical to that of Burgundy, whose Pinot Noir wines were world-renowned.

Bill and I wanted be part of this great Oregon experiment of growing Pinot Noir, the Burgundian red grape with a reputation for being difficult. We focused on planting a vineyard. Starting a winery seemed so far in the future, we never talked about it. The immediate challenge before us would be figuring out to how grow wine grapes in this new, untested region. If we succeeded, it would take all of our smarts as well as our physical strength and stamina.

After looking at possible vineyard sites in the hills of the northern Willamette Valley, we found what seemed the perfect piece of land in the Dundee Hills, about thirty miles southwest of Portland. The area, known for its giant, sweet Brooks prune plums and hazelnuts, is a series of gentle hills ranging from three hundred to a thousand feet in elevation. Our eighteen acres, at the five-hundred-foot level, had been an orchard, destroyed by the Columbus Day Storm, a powerful windstorm famous for its devastation. The old prune trees sprawled across the land in haphazard fashion, few still upright. Local lore was full of stories of the damage and death caused by that tempest, which we assumed had happened recently because it was such a common point of reference for local farmers. We were shocked to learn that it had occurred in October 1962, almost a decade earlier. The stories told with so much immediacy showed the long-term impact of weather on a farming community. We weren't deterred. Perhaps because we hadn't lived through its ferocity, the storm seemed a remote, one-time event.

The old orchard had been waiting for us, the downed trees obscured by a labyrinth of blackberry vines and common vetch that had blanketed the hillside over the years. Knowing that fruit trees had once flourished, and that Dave and Diana Lett's new vineyard was just down the road, cinched our decision to buy the land. Even with our limited knowledge, we knew that the presence of an orchard meant the hillsides would be frost-free in early spring when those trees blossomed and thus would be safe for grapes, which leafed out at the same time. We bought the land for eight hundred dollars an acre and hired a local farmer to clear it. It had been just five months since the subject of a vineyard had first come up.

From the beginning, the vineyard was Bill's baby. I mirrored his excitement and didn't want to disappoint him, but it was years before I experienced the passion that he felt from the start. I didn't flinch at the challenge, the commitment, or the money we put into the project. But it took time for me to feel that it was a genuine partnership.

Our rented house in southwest Portland, so far from our property, became increasingly inconvenient. With Bill teaching at Portland State University, we had only weekends to work the land. We found a farmhouse to rent about a mile from our property, and our family— Bill and me, baby Nik, and our cats, Cadwallader (Caddie) and Tigger, moved there in May 1971. The house had a long, narrow front yard ideal for rooting grape cuttings in nursery rows. The small bushy plants would then be planted as dormant rootings the following spring.

California, with its nascent wine industry, was then the only source for wine grapes, so when Bill visited his folks in Oakland, he and his dad drove to Wente Vineyards in Livermore, hoping to buy some of Karl Wente's certified, virus-free Chardonnay cuttings. Bill was thrilled when Karl himself greeted them warmly in his small office. "Gonna grow grapes in Oregon, eh?" he said. "Great idea. I always wondered why no one was trying the cool-climate grapes farther north. I think you have a chance to make some great wines up there." These words of encouragement from a successful third-generation winegrower further motivated Bill. He and his dad returned home with cuttings of all the varieties we thought might grow in our cool climate— Pinot Noir, Chardonnay, Pinot Blanc, Riesling, and Müller-Thurgau (a cousin of Riesling). Bill always remembered Karl Wente's welcome and encouragement, but never saw him again. The great man died suddenly at age forty-nine, six years later.

The big white farmhouse we rented sat beside the old state highway, a picture-book place with its tall, shady trees along the front and old, untended cherry and prune orchards along the sides and back. But any romantic notions we had about country living quickly dissipated. From across the narrow road, one of the area's major turkey farms assaulted every one of our senses from the day we moved in. Hundreds of white turkeys lined up at the fence to clamor at us, red jowls bobbing and beady eyes staring. From time to time huge trucks went by carrying stacks of large cages crowded with turkeys. White feathers floated to the ground long after they had passed. The odor of turkey manure, ranging from pungent to gagging, depending on the heat and wind direction, maintained a constant presence. The gentle breeze that cooled me while I worked in the vegetable garden also enveloped me in the rank smell of turkey.

Bill and I had often talked about what fun it would be to buy an old farmhouse and fix it up. Realizing what it would take to make our rented farmhouse comfortable ended that fantasy. We were told that our house, like a number of others in the valley, was the work of some barn builders who came through in the early 1900s. They built houses the way they constructed barns—framing studs set more than two feet apart, little attention to detail, no insulation. My homemade cotton curtains fluttered in the wind even with the windows closed, and the smell of turkey manure leaked in through the cracks. Over the years, residents had added sections to the original house, so that by the time we moved in, what had once been an animal shed in the back had become part of the house.

The cats roamed freely through the abandoned orchards, sleeping by day, hunting by night, and wreaking havoc on the mouse and gopher population. After Tigger was run over one gruesome night, Caddie did the work of two. She was a fearsome hunter and ate most of her prey outside, leaving the front teeth, whiskers, and large intestine on the doormat to show us her prowess. But occasionally she thought they'd taste better inside; one night she leapt up and came flying through the open window above the head of our bed. I opened my eyes in time to see Caddie, clutching a giant gopher in her mouth, pass over me, inches from my face. I listened to her chewing her prize for a few minutes, and then turned over and went back to sleep, making a mental note to watch where I stepped in the morning.

For the first few months, until the cats pared down the population, the mice were the most active inhabitants of our house. I learned to put my feet in my slippers slowly after once feeling a living fur ball cowering in the toe. When my mother visited from Wisconsin, I sat with her at the kitchen table trying to keep her engaged in conversation so she wouldn't see the mice scampering across the floor. She turned and saw them, of course, as soon as I stopped talking to take a breath. They only reinforced her belief that Bill and I were living in the wilderness. She must have enjoyed herself anyway (or else felt I really needed help), because by the end of the decade she and my father had moved to McMinnville, seven miles from us, where they spent the rest of their lives.

Our house stayed warm because we kept the huge brick fireplace in the living room going fall, winter, and spring. We had plenty of firewood from downed trees, and a big fan in the fireplace sent waves of heat through large vents to warm the rest of the house. We splurged on new carpet for the living room, a gold shag found at a discount warehouse. Shag was in fashion, and we bought a special rake to make the long threads lie in the same direction. But even with the carpet neatly combed, the place was never more than tolerable. We were near our vineyard and the rent was only a hundred dollars a month, so we put up with it.

As an urban girl, my gardening experience had consisted of growing a sweet potato propped on toothpicks in a glass of water, a grade-school science project. In Oregon, surrounded by fruit trees and plenty of land, I felt compelled to have a vegetable garden. I went wild with the Burpee seed catalog, inspired by page after page of captivating photos of pristine vegetables. The seeds I planted would surely grow into that picture-perfect produce if I followed the instructions on the seed packets. But did "plant in full sun" mean I should plant the seeds on a sunny day, or in a sunny spot? One gardening book advised, "Harvest during the full moon." Should I pick my vegetables under moonlight, or could I pick them in daylight if there was to be a full moon that night? I laugh now, but at the time I was genuinely confused.

That first spring, after savoring the catalog descriptions all winter, I planted everything that looked interesting, from peas to pumpkins. I kept the growing season going right into fall, but I was way out of my league. Overwhelmed by the successes—I'd never seen so many zucchini—I was also befuddled by pest problems. I had no idea whether the cute little bugs I saw crawling around the plants were going to help me or destroy the garden. I knew ladybugs were good, but how about the ones with black spots that were yellow instead of orange? Captivated by the wonder of working with the earth, I came back every year with a little more knowledge and renewed hope. My garden taught me that every year gave me another chance, the secret to a farmer's optimism.

While our grape cuttings in the front yard sprouted leaves and roots, we searched for vineyard equipment we could afford, which meant it had to be secondhand. The weekly agricultural paper listed the farm auctions and used equipment for sale everywhere in the valley. We needed a tractor and other equipment, so Bill and I, with Nik in the backpack, attended farm auctions almost every weekend. When we found the right tractor at the right price, an early 1960s Massey Ferguson orchard model, we happened to be at an auction at the other side of the valley. The only way for us to get it home was for Bill to get on the tractor and drive it. As he bounced along country roads in the open air at less than fifteen miles per hour for the two hours it took to get back, Bill didn't need my sympathy. So proud was he with our new purchase, he confessed he felt like a king piloting his carriage. Nik and I rattled along behind him, in case the old tractor broke down, in our '54 green Chevy pickup, which we called Truckeroonie.

Truckeroonie had been Bill's first vehicle, bought while we were at Stanford. Despite a two-year rest while we were in Chapel Hill, it was feeling its age. Bill commuted to Portland in the VW camper, so when Truckeroonie broke down, I was at the wheel. I learned never to go out in it without rain gear, rubber boots for walking in the mud, and a backpack for Nik. I will always be grateful to Hank Paul, the local mechanic in Dayton, the nearest town, who got used to my sudden appearance in his shop. His scruffy little white dog, with the shaggy hair over its eyes, always scampered out to greet me. Hank would stop what he was doing; Nik and I would climb in Hank's big pickup, with the dog; and we would drive back to wherever Truckeroonie had stalled so Hank could get it going again.

With its old green cab, worn leather seat, and long wobbly stick shift, Truckeroonie had taken us camping in the California redwoods country, where we had slept under the towering trees, and to the San Francisco Opera House, where we had watched Rudolf Nureyev make jaw-dropping leaps across the stage. Truckeroonie was our transportation, whether I wore dirty jeans and hiking boots or a slinky black dress and high heels. One day, Bill came home with a shiny new sky-blue pickup. We sold old Truckeroonie to a farm kid excited to get his first wheels. I had a lump in my throat watching him drive it away.

Always on the lookout for used equipment, when we heard that the local pole-bean farmers were switching to bush beans, we jumped at the chance to buy their used poles and wire. We sorted through piles of old bean stakes to find the strongest, straightest ones, and then Bill soaked them in foul-smelling, poisonous pentachlorophenol so they wouldn't rot when he put them into the ground.

Not all our penny-pinching deals worked out. The spring after Nik was born, Bill bought an old Cat 22, a small Caterpillar bulldozer. The farmer guaranteed that it was almost ready to go. The cans of parts sitting on it, he assured us, would go together quickly. For the next two months, Bill and his dad spent many hours in that farmer's field, forty miles from home, trying their best to put the thing together. Nik and I started out going along, but got bored sitting in the field watching them try to match the pieces. They got it running enough to load the little crawler on a trailer, along with miscellaneous cans of parts, and brought it to the vineyard. When, at long last, Bill proudly tried it out, he discovered it would turn only to the right. Neither he nor those he consulted ever did get it to work right. It was a long time before he was able to chuckle at his great money-saving scheme. We sold it for parts to someone equally ambitious about making an old Cat 22 run again.

Bill orchestrated our first vineyard planting in the spring of 1972. Bill's family—aunt and uncle, cousins, and sister—came to help. When we were ready to put the plants in the ground, I drove the tractor, with Nik in the backpack, freeing Bill to carry the heavy bundles of dormant plants and pails of fertilizer. My job was to drive down the row, stop at the right spot, and drill a hole. The auger was mounted on the back of the tractor, so lining it up with the marker stake required prolonged twisting to look behind me. Nik had a great view of all the activity, but at seventeen months he was not happy being

August 1971. Bill Blosser (left) and me (right), with eight-month-old Nik on my shoulders, taking a break as we work on our new vineyard property. Bill is wearing his French vigneron beret.

cooped up and his weight in the backpack made my job even more tiring. My back ached after the first hour.

I was rescued by Bill's parents, Betty and John Blosser, who took their vacation time to drive up from Oakland and work in the vineyard for a week. Bill's dad, an orthopedic surgeon, had a grin from ear to ear as he took my place. He loved driving the tractor. I never heard him complain about the twisting, or about back pain. Grandma Betty freed Nik from the backpack, played countless games of patty-cake, fed him, and made sure he napped. I gratefully accepted her help. From then on, until they finally moved to Portland, John and Betty came up every year, and we intentionally postponed major projects until they arrived.

We planted five acres that first year—one White Riesling, one Müller-Thurgau, one Chardonnay, and two Pinot Noir. When it was all over, we walked to the top of the hill and surveyed our new vineyard. I stood next to Bill, who had Nik on his shoulders, and looked out over the valley. Little sticks poked out of the reddish dirt in neat rows, and the freshly turned soil smelled clean and sweet. I was sweaty and hot, but a chill went up my spine. We had done it. We had literally put down roots.

WHEN PEOPLE ASKED, AND they always did, why and how we ever decided to start a vineyard, I was slow to answer because I really wasn't sure how it happened. I said we were part of the back-to-the-land movement of the early 1970s. I said it was because we had more guts than brains. But I winced inside as I answered. Yes, starting a vineyard was unconventional, even outlandish, but neither of us were known for eccentric or bizarre behavior. We weren't flower children or hippies, although our kids like to portray us that way. I picture us as a fresh-faced young couple, well educated, solidly middle class, and looking to be engaged in life with a purpose.

It is only with the perspective of time that I realize, looking at the bigger picture, that Bill Blosser and I were bit players in a drama far larger than we knew. We shared a small part of the incredible entrepreneurial energy that enveloped the world when we were young and ready for adventure.

The decade of the first plantings in Oregon vineyards, 1965–75, was one of political and social upheaval. When those of us who lived through it look back, what stands out are the Vietnam War, civil rights, and feminism that dominated the news. Race riots, antiwar protests, political assassinations, and bra burning were what we saw every time we turned on the TV news. What we didn't see, but experience today in every facet of our lives, was what was happening behind the scenes in the business world, which was facing its own upheaval.

Radical thinking flourished in more than politics. This was a decade in which young entrepreneurs started looking at the world differently. Innovative companies that became household words got their start. Apple, Starbucks, Microsoft, Nike, and many more all began in that decade. Laptops, lattes, cell phones, high-end sneakers, word processing, gourmet home cooking—all these things that have become part of our lifestyle had their birth or blossomed in the decade between 1965 and 1975. It was an extraordinary time on all fronts and we are still reeling from the momentum created.

When Bill and I decided, in 1970, to start a vineyard—out-of-the-box thinking for two history majors—we were manifesting the innovative energy of the time. Like the Eraths, Letts, Adelsheims, Campbells, and Ponzis, who also dreamed of European wine grape vineyards, we were each following our own dream, not realizing we were part of a global phenomenon.

———

IN 1973, BILL AND I decided it was time to move out of our drafty rented farmhouse. We had lived the seven years of our married life in rented housing, never more than two years in the same place. I was pregnant with our second child, and we wanted a home of our own. We tried to buy a house nearby, but there weren't many and none were for sale, so we had to build. A sloping corner of our vineyard, not good for grapes, would work for a house. Bigleaf maples and Douglas firs lined the west side, but we could look east, north, and south over the vineyard from the second floor.

The library's books of house plans showed us boxy houses that seemed too conventional. Far more enticing were plans for vacation homes. These had imaginative shapes and angles that could be fun to live in. We chose an octagonal pole house. Neither of us had ever seen such a house, but it sounded interesting and we liked the idea of views from eight sides.

We hired a contractor from a nearby farming community, whose workers came from a local commune. We planned to have them only frame the house. We would do the rest ourselves and Bill took six months off to work on the house. He installed the whole electrical system and beamed with pride and relief when it passed inspection. To save money when he put up the drywall, he carefully cut and fit small pieces into the odd angles that an eight-sided house created. It took so much time that we decided to hire professionals to do the taping and ready it for painting.

The men we hired couldn't believe that Bill had used so many tiny pieces and never stopped complaining about all the odd shapes they had to tape. I did much of the painting of the walls, propping myself against the ladder with my increasingly pregnant belly. We moved into our almost finished home just in time to celebrate Christmas. One month later, Alex was born.

We were thrilled to finally be in a home of our own, but it didn't take long to discover that while an octagonal house looked good on paper, it was full of angles that made rational furniture arrangement almost impossible. None of the rooms had the square corners required to accommodate a cupboard, a TV, or a chair comfortably. Our main living area—living room, kitchen, dining area, master bedroom, and large deck—was on the second floor, overlooking the vineyard. The kids' bedrooms were on the first floor. Below that, a daylight basement opened to the carport. We framed in space for a motorized dumbwaiter, with the idea that I wouldn't have to carry groceries up two flights of stairs. But in the eighteen years we lived there, we never got around to building it.

As the second child, Alex had the advantage of my having been broken in by Nik. The youngest of four siblings, I never babysat or even paid much attention to children. I had no idea how to handle babies and was nervous that I would do something wrong and wouldn't be a "good mother."

In the rented farmhouse, I was generally alone all day, sometimes in total silence except for Nik's wailing and the creaking of the rocker where I sat holding him, unable to stop the tears of helplessness flowing

Checking out the vineyard on a sunny day in early spring before the vines leafed out. Bill has four-month-old Alex in the backpack. Three year-old Nik is in between me and Bill's father, John Blosser.

down my cheeks. Nik just kept crying. I changed his diaper and nursed him, held him, rocked him, and sang softly to him. What could it be? I reread my paperback copy of Dr. Spock's book until it was falling apart.

It took me a long time to loosen up enough to enjoy my baby. Later I understood that his crying reflected my insecurity, and I carry a rueful tenderness in my heart for Nik who, as the first child, had to bear my learning curve of motherhood.

As I relaxed, I was surprised to discover how interesting, how much fun, and how individually distinctive my children were. My two boys were born three years apart: Nik, reserved and intellectual, with an unexpected silly streak; Alex, gregarious and unconventional, with an unexpected intellectual streak. They complemented each other, and the older they got, the more fun they had together. I found motherhood deeply satisfying, but never easy.

With the vineyard in its infancy and only a few acres planted, I had time to get involved in non-farm activities. I joined the McMinnville chapter of the American Association of University Women (AAUW) and through my new friends learned of a teaching opportunity at Linfield, a small liberal-arts college nearby in McMinnville. I grabbed the chance to indulge my interest in American history and do the work I had trained for. Hired as an adjunct professor, I taught for the next two years, first History of the American Revolution, and then History of Women in the United States. I had my own office in the History Department and worked so hard that I managed to turn teaching one class into a full-time job. The whole experience—planning and giving lectures, talking to students, being one of the faculty—was intellectually invigorating. The department chair gave me the freedom to formulate the syllabus for the courses, and I felt as if I were in graduate school taking a tutorial, except that I was also teaching it. The material was always fresh in my mind because I was absorbing it only days ahead of my class. Here was the stimulation I craved, and I stayed until it became a luxury I couldn't afford. I was needed in the vineyard.

———

PEOPLE IN THE LOCAL farming community were curious about us since none of the farmers had experience with wine grapes. Our first contact with the community was Carrie and Les McDougall, a retired couple who lived in a pink, ranch-style house on the large lot adjoining the top corner of our property, the site of our first planting. Summer evenings we'd see them settled on folding lawn chairs in the driveway in front of their house and we'd join them when we finished work. The four of us talked about farming and looked out across our rows of grapevines, past a few big maple trees, and down onto the patchwork of farms on the valley floor. The distance made it seem peaceful, but farmers work long days, and the valley was full of activity.

"Golly, look at that," Carrie would say, pointing to a tiny tractor moving slowly across a light green field in the distance. "I guess George is letting little Sam drive the tractor now." Then Les would pipe up with "Look, over there," and nod toward a spray of water moving back and forth across a faraway patch of dark green. "Phil's irrigatin' his beans again tonight. Must have a good contract this year with the cannery." They'd point out a crew moving the water lines in a field of broccoli and tell us how a young man had been killed when the long piece of irrigation pipe he was moving crossed an electric line. From their lawn chair lookout, the McDougalls knew what was happening on every parcel of land.

Over the course of the 1970s, we bought several parcels of producing orchards from other neighbors, Ted and Verni Wirfs, who became our good friends as they slowly retired from farming. Ted showed his tractor skills helping us during grape harvest, hauling full totes of grapes from the steepest parts of the vineyard down to the winery. His expertise proved invaluable when it rained and the wet, slippery hillsides made maneuvering treacherous for less experienced drivers.

Verni knit Christmas stockings personalized with the names of each of our kids, provided us with one of her kittens when we wanted one, gave me starts from her unusual African violets, and showered us with a large box of her seasoned pretzel/cereal snack mix every Christmas.

Ted had an endless repertoire of stories about his years of farming, and he and Verni became a source of comfort and encouragement. After visiting with them, the problems we were struggling with always seemed more manageable. They lived from harvest to harvest with a curious combination of fatalism and optimism—making the best of whatever hand Mother Nature dealt and then welcoming each new year as a fresh start and another chance. As novices, we were grateful both for their advice and because they took us seriously. Many local farmers stopped short, looked at us sideways, and narrowed their eyes when we told them what we were doing. "You're growing what? Why're you doing that? Nobody's done that around here." Ted and Verni won our hearts and our loyalty by supporting us with their farming knowledge and their friendship.

I met many of the local farm wives when I accepted Verni's invitation to join the Unity Ladies Club, which took its name from the local Unity School District, which had actually ceased to exist long before most of the club members were born. The ladies were older than I was, ranging in age from forty to nearly eighty. Each month a different member hosted and her dining room table, covered with a lacy crocheted tablecloth, would be laden with plates of freshly baked cookies, homemade pies or cakes, local walnuts and hazelnuts, and the obligatory dish of mints.

We chatted, sipped coffee or sweet punch out of flowery china teacups, and ate primly off the hostess's best china. It was a Norman Rockwell painting and reminded me of the fun I had as a little girl having tea parties with my dolls and my mother, pretending I was grown up, and a lady. Here was the real thing. The ladies were very kind to me. When I was pregnant with Alex, they surprised me with the first (and only) baby shower I ever had.

Most of the women had lived their entire lives in the area and our conversation focused on their interests—mainly families, health problems, and crops. Meetings always had their share of "Did you hear about . . . ?" Ruth Stoller, wife of one of the major turkey farmers, held the unofficial title of county historian, and entertained us with tales of local towns. In the early 1900s, stern-wheelers had brought people up the Yamhill River from Portland, giving Dayton, a little town near us, the name for its main drag, Ferry Street. Ruth showed us old pictures of passengers on one of the stern-wheelers, women in long dresses and bonnets and men wearing vests and straw hats.

The club leaders were the wives of the wealthiest and most

successful farmers, the ones who raised turkeys, row crops, wheat, berries, or tree fruits. No one would have guessed, then, that within twenty years all the turkey farms, and most of the orchards and berry fields, would be gone, and nurseries and vineyards would be the area's primary agricultural industries. By the turn of the twenty-first century, not a single turkey was being raised for sale in the county.

At the Unity Ladies Club in the 1970s, we weren't looking to the future. We savored the moment, gossiping, exclaiming over the hostess's culinary skills, drawing names for our "secret pals" each year, and exchanging homemade Christmas and birthday gifts. There was no reason to think our world would be any different in years to come. We could not have imagined how significantly the landscape would change over the next two decades.

———

AFTER BUYING TED AND Verni's orchards, summer and fall turned into a continual harvest. We needed whatever income we could generate, so we kept the producing orchards going until we could afford to replace them with grapes. Life went like this: cherry harvest in late June, peaches July through August, prunes in late August, grapes in September and October, and walnuts in November.

The best part of our newly acquired orchards was that tree-ripened fruit introduced me to delicious new tastes. Before we owned the orchards, for example, I had only eaten canned Royal Anne cherries, which my mother would serve as a special dessert. How much better they were fresh and ripe off the tree. The whole family would go down after dinner and wander from tree to tree, plucking the biggest ones and popping them into our mouths for dessert. "Let's go down and graze in the cherry orchard," one of us would suggest and we'd all troop down the hill. I had also never eaten a tree-ripened peach. I couldn't believe how much more flavorful it was than any I had bought in a store.

I felt it my duty not to let anything from our orchards go to

waste. We were overloaded with fruit, even though I canned, froze, pickled, and made jam, preserves, and brandy. It became too much of a good thing. After about two years I admitted defeat. Worn out, it was a relief to finally accept that I simply could not use, or give away, all the fruit, and that I would have to let some drop to the ground.

The first orchards we took out were the peaches. They were the most difficult to grow and we didn't have a secure market for them. Even after we had taken out all our trees, I liked to help Ted and Verni pick and sort their peaches for the fresh market. It was too big a job for the two of them, and they were so good to us that I was glad to help. Harvest started about five in the morning, while the peaches were still cold and firm and wouldn't bruise from handling. We strapped on harnesses attached to large aluminum buckets so we had both hands free to pick. Unlike cherries or grapes, which could be harvested all at once, peaches had to be picked as they ripened, every few days. Everything about growing peaches was difficult, from fighting disease to propping up the trees laden with fruit, to the ordeal of picking. After experiencing a growing season, Bill and I concluded the only reason to go through all this was to enjoy the taste of a fully ripe peach. Besides being sweet and juicy, a tree-ripened peach has a perfume, intense and captivating. No other fruit we grew enveloped the senses so completely.

This was one place I couldn't include the kids. Alex wanted badly to help me pick, but his hands were too small to get around the whole peach and twist it off without either bruising it or tearing the skin. Sometimes he would walk down to the peach orchard, about a quarter mile away, to find me when he got up. I think he knew we would be close to finishing and Verni would have something good for him to eat. We always finished the picking morning with freshly baked coffee cake. We sat as long as we could, until finally someone would say, "Well, guess it's time to get back to work." Alex and I would trudge back up the hill.

Cherry season had rituals of its own, from bringing in the bees in

March to delivering the harvest to the processor in early July. There was nothing easy about any of it with the big old trees that comprised our orchard. Work began in the spring, as soon as we had a few dry days and could get in to work the soil. When the trees bloomed in March, we brought in beehives to pollinate the blossoms. We hoped for sunny days, but too often it was so cold the bees wouldn't come out of their hives, and the beekeepers had to come to the orchard to feed them.

Full bloom in the cherry orchard enchanted me. Delicate white blossoms with a touch of pink covered the trees, giving them a gauzy, ethereal quality. Standing in the middle of the orchard surrounded by twenty-foot trees with frothy white, sweet smelling blossoms, listening to the steady hum of the bees doing their job, the cares of daily life receded.

Our aged cherry trees had thick trunks. Their branches hung low, making picking from the ground easier. The Latino crew we hired to harvest arrived early to cook breakfast before work. The smell of tortillas and onions greeted us as we came down to start the day. These men worked hard but still had time for animated conversation and jokes, and the sounds of their lively camaraderie filled the air. Each picker worked with a two-gallon aluminum bucket, a harness, and a wooden ladder. After the cherries were dumped into large wooden totes, we loaded them on our truck and took them to the brine plant at the end of the picking day.

Delivering handpicked cherries was a ritual of its own. After I got proficient driving our twenty-foot flatbed truck, I would make the trip with one of the kids—Alex always wanted to come—and our dog, Bagel, who was willing to go anywhere as long as she could ride. Thirty totes, three layers of ten totes each, put our truck at its maximum load. I tied the cargo down and drove slowly to avoid sudden stops.

During the peak of harvest, there would be a string of trucks at the cannery at the end of the day, waiting to be unloaded and sampled. Small pickups, straining under the weight of one tote, alternated with large flatbed trucks carrying many layers of totes. We sat in the long line, with the doors open to catch the breeze, and waited for our turn. The slow-moving line of trucks laden with fruit moved in a choreographed dance with the fast-wheeling forklifts unloading totes.

Payment depended on how well our cherries fared in the grading, which took place while we watched. The forklift brought several totes over to the grader, who put handfuls from random totes into a small bucket, and then examined each cherry. I held my breath with every one. Perfect cherries with stems went to the drinks-cocktail market, fetched the highest price, and went into pile number one. The second pile was perfect cherries without stems, suitable for the baking market. The third pile was rejects—cherries that were split or showed any rot—for which there was no compensation. My heart sank at every reject. After sorting, the grader weighed each pile, calculated its percentage of our sample, and applied that percentage to our whole load. Growers tried to top-dress their totes, putting the best cherries on top, but the graders knew to dig down to get the samples. During cherry harvest, the cannery stayed open to receive cherries long past dark, often until midnight.

We farmed the cherries longer than the other fruits. In 1987, with relief but also nostalgia, we took out the last cherry trees. Finally, we could give our entire focus to our vineyards. But alas, there was no more grazing in the cherry orchard after dinner.

———

BILL AND I WERE on a steep learning curve. From the time we cleared our first piece of land in 1971 to building the winery in 1977, everything we did—starting a family, farming orchards, building a house, planting a vineyard, starting the winery—was a new experience. As soon as we put the vines into the ground, we were on an express train, with nature at the wheel. Everything needed our attention at the same time. Life was so full, and moving so fast, that we didn't have time to reflect on the wisdom of our undertaking. We fell into bed and slept soundly every night, waking only when a baby cried.

My father's business success in Milwaukee, Wisconsin, enabled him to indulge his love of wine and become our partner in 1974. He invested as soon as he was convinced we were serious about our project. He invested only a bit of cash, but he encouraged us to expand by guaranteeing loans for us at the Milwaukee bank that handled his business. His help was crucial, because local banks thought we were just as crazy as everyone else did and refused to lend money to such a risky project. With my father's help, we were able to buy adjoining parcels of land as they came up for sale. We benefited from having our vineyards contiguous. On the other hand, financing our operation so completely through debt left us undercapitalized and financially vulnerable, a condition that plagued us for years.

Daddy envisioned a family winery where we could ferment the grapes we grew and craft them into fine wines on our own land and by our own hand. Bill and I, barely able to keep the vineyards and orchards under control, were daunted at the thought of adding a winery. But spurred on by my father, Bill started researching startup costs and building materials and hired a marketing consultant to help estimate income and costs for the first ten years. He hired a winery design consultant to help lay out the winery and select equipment. As Daddy's enthusiasm grew, he talked my three older brothers into investing.

The next step, getting permission to site a winery on our property, became an unexpected hurdle. The land use regulations we both strongly favored became our stumbling block. Because of his training, Bill was a firm believer in land use planning and didn't mind having to go to the county planning commission for approval to construct a winery on farm property. Oregon had just buttressed its land use laws, the legacy of Governor Tom McCall, one of the state's most colorful and well-loved politicians. McCall took a forceful stand on controlling growth that gained national attention. In a CBS interview in 1971, he quipped, "Come visit us again and again. This is a state of excitement. But for heaven's sake, don't come here to live."

When Governor McCall pushed the Oregon legislature to pass a state land use bill in 1973, mandating that each county decide how the land within its boundaries should be used—what should be designated agricultural, residential, commercial, or industrial—Bill put his planning degree to use by getting involved. His goal was to convince county planners to designate the hillsides where we had vineyards as agricultural, rather than as residential "view property," which was the route they were headed. Hillside soils, with their lower fertility and excellent drainage, suited wine grapes, and gave the vines natural frost protection because they were a few degrees warmer than the valley floor. The small group of winegrowers worked together to convince the county that vineyards were the wave of the future and the hillsides should be designated agricultural.

The designation of hillsides as agricultural, with twenty- and forty-acre minimums, became vital protection for the wine industry. The efforts of the early winegrowers meant the hillsides in Yamhill County would become dotted with vineyards instead of trailer parks or subdivisions. In neighboring counties, where the growers were less active in shaping the law, hillside housing developments encroached on farms and vineyards as the population of metropolitan Portland expanded.

Oregon entered the twenty-first century as the only state in the nation with a comprehensive land use program. Governor McCall's land use initiative, Senate Bill 100, passed at an extraordinary time in Oregon's history, when visionary and strategic politicians from both political parties found a way to work together, thinking of future generations and the betterment of the state. Its implementation coincided neatly with the development of Oregon's new wine industry.

As we moved ahead with our winery plans and applied for the land use permit, we saw a side of Yamhill County that we had known was there but hadn't paid much attention to—teetotaling religious fundamentalism. Without our knowledge, a few fervent winery opponents carried around petitions requesting that the county deny our permit. While the petition said nothing about God, religion, or the evils of alcohol, we found out that the leaders of the petition drive were either Mormons or members of the Church of God, a fundamentalist Christian denomination. Both groups were vigorously anti-alcohol. As long as we only farmed, we were accepted into the community. But the winery we were proposing represented something new and threatening. We suddenly found ourselves thrust into the role of outsiders.

Our neighbors' imaginations ran wild thinking about the terrible possibilities. "Do you want drunks from the winery roaming the hills?" the petition carriers would ask their neighbors. They mentioned rape. "Our homes and women wouldn't be safe." Petitioners asked their neighbors to imagine the flashing neon signs that would undoubtedly be on top of our winery to attract people off the highway a quarter mile away. In sum, a winery would be a blight on the neighborhood, threaten the well-being of their families, and endanger their quality of life. If I had believed all the things they said would happen, I would have been against us too. The petition recorded fifty-three signatures. I was saddened to see the signatures of some of my Unity Club friends. No one had talked to me about their concerns—they had just signed.

Adding fuel to the religious opposition was political opposition roused by Bill's work on the county land use plan. Saving hillsides for agriculture might have been good long-range planning, but it infuriated farmers who had wanted to divide their land into smaller parcels or build more than one house on it. After working on the county plan, Bill was appointed to the Yamhill County Planning Commission, whose task was to uphold the new plan. He recused himself when we applied for our winery permit. People who had been denied their petitions saw a chance for revenge. One opponent stated flatly, "Blosser kept me from getting my request; I'm sure as hell going to keep him from getting his."

The hearing before the Yamhill County Planning Commission,

41

February 17, 1977, took place in the basement of the Yamhill County courthouse. The low-ceilinged hearing room was packed when we arrived. I wondered what had brought out all these people and was shocked when I found out they were there for us. Or rather, against us. We were blindsided. The fierce looks on people's faces made it clear that Bill and I were the enemy and it was their mission to defeat us. Our permit request was the second item on the agenda. The commissioners never got to the third item; our hearing took up the rest of the evening.

The anti-winery faction had turned out in force, bringing an attorney, people to testify, and their petition full of signatures. Many of the complaints had nothing to do with the proposed winery but spoke to vineyard issues—the use of noisy air cannons to scare away birds, fear of the migrant workers employed during harvest. "Technical" reasons for opposition were that a winery would lower the water table by using too much water, cause pollution, lower property values, create traffic jams, generate offensive odors with fruit waste, promote drunkenness, be a visual blight in the neighborhood, and be incompatible with the existing development in the area.

Bill quietly and methodically presented our case and painstakingly rebutted the opposing testimony, point by point. He had put in a full day of work in Portland and barely had time to grab dinner. Alone and vulnerable in the face of such intense opposition, I could see him struggling to stay calm and not rise to the emotional pitch of his opponents. Surrounded by a sea of angry people, wishing I were anywhere else, I listened to people around me condemning our project. I could feel my shoulders hunching up around my ears.

A tension-relieving moment came when Howard Timmons, a retired farmer who owned a large parcel at the top of our hill, stood up to testify against the noise from our bird-scaring air cannon. He was feisty and agitated about how bothersome that was. When he finished, Bill asked him to clarify one of the allegations. Silence. The audience looked expectantly at Howard until his wife, Hazel, finally interceded to explain that he hadn't heard the question; he was almost deaf. People couldn't help laughing, even though Howard had most certainly damaged their case. The absurdity of Howard complaining about the air cannon he couldn't hear epitomized, for us, the whole anti-winery campaign.

After three hours of testimony, the planning commissioners, apparently perplexed by the strength of the opposition, questioned their staff, which had recommended approval. After making sure the opponents' arguments were unsubstantiated, they voted unanimously to approve the project and send it on to the Board of Commissioners for approval.

When we got home, Bill was exhausted and I was still so upset that I rolled Bill's exercise bike into the living room, hopped on and pedaled as hard as I could, venting the anger I had controlled at the hearing. The personal attack and questions about our morality had hit a nerve. The testimony on religious grounds such as, "I am against the winery because of my Christian family values" implied that because we wanted to start a winery we were immoral. Their condescension and sanctimony infuriated me. Their behavior struck me as very un-Christian. This was my first encounter with outspoken prejudice in the name of God, and it was a rude awakening.

At the commissioners' hearing two weeks later, the anti-winery faction was back in force. This was their chance to appeal to the three men who had been elected to the Yamhill County Board of Commissioners and had the final say over policy issues. The commissioners listened carefully to their constituents and did not automatically adopt the recommendations of the planning commission. We knew our opponents had a good shot with their appeal. Each person who testified against us presented a picture or map showing how close they lived to the proposed winery and pointed out the dangers they faced—waste and water runoff flowing onto their property, increased traffic driving by their residences, a sinful business corrupting their family life.

But this time we came armed, bringing neighbors and other winery and vineyard people to speak on our behalf. I had eighteen signatures on a petition requesting that any decision by the Board of Commissioners be based on facts, not fears. Most people had signed our opponents' petition simply because either a neighbor had asked or they were scared by the scenarios the petitioners had described. The small core of people who set out to defeat the winery proposal had stirred up a lot of commotion and I realized I needed to do damage control.

Immediately after the planning commission hearing, while Bill was at work in Portland, I had gone to visit the neighbors to explain what we wanted to do. After my visit, most wanted to stay out of the fight entirely, realizing that our winery would not cause the problems they had been led to believe. By presenting a map showing the locations of neighbors who were opposed, in favor, and neutral, Bill was able to demonstrate that more homeowners in our immediate area were in favor of our application than were opposed. Bill's quiet dismantling of the opposing testimony contrasted sharply with the emotional, often illogical testimony of those against the winery.

The commissioners, probably baffled by all the turmoil over what seemed a straightforward issue, postponed their decision for two weeks. Finally, they came out in favor of our application for a land use permit. We celebrated, but the fight was not quite over. The hard core of the opposition appealed the county's decision to the courts, throwing us into a quandary. We had been waiting for resolution before starting construction. If we waited until the appeal wended its way through the courts, we would not have the winery ready for the 1977 crush. We were pretty sure the courts would uphold the county's decision, but what if they didn't? We decided to take the risk. When a court decision in our favor finally put an end to the long, emotional battle, we could move full steam ahead.

Our experience paved the way for future wineries; the county made the establishment of a winery on land with a minimum number of vineyard acres an outright permitted use, on the assumption that a winery facility was needed to process the fruit. Later wineries did not have to face the same kind of opposition that we did.

Once the winery was built and the neighbors saw their fears were groundless, they took pride in it. Within fifteen years, the wine industry had gained sufficient status that land that had cost eight hundred dollars an acre when we started was selling for as much as fifteen thousand dollars an acre. Soon after that, it more than doubled and is still rising. The same people who fought us started actively promoting their properties as vineyard land, with premium price tags. Years later, in exquisite irony, the poorly producing wheat fields Howard Timmons fought to protect from the wine business sold for a bundle to become high-value vineyards.

On October 10, 1977, the day finally came when our first block of grapes was ready to pick and we could start the winery's first vintage. Our twenty-person crew started at seven in the morning and didn't stop to eat until they finished, working as if they'd each had a shot of adrenaline. Wielding curved knives with wooden handles and leather wrist straps, they grasped the grape clusters and cut the stems with swift, short strokes.

In the quiet early morning, as the picking began, the only sound was the clusters thudding into empty buckets. As the pickers got into a rhythm, the noise level rose. Soon the air was alive with the sounds of pickers running and shouting to each other, grapes sloshing into the totes, tractors chugging back and forth. Each picker had two plastic five-gallon pails, and each time he emptied them into the wooden tote at the end of the row the contractor gave him a ticket to turn in for pay. The pickers ran, even with full pails, shouting their numbers to the contractor, stuffing their tickets into their pants, hustling back to pick. The contractor barked instructions and warnings (in Spanish): "Don't pick so many leaves! Fill your buckets to the top! Pick the whole vine! You're leaving too many clusters on the back side!" The pickers were mostly men, but some women came, and a few brought children who hung around with their parents. Pickers sometimes missed whole vines or skipped clusters that were hard to reach. I didn't want to waste a single grape of our first vintage and walked up and down the rows with a bucket picking the fruit they had overlooked.

We tried to sort the grapes as they went into the totes, taking out the leaves and any clusters that looked underripe or diseased. Most of the time I stood at the totes with the contractor to monitor the picking. Ted Wirfs brought his tractor to help our vineyard foreman, Wayne, lay out the totes in the morning, and then ferry them to the winery as they were filled. Nik and Alex, then six and three, were in on the excitement; I had hired a babysitter to be with them so they could participate in our first vintage. Clad in rubber boots, blue jean jackets, and baseball caps, they watched big-eyed.

One by one, over the course of the month, the other blocks of grapes ripened too. The dark purple, small-clustered Pinot Noir grapes went directly from the stemmer-crusher into large, open-topped wooden vats to ferment. Three times a day, Bob McRitchie, our wine-maker, and Bill took turns standing on a wooden plank laid across the top of the open fermenter, to punch down the cap of grape skins that had risen to the top. To do this they had created a tool—an inverted dog dish attached to a long piece of PVC pipe.

When fermentation was complete, they pumped the Pinot Noir back into the press and pressed the juice off the skins. Then the young wine went into small French oak barrels for aging.

We finished harvesting our Chardonnay and Riesling, the last of the grapes, on October 22. By then we were starting the picking day bundled up against the cold. The fall rains were threatening to settle in for the duration. But the grapes for our first vintage were safely in.

Deciding what to call our new winery turned out to be surprising difficult. I was certain there was a perfect name that would call out to customers in wine shops and make them want to grab our bottles off the shelf. We just had to will that name into our consciousness. We thought of names that highlighted local towns, the hillsides, the vines, the river, the creeks. Nothing had the right magic. I concluded we simply weren't creative enough. The marketing consultant Bill had hired consoled us. This winery was our baby, he said. Giving it our family names would let potential customers know that real people were involved. "Remember that slogan for lacy women's bras? 'Behind every Olga, there's an Olga'? Put your names on the line—both your names, since you're equal partners."

So Sokol Blosser it was. After all, we told ourselves, Orville Redenbacher, the popcorn king, and Smucker's, the jam people, had used their odd family names. That didn't keep them from being successful. We could do it too. Bill's friends teased him about putting my name first, but it was the right marketing decision. We were going to use the initials SB as part of our winery logo.

Once we had our name, we engaged a Portland graphic artist, Clyde Van Cleave, whose work we liked, to design a wine label for us, which we used, with only color modifications, for the next twenty years. The label was about three inches by three inches, with a rounded top that arched over the SB logo. Later, the black and brown lettering on textured beige paper seemed drab, but at the time we thought it fresh and exciting.

Located on a busy state highway, we had great visitor potential. We decided to build a tasting room, although no other Oregon winery had more than a converted garage for the public to visit. Our marketing consultant advised us that a tasting room would be an indispensable public-relations tool as well as a retail sales opportunity. It turned out to be one of the best pieces of advice we received.

A mutual friend introduced us to John Storrs, a Portland architect noted for his imagination and ability to design for the natural setting. John had designed several Oregon landmarks, the best known of which was Salishan Lodge, a resort on the coast that had become an instant mid-twentieth-century architectural classic. Tall, boisterous,

Our first wine label, with the SB logo and our winery name front and center. An exciting moment to see it on a bottle of our first Pinot Noir vintage.

and charismatic, John always dominated the space he was in. "Blueprints are just a formality," he declared. He designed as he built. We enjoyed him and watched as he wandered around changing things after construction had begun—an opening here, a window there. He drove the builders crazy with his unconventional style. They grew to dread his visits, as they knew he would find something he wanted redone. But the result was better for it.

In the summer of 1978, Sokol Blosser opened the first Oregon tasting room designed specifically for that purpose. The gray stucco building hugged the knoll and coordinated well with the gray concrete winery building. The existing large oak and maple trees and landscaping

I ran the tasting room on weekends for the first few years. Behind me on the wall is a framed needlepoint my mother did for me. Underneath that are our first medals from wine competitions.

with native plants provided color and contrast. On a clear day, Mount Hood loomed majestically, perfectly centered in a large east-facing window. Besides a tasting area, we had a small kitchen, a tiny one-person office, and the requisite two bathrooms. The back door opened to a breezeway that connected the tasting room with the winery.

There was another door in the main tasting area, six feet off the ground, anticipating the big deck we wanted but couldn't afford. That door remained nailed shut for the next twenty years until, in the late 1990s, the deck was finally added.

Once we had the tasting room, the challenge was to get people to visit on weekends, when we were open. Wine touring in Oregon was not yet in vogue. We sent out mailers to friends and friends-of-friends and threw a big party. Slowly the word spread. I spent weekends behind the bar welcoming people and pouring free tastes that we hoped would lead to sales. It was months before we could hire any help and years before we could be open more than weekends. The kids were always with us. During cherry season the first year, seven-year-old Nik demonstrated his entrepreneurial skills by showing up with fresh cherries from our orchard to sell to customers. Taking his cue from the way we worked the tasting room, he offered free tastes. He never failed to sell out.

———

THE EARLY WINEGROWERS IN the Willamette Valley were a close-knit group. We shared information and cooperated to chart a course for the new wine industry. This willingness to work together for the good of the whole became a distinguishing feature of Oregon winegrowers from the start. We understood our actions would shape the future and thought hard about what we wanted the Oregon wine industry to look like.

The whole industry, which was ten to twelve people in the early years, met regularly in each other's living rooms, sitting around on mismatched thrift store furniture, a decor which we called "Contemporary St. Vincent de Paul." First, we shared news of hot deals on equipment or supplies. Then, after passing along the address of a farmer who had stakes, wire, or used equipment for sale, we talked about what legislation we might need to protect our fledgling industry. Not every session ended in consensus, but we kept meeting until we reached it.

One issue with lasting effect was tightening Oregon's labeling regulations. At the time, federal wine-labeling regulations were lax, shaped by the practices of industrial producers in California and New York. A winery could legally give a wine a varietal label, such as Pinot Noir or Chardonnay, when as little as 51 percent of the grapes in the bottle actually came from that variety. We didn't want wineries compromising our reputations by labeling a wine "Pinot Noir" when 49 percent of it was made with less expensive grapes. Using cheap table grapes like Thompson Seedless would have been legal. We wanted the world to know that if the wine came from Oregon, virtually all the grapes would be the variety printed on the label.

Dave Adelsheim wrote up the regulations we had all agreed to and presented them to the Oregon Liquor Control Commission (OLCC), the state regulatory agency. The OLCC was not eager to have stricter laws than those required by the federal government, but with the whole Oregon wine industry behind the changes, it agreed. By the late 1970s, when our new regulations went into effect, any Oregon wine with a varietal label had to contain at least 90 percent of that variety. We made an exception for Cabernet Sauvignon, requiring only 75 percent, because in the grape's French home, Bordeaux, similar varieties were often blended into the wine. Oregon's stringent new labeling requirements influenced the federal rules, but not for another ten years. At that point federal regulations raised the requirement for varietals from 51 to 75 percent, better for consumers, but still far below Oregon's standard. California and Washington winegrowers accepted the federal regulations. Only Oregon had tighter restrictions.

Another piece of the new regulations concerned generic wine names. As growers of Pinot Noir, the grape of Burgundy, we were outraged that some large California wineries would put a blend of cheap red grapes together and call it "Burgundy," trading on the prestige of Burgundian wines and intimating that their product would taste as if it had been made of Pinot Noir grapes. So we devised a regulation that said Oregon wines could not be named for a geographic region unless all the grapes actually came from that place. This precluded labeling wines Burgundy, Chianti, Chablis, or Champagne—all names of wine regions in Italy or France. In reaching consensus on labeling regulations and persuading the government to implement them, the Oregon winegrowers demonstrated a level of cooperation and commitment rarely found in an industry whose members are ultimately in competition.

―――

IN THE EARLY MONTHS of 1979, when Nik was eight and Alex was five, Bill and I suddenly realized that our boys were growing up fast. Bill commented he missed having a baby around and I surprised myself by admitting I did too. Impulsively, I stopped taking birth control pills and was soon pregnant. The boys were excited, since they were old enough to have proprietary interest in a new brother or sister. We had planned to tell Bill's parents at a family gathering, but Alex, full of importance with his new knowledge, blurted out, "Mama's going to have a baby!" to Grandma Betty and Grandpa John before we even got through the front door.

Because I would be thirty-five when the baby arrived, the age after which pregnancy was considered riskier, my doctor recommended that I undergo a new procedure, amniocentesis, to check the health of the fetus. I had the procedure, then waited six weeks, which seemed an eternity, for the report. After reassuring me about the baby's health, the nurse who called asked if I wanted to know the baby's sex. When she told me I was going to have a girl, I burst out crying. I hadn't realized until then how much I had wanted a daughter.

Our baby girl arrived in December 1979. Alison was so much younger than her brothers, I worried they would boss her around—a predicament I knew well, growing up with three older brothers. But Alison seemed born to take charge and quickly proved she could hold her own. One night, when Bill and I had prevailed on the boys to babysit, we returned home to find four-year-old Alison clutching a large wooden spoon while playing Lego with her brothers. We knew something was up.

It turned out that after we had left, the boys had gone off to play, leaving Alison alone. She didn't like being ignored and decided she wasn't getting the babysitting to which she was entitled. So she got a wooden spoon from the kitchen and ran after them with it until they paid attention to her. They were more amused than scared, but they gave in and played with her. The episode firmly established Alison's reputation for not taking any guff, and Alison threatening her older brothers with a wooden spoon became a family joke.

We had started the decade with a new baby, a wild business idea, and a bare piece of land. By the end of 1979, we had three children, a mature vineyard, and a fledgling winery. What a decade it had been.

....

Mac & Cheese

In the 1970s, Bill was commuting to Portland for work and got home just in time for dinner, so I had all the cooking duties. One of our staples, which the kids loved, was homemade macaroni and cheese. It's still a comfort food for them and their families today. When I told cookbook author Marie Simmons how I put the dish together in those early days of the vineyard—a quick one-pan recipe that didn't require a separate sauce—she helped me re-create this recipe. Sokol Blosser Pinot Gris would be a great pairing.

Makes 6 to 8 servings

1 teaspoon coarse sea salt, plus salt for cooking the pasta

2 cups elbow macaroni

2 tablespoons butter

2 tablespoons all-purpose flour

1 teaspoon dry mustard

3 cups whole or two-percent fat milk

2 cups shredded Monterey Jack cheese

2 cups shredded sharp cheddar cheese

Bring a large saucepan three-fourths full of salted water to a rolling boil over high heat. When the water is boiling, stir in the macaroni and cook until it's almost tender (taste a piece), 8 to 10 minutes; the macaroni will continue to cook in the sauce. Drain the pasta through a colander and return it to the hot pan.

Immediately add the butter, flour, mustard, 1 teaspoon salt, and the milk to the pan and place over medium-high heat until the liquid begins to boil. Reduce the heat to medium-low and cook, stirring constantly, until the sauce is smooth and thick, about 5 minutes. Add the cheeses and stir until well blended.

Remove the mac & cheese from the heat and serve right from the pan. Or, for a casserole, pour the macaroni and cheese mixture into a buttered shallow baking dish and bake in a 350°F oven until the top is golden, about 20 minutes.

CHAPTER TWO

A Sense of Place

My father, who loved to say that the best fertilizer is the farmer's footsteps on the land, had been urging Bill to devote his full attention to the vineyard and winery. In early 1980, shortly after Alison was born, we decided the winery could afford to pay its president, so Bill quit his job in Portland to be the full-time winery president. Every morning after breakfast, he walked to work, through the vineyard, down the hill to the winery. I watched him disappear among the vines, wearing jeans, and vineyard boots, and carrying his briefcase—the only vestige of his city job. His suit and tie collection hung in the back of the closet, reserved for sales trips and meetings with the banker. He no longer spent two hours commuting, and it felt as if he were closer, but really it meant he could spend more time working.

Having Bill at the winery on a daily basis changed our dynamics. I had been running the tasting room pretty much on my own. With Bill there I was less autonomous, and I didn't want him to be my boss. He understood and we looked for an arena that could be mine. Why not running the vineyard? I kept the books and wrote the checks; I could learn to do the physical work, too. We decided I could shift my focus.

I knew this would be an adventure since my only claim to farm life is that when I was born, in 1944, my parents, Phyllis and Gus Sokol, lived at Melody Farm, in Waukesha, Wisconsin. In 1942, to counter the austerity measures of World War II, they gave up the city life they had always known and moved with their three sons to the country, where they could grow their own food. Their farm life, with its classic white-washed brick farmhouse, orchards, and barns, bordered by a split rail fence, lasted only seven years, but it loomed large in our family lore.

Stories of my mother driving a horse and buggy to the local store during wartime gas rationing and my father keeping chickens, pigs, and horses kept the memory alive, but my personal knowledge of farm life was nil. By the time I was four, we had moved back to the city. I grew up as a middle-class urbanite. My early memories include helping my father choose which patterned silk tie to wear with his suit for his workday; hearing my parents talk about the theater and concerts they attended; falling asleep listening to the adventures of Gene Autry on the big radio next to my bed; and smelling my mother's perfume and feeling the tickle of her fur coat on my cheek as she leaned down to kiss me after coming home from an evening out. I can't imagine either of them harnessing a horse or mucking out a chicken coop.

But managing our orchards and grapes put me in the vineyards every day for much of the 1980s. Wayne Cook, the young man we had hired as our foreman, patiently trained me on all the equipment. Although I was his boss and twelve years his senior, he took time to show me things—little things, like where to find the grease fittings on each piece of equipment and how to refill the grease gun from the bulk grease barrel, and big things, like how to use the forklift to load totes of grapes onto our big flatbed truck, tie down the load, and start moving. I started with almost zero knowledge, so was grateful that he was never arrogant or overbearing.

Little by little, I learned what needed to be done, how to get the equipment ready, and do the work myself. I gathered a store of information about things that I had never before even wondered about. I'd never had an urge to know how to attach a piece of heavy equipment to the back of a tractor, but now I learned how to maneuver the tractor into position so I could do it without heavy lifting. I'd never imagined driving a twenty-foot flatbed truck, but now I learned how far into the intersection to go before starting to turn a corner. I absorbed the rhythm of the vineyard year and what needed to be done each season in the orchards and vineyards—pruning, fertilizing, spraying, canopy management, crop estimates, harvest procedures. I took a farm management class to get a better understanding of the business side.

I threw myself into my vineyard work, wishing I could inhale all the new information and relishing my new skills. Crouching to lubricate a piece of farm equipment, my overalls covered with dust and my hands and nails stained dark brown from the grease, I'd suddenly wonder what my high school friends would think if they could see me now. My parents proudly displayed a photo of me as a debutante in which I looked out from the sterling silver frame, elegant in my white strapless gown and elbow-length kid gloves, my hair in a French twist. It was about as far from my vineyard life as I could imagine. The image made me smile, not only at the contrast but also at the unexpected turns my life had taken. I would not have changed places with anyone.

Something happened to me when I got out into the vineyard. It both freed my spirit and tied me to the land. Being responsible for the farm focused my attention and stimulated my mind, but being in the orchards and among the vines penetrated right to my gut, giving me a sense of oneness with the land and a fulfillment I had never imagined. I could have lived my whole life in a city and never discovered those feelings. Until then, I'd participated with more fervor than I felt. After taking over the vineyards, I finally began to take emotional ownership of the project that had been swirling around me and dominating my life for a decade. My passion for our venture grew steadily from then on, until finally it surpassed Bill's.

Even now, I can close my eyes and imagine myself walking down a row of vines early on a summer morning. My feet are wet from the dew soaking through my boots. The air is fresh, cool on my skin, and very still. The vines are bright green and lush with new growth. The sun, just touching the vines, will soon be intense. If I am lucky I will spot a nest, probably from one of the bright yellow goldfinches, hidden in the vine canopy.

Or, I imagine it is the end of a summer day, when the sun casts long shadows in the vineyard and all the colors look deeper and richer. Above me, the swallows swoop and swirl, snatching bugs out of the air. A small breeze makes the growing tips of the vines wave gently. I can feel the heat of the day fade as the sun starts to set and a hush settles over the land.

In October, during harvest, the vineyard starts the day shrouded in mist. Viewed from the vineyard's highest point, only the tops of the tallest Douglas firs poke through, reminding me of a Japanese landscape painting. In the foggy wetness the pickers start, breaking the dew-covered spiderwebs that stretch across the rows. By noon, the day will be gloriously sunny, with the crispness in the air that is autumn.

In winter I see the skeleton of the vineyard, the trunks and canes of the vines stark without their leafy cover. Its austerity is striking, whether cloud-shrouded and bleak with rain, or snow-covered and glaringly bright. The vines sleep a long time, from December to April. By then I am eager for the vineyard to come alive. My heart sings as the swollen buds start to unfurl into tender green leaves, pink-hued around the edges. Baby clusters emerge with tendrils like tiny curls. The birds start nesting again. The air feels soft. What will this season bring? It could be a great year. A farmer's hope is always highest in the spring.

Each new vineyard year starts in the winter, when the vines are dormant, with our crew pruning away most of the previous year's growth. It is done in January, February, and March, when the weather is miserable—pouring rain, cold and windy, or just gray. Layers of long underwear and flannel underneath yellow rain pants and slickers, rubber boots and fingerless wool gloves completed the well-dressed pruner's look.

During my years in the vineyard, pruning season was one of the most sociable times, despite the fact that it took place during the worst weather of the year. In addition to our own small crew, I hired three or four extra people each winter to help.

On rainy days, we would prune with our hoods up and our heads down, each in our own row, with only the sound of the loppers breaking the silence. But when the rain stopped, we would throw back our hoods and the conversation and singing would start.

At noon we would sit in the vineyard office—the basement of our house—while we dried off and warmed up, the ambrosia of wet rain gear, tuna sandwiches, corn chips, and fresh oranges permeating our conversation. Someone had given me a book called *Totally Tasteless Jokes* and we took turns reading it. The jokes were pathetic and we mostly moaned at them, but then one would strike us as hilariously funny and the laughter felt good. Occasionally—just often enough to keep us from rain-induced depression—the sun came out and the whole world looked different: blue sky, bright sunshine, and snow-covered Mount Hood looming over the vineyard, its majestic peak alternately tinged with pink, gold, or blue. What a glorious feeling to be working outside! How lucky we were to be working in the vineyard! We strode up the rows more boldly and sang louder on those days.

Soon after I started in the vineyard, we witnessed Mother Nature's stunning power. On the morning of May 18, 1980, Mount Saint Helens erupted with a force that sent a plume of ash fifteen miles into the air and created the largest landslide in recorded history. A wall of logs and mud flowed down leveling everything in its path—forests, homes, roads, bridges, wildlife—and leaving miles of desolation blanketed in gray ash.

It was a Sunday and the five of us had been to a birthday brunch for Bill at his parents' home in Tigard, about seventy-five miles from Mount Saint Helens. Shortly after leaving their home, we saw the effects of the eruption. We sat in the car at the top of a hill and watched in awe as the mountain sent up a huge, roiling cloud of ash. The actual explosion surprised everyone, although the possibility of an eruption had been in the news for weeks. We had watched endless television interviews with people forced to evacuate their homes. Those who refused to leave vanished without a trace. Ash drifted far beyond the area desolated by the eruption. In Portland, the gray dust clung to grass and shrubs for months. A thin layer of ash even landed on our vineyard, but it barely covered our hillside and didn't cause any harm. We drove to Hillsboro, northwest of us, where the ash was almost an inch deep, and Nik and Alex gathered it in buckets to keep as souvenirs. Then they got the bright idea of putting it in little bags to sell to tasting-room visitors. They sold out so I never had to deal with buckets of leftover volcanic ash. Local farmers plowed in the ash, the crops suffered no harm, and the 1980 eruption of Mount Saint Helens took its place in local lore next to the Columbus Day Storm of 1962.

We did many experiments in the vineyard and the one for which I had the highest hopes turned out to be our biggest failure. We got the idea of using geese in the vineyard when we heard they were used to weed the fields at mint farms—they ate the weeds and left the mint. I envisioned a pastoral scene with fat, happy geese wandering around the vineyard, feasting on weeds and leaving the vines to grow healthy and lush. Here was an idea that had everything going for it. It was more environmentally friendly than spraying herbicide or running equipment to mow or till, and it would save time and money. We chose a block of vines that we could fence relatively easily—three acres of Riesling adjacent to our house. We could watch the geese from our deck.

There were some immediate obstacles. We needed to fence, but we also needed to get a tractor up and down the rows to spray for mildew and botrytis (rot). We met this challenge with a makeshift chicken wire fence that had to be removed when we needed to spray, which was every ten to fourteen days all summer. But we figured all this extra time and energy was a small price to pay for such a great idea.

Two dozen white Chinese goslings arrived at our house in March. I had never had any farm animals and couldn't wait. When we opened the box, forty-eight tiny bright eyes looked up and gave us little goose smiles, accompanied by considerable twittering. We bonded immediately. They were so little that we put them in a small pen until they got bigger and we got the fencing in place. They came waddling, honking eagerly, whenever they saw or heard us. We chuckled at their antics.

In April, when the vines had not fully leafed out but the grass and weeds were growing fast and at their tender and tasty best, we embarked on our great experiment. As far as we knew, no other vineyard in Oregon had even thought of trying this. We put the geese in among the vines, in a section that has been known since as the Goosepen Block. The young geese loved their new freedom and wandered around giving all the various plants the taste test. I expected they would develop a taste for the leafy weeds. The vines would be too high for them to reach, anyway.

Our plan started to fall apart right away. The geese just wanted to be near us. When we went out onto the deck to see how they were doing, they'd come running over and line up along the fence, honking at us. When we weren't outside, they would sit quietly at the fence and wait for us to reappear. I tried going into the vineyard and showing them the far reaches of the block. They dutifully allowed me to herd them, and then they went back to their positions along the fence line facing our house. We thought maybe the geese would cover more of the block after they had eaten all the weeds in the section near the house. It never happened. They spent the rest of their lives trying to be near us, while the weeds grew freely. We knew it was time to act when the young geese got big enough to reach the grapes hanging on the vines.

In the end, we chose one pair to keep, and the rest of the geese ended up in our freezer. I cooked one, but we couldn't bear to eat it. They stayed in the freezer for years. I was simply unable to bring myself to deal with them. It wasn't until we moved, and I had to empty the freezer, that I finally closed the chapter on the geese—except, that is, for the two goose-down pillows that Bill had given me for Christmas. For many years we laid our heads on the fluffy remains of our unwilling weed eaters.

The pair that we kept, dubbed Papa Goose and Gertie, grew large and elegant. At first, they hung out in the front yard and liked to camp on the front doormat. The whole front porch was soon awash in goose poop. Not good. We fenced an area off our deck that became their pasture, then built a little pond and a house for them. I even bought a series of exotic ducks to keep Papa and Gertie company.

Our most successful vineyard experiment was far less glamorous: testing various grasses as potential cover crops between the grape rows to prevent erosion. Ours was one of a handful of vineyards that worked with the US Soil Conservation Service and Oregon State University to test a variety of perennial and annual grasses. We later learned that the level of cooperation between these two groups for this project was unprecedented. Apparently, it was uncommon even to have two different departments at the university working together.

My goal was to find a grass that would prevent erosion, would not compete with the vines for water since we didn't irrigate, and would be stalwart enough to withstand equipment driving over it. From among the eight different perennial grasses we tried, we identified a sheep fescue called Covar that did all those things and, in addition, never grew more than four inches high. I sowed that wonderful little grass as a cover crop on our whole vineyard, as did many other farmers. The US Soil Conservation Service recognized my work in 1984 by honoring Sokol Blosser as Cooperator of the Year for the Yamhill Soil and Water Conservation District. We were to be recognized and presented a plaque at the annual awards dinner. Bill and I both went to the dinner, but I might as well have been invisible. People looked right past me and came over to congratulate Bill and ask him about Sokol Blosser's project. They assumed the farmer and decision maker was the man, as of course it usually was among the local farmers.

Before and during harvest, it was always a challenge to keep the wild birds away. Cedar waxwings and robins especially loved the ripening grapes. Cedar waxwings move in large flocks, flying like a squadron of small planes. Their elegant descent on the vineyard, in perfect formation, belied the damage they were about to do. I admired their grace and they were easy to scare, so it was hard to dislike them. Robins were a different story. Plump and wily, robins acted alone rather than in flocks, but there were many of them in the vineyard, and they were voracious grape eaters. They would hide in the leafy canopy when they saw us, and then go back to eating when we had gone. When I walked the vineyard with our dogs, Bagel and Muffin, they always took it as a personal affront when they saw birds in the vines and took off after them, barking ferociously. But even their most energetic efforts did not solve the problem.

We had tried everything else to warn off the birds: driving the pickup around honking the horn, riding bikes down the rows and yelling, tying a helium balloon with a picture of a hawk to a trellis wire, turning on an electronic device that emitted bird distress calls, even shooting an air cannon.

Air cannons now operate off propane canisters, but they were more elaborate and difficult in the early days of our vineyard. Water dripping on carbide rocks in a sealed chamber created acetylene gas. When enough pressure was built up, a lever would cause a wheel to

I had just finished pounding posts for our new plantings and as I returned to the equipment shed, little Alison ran out to greet me. This remains one of my favorite mother-daughter photos.

strike a flint to ignite the gas and create a giant "kaboom." They were not reliable and had to be checked often. Maintaining those cannons meant working on hands and knees in the mud during Oregon's rainy fall season. Bill would light them in the mornings before he left for work and I would keep them going during the day.

I hated and feared guns, but finally I learned to shoot a shotgun to scare the birds; it was the only thing that seemed to work. In the early morning and in the late afternoon, the birds' feeding times, I'd go out with my shotgun and my ear protection in our little off-road vehicle called a Hester ag truck. A cross between a four-wheel ATV and a golf cart, it had big knobby tires to traverse the vineyards, a bench seat so two people could ride, and a three-foot-square bed behind the seat for supplies. When Alison was little, we went into the vineyard to scare birds every morning after the boys got on the school bus. I bundled her up and she sat in the supply compartment, holding on to the sides with both hands. We bounced up and down the vineyard rows, two fearless females protecting our crop. When it was time to stop and shoot, I put big earmuff protectors on her and popped the shotgun a few times. The birds left unscathed but the noise scared them and I had the satisfaction of doing something about the bird problem.

Harvest season is always the most stressful time of year. The birds can eat the whole crop, the weather is changeable, and I am acutely aware that the future of the wines hinges on my picking decisions. Every year has its own twists and turns, but when I think of harvests, my mind always jumps to the disaster of 1984—the harvest from hell.

That year an unusually cold and wet spring had delayed bloom until mid-July, almost a month late, so we knew harvest would also be later than normal. We would have to depend on Oregon's classic Indian summer to finish the ripening process. In early October, I walked the vineyard monitoring the grapes. Plump Pinot Noir clusters hung in neat rows along the fruiting canes. They had turned purple, the first sign of ripening, but they were still tart and did not yet have the taste I knew they could acquire. We needed at least two more weeks of good weather to achieve the quality we needed. We never got it.

The rain started a week later and seemed like it would never stop. As the cold gray rain pelted the vineyard, I sat inside, frustrated, helpless, and miserable. I tried to keep myself busy, but all I could do was look out the window and worry, hoping that the next day Indian summer would arrive. I passed the time by baking, then eating, cookies: chocolate chip, butterscotch chip, oatmeal. Between the rain and my overeating, I was a colossal grouch.

After a week of heavy precipitation, it finally stopped; I went out to inspect the damage. A rain-forest dampness hung in the foggy air. The ground was so soggy that I knew we couldn't get a tractor into the vineyard; it would have slid around on the hillside. The grapes tasted watery, their flavor diluted. The forecast was for more rain. I couldn't believe it. What had happened to our Indian summer? We had always wondered which season was most critical and the consensus had been that they were equal in importance. The harvest of 1984 showed us that one season mattered most: Oregon's typically long, warm autumn was the secret to its great grapes.

After agonizing whether to act now or take a chance the weather would improve, I decided to pull in the harvest. When we brought in the Pinot Noir, it had absorbed so much water it was almost 40 percent heavier than we had forecast. Then, the storm began again and we had to harvest the Chardonnay in the rain. I felt apologetic for the pickers who had to slosh uphill to the ends of the rows toting two buckets full of grapes, over thirty pounds each since we couldn't get the tractor onto the steep slope at the lower end of the rows. We paid them extra to pick under those terrible conditions, and our picking contractor had boxes of fried chicken for his crew when they finished.

The wine reflected the watery harvest. Since vintage-dating a wine (vintage records the year the grapes were picked) denotes a more premium wine, we decided to declassify the wine by producing only a nonvintage Pinot Noir that year. This was our way of letting people know we didn't think the wine was good enough to deserve vintage dating. I get a sinking feeling in my stomach every year that we get rain in September. A disaster like 1984 is always just a rainstorm away. When the sky is dark gray and the rain is coming down steadily, it's hard to imagine sunny weather returning. But it always has, except for that one year, wedged in between the two stellar vintages of 1983 and 1985. The memory reminds me how dependent on Mother Nature we are.

I worked enthusiastically with my vineyard crew for the 1980s. We farmed the vineyard and the orchards, and planted more acres of grapes when we took the orchards out. We created a wine grape nursery and sold our grape cuttings to new vineyards arriving in the valley. We researched cover crops, pruning, trellising, and canopy management. With all that attention, the farm became profitable for the first time by the end of the decade, twenty years after we started.

IN THE EARLY 1980s, when our small group of local wineries decided to band together to form the Yamhill County Winery Association, our first joint project was for each of us to host an open house at our winery during the three days after Thanksgiving. The weekend became a wine country tradition, copied later by county winery groups all over the state.

The original nine wineries (Adelsheim, Amity, Arterberry, Chateau Benoit, Elk Cove, Erath, Eyrie, Hidden Springs, and Sokol Blosser) advertised together in Portland, Salem, and Seattle newspapers to lure people out to wine country. People were glad to get out of the house and show off Oregon's newest industry to visiting friends and relatives. As the number of participating wineries grew, so did the number of visitors and the popularity of wine touring.

"Wine Country Thanksgiving" became our biggest retail weekend of the year. After the initial years of welcoming visitors in our small tasting room, we had to move the event into the larger winery cellar to handle the crowds. We served food, offered tastes of all our wines, lowered prices for the weekend, displayed holiday gift baskets, and brought in neighboring farmers to sell their chocolate-covered hazelnuts, flavored honey, marionberry preserves, and Christmas swags and wreaths. Holiday greens, wooden lattice, and bright red poinsettias helped mask the production equipment of tanks, barrels, catwalks, and refrigeration pipe.

Sometimes I wondered what it would be like to go away for the Thanksgiving holidays, or to be free for shopping or whatever we felt like doing. It wasn't an option. Wine Country Thanksgiving was too important to our business, so we made it a family event and tried to make it fun. In the early years, Bill's mother, Grandma Betty, took charge of the tasting room kitchen, which was separated from the main space by a long counter on which she kept a large coffee urn for nondrinkers and designated drivers. She was adept at chatting with visitors while attending to her main job, slicing French bread to go with the cheese on the food platters. Tired of arm cramps from slicing baguettes to feed the increasing crowd, she showed up with a gift for the winery—an electric bread slicer. Bill's father, Grandpa John, helped pour wine, stopping occasionally to chat with former patients who were delighted to see one of their favorite doctors. Usually they wanted to hang out at John's table and talk, and we had to rescue him to keep the tasting line from backing up.

Nik, Alex, and Alison did whatever they were able to do, making change at the admissions table as soon as they were old enough, and later, when they were older and stronger, restocking wine, washing glasses, and carrying cases out for customers. Before we had a full-time bookkeeper, we made a custom each night of counting the day's take. We brought the small gray metal cash box home and gave the kids the honor of doing the counting. They sat on the floor in the living room and learned, at an early age, how to put the bills in order, all facing the same way, how to count the change, arrange the credit card receipts, and fill out the cash-box records.

We were always on the lookout for vineyard or winery projects we could tackle as a family so the kids could be involved. One year Grandma Betty showed us an advertisement in a Christmas catalog for a package of shredded grapevines to be used as smoke flavoring for the grill. She brought it as a curiosity, but teenage Nik seized on the idea, and NGB (his initials) Enterprises was born. He tackled the production side, and I agreed to help with the packaging. We would sell it in the tasting room.

Production started that February, as Nik and Alex (NGB Enterprises' first employee) pulled the vine prunings out of the vineyard rows. They kept the Pinot Noir and Chardonnay separate and transported the big piles of prunings down to the shed to dry out. Nik used the money he earned working at the winery to buy a shredder to shred the prunings to the right consistency. The shredded prunings, which we called Grapevine Smoke, dried in wooden totes until the family (free labor) could get together to bag, seal, and label our new product.

I got carried away designing the packaging. I pictured people grilling with Pinot Noir Grapevine Smoke and then drinking Pinot Noir with their meal, so I decided to package the smoke and the wine together, in a two-bottle wine box. This required putting the new product in a long, narrow, special-order plastic bag that, when filled, would be about the size of a wine bottle. And if there was to be a card for the directions (simple: soak in water before putting over the coals on the grill), why not print recipes on the other side? I found a woman to create recipes for both the Pinot Noir and the Chardonnay. When she tried out the two different Grapevine Smoke samples, she called to say, "I never would have guessed how striking the taste difference was between the Pinot Noir and Chardonnay smoke. It's amazing!"

The final step was to have a colorful label designed and printed. I spent more time on this project than I had intended and did all the running around, since Nik wasn't old enough to drive. But I enjoyed the challenge. We sold the individual bags in the tasting room and made up gift boxes with the wine and matching Grapevine Smoke.

The next year we decided to offer our new product to Norm Thompson, a Portland catalog company whose slogan was Escape from the Ordinary. Nik and I visited the Norm Thompson headquarters to pitch the new package we had devised—a slatted wooden crate containing one bag each of Pinot Noir Grapevine Smoke and Chardonnay Grapevine Smoke shrink-wrapped so that the products, labels, and recipe cards were clearly visible. To our delight, their buyer loved it and ordered one thousand boxes.

We had made only a hundred bags of each type of Grapevine Smoke the first year, but Nik and I jumped at the chance to be in the prestigious Norm Thompson catalog, and ignored the logistics of increasing production by a factor of ten. Production went into high gear. Every weekend the extended family gathered in the equipment shed to tackle the mounds of shredded, dried grapevine prunings. As the rain pounded on the metal roof, we ran our little assembly line and managed to keep our good humor, as long as we could see progress. I applied our fancy self-stick labels to the plastic bags, then Grandma Betty, Grandpa John, and Nik, in white dust masks, filled them with the Grapevine Smoke. Bill ran the temperamental hot sealer to close the bags. Alex put the bags in the crates so they could go to Portland for shrink-wrapping. Alison was too little to do much but play and get in the way. The final product was impressive and we were proud to see it in the catalog. Nik made enough money to buy himself a used car. But that was the end of the Grapevine Smoke caper. Nobody was willing to do it again.

Growing up around the winery meant a lot of watching Mom and Dad pour wine for customers, talk about the wine, and sell it. Kids are nothing if not imitators, so I guess it was natural for me to want to copy them and sell something to customers, too. Since the cherry trees on our farm happened to be in season, I decided cherries would be what I would sell. The tasting room was open only on weekends, so if I wanted to do this, it would mean giving up watching Saturday morning cartoons, but I decided getting up early to pick the fruit and pack it in the little green pint fruit cartons, ready to sell to customers, would be worth it. I was probably eight years old. I thought I had told Mom what I was planning but she looked surprised when she found me setting up shop at a picnic table outside the tasting room with my baskets of cherries and free samples.

Then, one May when I was nine years old, our local volcano, Mount Saint Helens, spewed ash across the western US. My brother and I took advantage of this opportunity, collected buckets of ash, put it in little plastic baggies, and sold them to visitors as genuine Mount Saint Helens ash souvenirs.

My next venture was "Grapevine Smoke." Mom had heard about using chopped up grapevines for barbecuing to add smoke flavoring. This ended up being our most complicated venture to date, with recipes, a chopping and bagging operation, and ultimately placement in a catalog for home chefs. The Grapevine Smoke business earned me enough money to buy my first car, after I was old enough to get my driver's license. The catalog company eventually stopped ordering, I went off to college, and I gave the car to my brother, who I felt had earned it from all his labor helping me.

Nik Blosser
Chairman of the Board, Sokol Blosser Winery

The Newport Seafood and Wine Festival, which took place in the city of Newport on the Oregon coast in February, was another family event. The Newport Chamber of Commerce started the festival in the early 1980s to lure people to the coast during the winter, and we supported it for many years, spending the weekend at a local motel. Bill's folks went along. John helped us pour wine while Betty entertained the three kids. She took them to the aquarium, the wax museum, and the beach. I know her job was harder than ours. Every morning, before the festival started, all of us went to a local restaurant famous for their poppy-seed pancakes. It was as close to a vacation as we got for many years.

With all the tastings, festivals, and wine dinners, we ran out of time and energy for any other social life. But we always took time for family. Besides holidays and birthday celebrations, we had regular breakfasts and dinners with Bill's parents, and then with mine after they moved to nearby McMinnville in 1980. My grandparents had all died before my birth, so I never knew what I had missed until I saw how much Bill's parents and mine enriched our kids' lives. My kids knew all four of their grandparents, stayed with them occasionally, and looked forward to being with them.

My mother, Phyllis, was the kind of person I would choose for a friend. Outgoing and opinionated, she was a woman with a lively and cultured intellect, imparting her views frankly and authoritatively. As her friend, I would have laughed when we disagreed. But as her daughter, I became defensive and shut down when I felt her criticism.

Bill's and my wedding exemplified my emotional quagmire as I got caught in the crosshairs of trying to please both my mother and my fiancé. Their power struggle became a battle of wills over whether Bill would wear the new suit he had bought for the occasion or the white dinner jacket my mother insisted was proper wedding attire. There was no bringing them together. Each was determined to win, Bill on principle, mother on propriety. She had an image in her mind of how her daughter's wedding should look. It never occurred to me that she may have wanted the wedding she had been denied, married during the Depression by a justice of the peace.

When Mother and I shopped for a wedding dress, she pointed to an extravagant dress with a long train. Bill had told me he didn't want a fancy wedding, explicitly requesting a dress with no train. I chose what I thought was a compromise, a simple linen wedding dress with a slightly elongated rear skirt, forming a mini train. It was too much for Bill and not enough for Mother. Such a small thing, but emotions ran high. Both were annoyed and I was miserable. In trying to find a middle ground, I had pleased neither.

The dress may have been what made Bill put his foot down on wearing his dark blue suit instead of a white dinner jacket. "I've given in on everything else," he told me. "Your mother's pushed me far enough. I'm going to take a stand on this one." Trying to please both, an impossible task, left me disheartened and depressed at a time that should have been joyful. Mother got my brothers to work on Bill and made sure a white jacket was rented so it would be ready when they succeeded, which she knew they would. I do not have good memories of either the wedding or reception, although my mother was thrilled with both and always spoke of it as the party of the century. My oldest brother's wife explained to me later: "Your mistake is that you thought this was your wedding."

When I had children, Mother wasn't shy about commenting on their behavior. If one of my kids did something she didn't approve of—was too clingy, interrupted someone, fussed at the dinner table—she would point it out, along with an example of someone whose kids were always well-behaved, usually one of my brothers. If she didn't like my hair or my outfit, she said so. She told me she was helping me be a better person, but it felt as if she were always telling me what to do. Her constant judgment and advice made me feel inadequate, or stupid, or both. Consequently, when I needed comfort, I went to Betty Blosser.

How lucky I was to have a mother-in-law who reversed the stereotype by being unfailingly encouraging and supportive. I could never decide whether she simply didn't see the things my mother was criticizing or saw them and just chose a positive approach. Betty Blosser treated me as though she thought I was the best thing that had happened to her son. She was intuitive about how people were feeling and what they needed. One year when Bill was out of town for my birthday and I was feeling forlorn and forgotten, she drove out, scooped me up with the kids, and took us out for a birthday dinner. It cheered me immensely and was typical of her thoughtfulness.

She had a knack for giving just the right present and continually amazed me with gifts I loved and hadn't thought of asking for. She would call me before Christmas to ask, "Do you think Nik is ready for his own tool set (or wagon or bicycle)?" Her ideas always entailed something that would encourage activity, motor skills, and creativity. Occasionally she did go over the top—like the Christmas she gave Nik and Alex yellow hard hats with built-in sirens and flashing lights on top. She was smart enough not to ask me in advance about those. The boys loved them and we couldn't wait for the batteries to run down.

Bill and his father were at their best when they were working on a project together, and, fortunately for their relationship, there seemed to be an inexhaustible supply of those. They didn't hesitate to take on big projects. One year they installed a fireplace in our house. Another year they built a twenty-foot flight of stairs off our deck.

Because my family, the Sokols, had invested financially in our project, when we were with my family, talk inevitably turned to winery finance. The kids enjoyed being with my parents, dubbed Grandma Phyllis and Grandpa Gus, but for me the financial issues always hovered in the air. After talking my brothers into investing and getting the winery started, my father faded into the background. Years later, we realized he had been entering the early stages of Alzheimer's—the disease that would turn my humorous, vibrant father into an empty shell of a person.

As my father seemed to slowly disappear, my brothers, who had never been enthusiastic about the winery, became reluctant and demanding investors. Ronnie, the youngest of the three, took Dad's place as the strategist and power broker. He lived in France, but even from a distance he exerted decisive influence. My mother and father trusted him totally and accepted his judgment on everything. As an attorney who had done major legal and financial work for my father's business, he saw himself as the protector of the family's investment.

Bill's ten-year financial forecasts, which had seemed conservative and reasonable at the time, predicted profitability in five years, by 1982. When the time came, we weren't even close. Selling Pinot Noir from a new wine region was considerably more difficult than anticipated. The general economic recession of the early 1980s dealt us a double wallop by depressing what sales we did have while simultaneously inflating interest rates. As president of the winery, Bill bore the brunt of the criticism from the Sokol family members who comprised the winery's board of directors. Although they recognized that the economy was in recession, my brothers felt misled because things hadn't turned out as Bill had predicted.

The implication was that if Bill had done a better job, the winery would be profitable. We were constantly on the defensive. It was a painful partnership for me, caught between my family and Bill. I had

When Bill returned from a sales trip to Maine, he brought back live lobsters and called me from the airport to start the kettle to cook them. It was such a special dinner for our family, we took time to photograph it for posterity. Note my long hair. When I managed the vineyard I let my hair grow. Alex later dubbed it my Mother Earth phase when he pointed out how my hairdos changed as my roles changed.

never been assertive with my older brothers and was easily shot down when I tried to defend Bill. And because this was my family, I couldn't feel the unmitigated rage that Bill felt at our predicament.

One reason the recession hit us so hard was that we were financed almost entirely by short-term debt. Bill and I had lobbied hard and succeeded in convincing the head of US Bank in McMinnville that we should get a long-term Small Business Administration (SBA) loan—almost unheard of for a winery at that time. Procuring the SBA loan ourselves, without having to rely on my father, had been an important step in freeing up the Sokol family money. The mountain of paperwork resulted in what we thought was a great deal—an interest rate of 3 percent over prime. When the prime rate rose from 7 percent to 20 percent, we choked on the payments. We couldn't stay in business very long paying 23 percent interest on most of our debt.

We needed to do something fast. The family stepped in and kept us in business. We paid off our ill-fated SBA loan by borrowing from a retirement plan my father, under Ronnie's guidance, had set up for my mother. While it saved the winery from going under, it only made matters worse with the family. We knew that somehow, as soon as we could, we had to relieve the Sokol family of winery ownership. We tried not to let tensions over business and finance get in the way of our family life or the kids' relations with their grandparents, but it was on our minds constantly and it was hard to keep the discomfort hidden. Relief came when two vineyard friends, Hyland Vineyards and Durant Vineyards, bought out my family. We had new partners, new optimism, and a measurable lessening of family tension.

———

ENJOYING OUR KIDS ALWAYS helped us forget the business problems. We made a point of having dinner together, and on winter evenings we played Uno or Monopoly, built Lego trucks and spacecraft, did jigsaw puzzles, or read stories aloud. When Bill read *Charlie and the Chocolate Factory*, one chapter each night, we all claimed favorite listening spots and looked forward to the next installment. Shel Silverstein's poems were another favorite, especially the one about Sarah Sylvia Cynthia Stout, who wouldn't take the garbage out. The kids, who by then had chores, could relate to that tale.

When I started working in the vineyard full-time, Bill suggested that he and I share the cooking duties, trading off weekly. It was a wonderful and welcome idea, which resulted in upgrading our meals, since neither of us wanted to be considered the lesser chef. Our dinners continued with our staple, macaroni and cheese, but ran the gamut from tuna casserole to a whole variety of dishes made with ground beef—tacos, spaghetti, or meatloaf—all homemade and often inventive. By that time, we were too busy with the vineyard and orchards to have a vegetable garden, but we did use the fruit from our orchards.

Nik and Alex were assigned chores too, which rotated weekly. Doing dishes and taking out garbage was one set of chores; washing, folding laundry, and setting the table was another. The rotation was posted on the refrigerator to take care of any "Oh, was this my week to set the table?" excuses. When we began, Alex had to stand on a chair to do the dishes. Later, Alison was added to the chore list, and the boys learned to cook dinner, using one of our cookbook staples in those days, Peg Bracken's I Hate to Cook Book. Maxie's Franks were a family favorite.

Enforcing the chores took a great deal of effort, including nagging, bribing, and demonstrating the consequences of failure. We kept at it and, for the most part, it worked. As teenagers, Nik and Alex composed a two-page mathematical calculation proving that we had worked them and their sister so ruthlessly that they had only two free hours a week. They presented it to us with great glee, showing no signs of being downtrodden.

— —

WITH MY TRAINING AND interest in education, I had started worrying, when Nik was still in diapers, about how good the school system was in our rural district. I attended budget committee meetings to get an idea of the school administration's priorities. After a short stint on the committee, I was elected to the school board. All but one of the other board members were men—prominent local farmers who spoke with authority but, I came to realize, really had no idea what they were doing. I served two terms over eight years, facing the same thorny policy and funding issues local school boards everywhere deal with. Our board hired two new superintendents, struggled annually to convince the voters to fund the school programs, implemented a Spanish-English bilingual program, tried to supplement the academic program for gifted students, and dealt with community turmoil over sex education in the schools and the salacious language in library books.

The school district, which covered fifty-nine square miles, contained only two hundred students. Kindergarten through grade twelve were housed in two red brick buildings a quarter mile apart along Ferry Street in Dayton. The grade school building housed the administrative offices. The junior high and high school had a berry field in front and a football field, encircled by a dirt track, in back. A large percentage of the students qualified for the free lunch program. The student body was not ethnically diverse, primarily Caucasian with about 20 percent Hispanic. The whole community turned out to cheer for sports, especially their state champion football team. Finishing high school was the goal for most students. Only a few went on to four-year colleges.

Long before he was tested, we suspected Nik would soon be bored by the meager supplemental programs that Dayton offered. It didn't seem like a big deal that he was reading in kindergarten, but it did cross my mind that it might be unusual for him to amuse himself when he stayed home sick from school by reading the encyclopedia and our small library of Time-Life science books. One night when Nik was still in elementary school, perhaps fourth grade, I came home from a school board meeting to find the house entirely dark and silent. I was startled to discover Bill in the living room, sitting upright, as still as a statue. "What happened?" I asked anxiously. Out of the darkness came his answer: "Nik beat me at chess."

We found opportunities for Nik to supplement his schooling and were rewarded when it was time for college and he was accepted by both Princeton and Stanford. After anguished indecision, he opted for Stanford, trusting that if it were good enough for his parents, it would be good for him too. He decided on a double major in English and aeronautical engineering. I told him combining those two would enable him to write instruction manuals that people could understand.

As the second child, Alex had to find his own niche. Not doing his chores helped him find it. When he was about ten, he missed the morning school bus because Bill had made him finish washing the dishes, which he had failed to do the night before. I had been out in the vineyard and returned to find Alex crying. "Mom," he pleaded, "drive me to school. I can't walk. I'm going to be late." My heart went out to him, but I knew I had to back up Bill. I suggested he ride his bike. Off he went down the hill, one miserable little boy, scared to go all alone, knowing he would have to cross a busy state highway in the course of the four-mile ride. After he left, Bill climbed in the truck and followed, out of sight, to make sure his son arrived safely.

I was watching for him when he pedaled into the driveway later that afternoon. "Mom," he panted after navigating our steep hill, "I did it! It wasn't so bad." He stopped and then announced triumphantly, "I think I'll ride my bike again tomorrow." That summer he joined a bicycle club and took long rides every weekend. At twelve he joined a racing team and got an underage work permit so he could work part-time repairing bikes at Tommy's Bike Shop in McMinnville.

As a teenager, Alex's specialty was track racing on the velodrome and he placed third in national competition among fifteen-year-olds the year he went. At his peak during the summer, he spent all his waking hours working at the bike shop, racing, working out, or eating. We would go out for a big family dinner and come home stuffed, but Alex would go straight to the cereal cabinet for more. He seemed to be solid muscle, and it was impossible to fill him up. I asked a professional photographer who had done work for the winery to photograph Alex at a race. I imagined Alex, someday in the future, patting his expanded girth and showing his kids this picture of his past glory. Indeed, when Alex had a home of his own and two boys, I was pleased to see the framed photo of him in prime racing condition hanging in the boys' room. I wonder what would have happened if I'd given in and driven him to school that day.

···

Bill's Meatloaf à la Gascogne

When we bought our vineyard land, we inherited five acres of Brooks prune plums, a specialty of the Willamette Valley. Extra-large and luscious, they are enjoyed both fresh and dried. When we had difficulty selling our harvest to the fresh market, we took what remained to a local processor to have them dried. One year, we ended up with fifty twenty-five-pound boxes of beautiful dried plums. We couldn't eat our way through them, but one night, as Bill was about to make his mother's standard meatloaf recipe, he decided to add some Gascon flair by adding some of our multitude of prunes. It didn't take long for our eagle-eyed boys to question the unexpected soft black lumps in the meatloaf. If they had been French, they might have accepted that prunes and meat were a classic culinary combination. But unused to such delicacies, they reacted with suspicion that their father had tried to sneak something over on them. "Yuck! What is this?" they cried. Bill confessed. The meatloaf was actually very good, and since then we have seen similar recipes in magazines and websites. Depending on your preference, you can either dice the prunes for chunks of fruit, or finely chop them with a blender or food processor for a subtler fruit accent. Pinot Noir would be a great accompaniment.

Makes 6 to 8 servings

> 1 cup fine dry bread crumbs
>
> ⅓ cup whole or two-percent fat milk
>
> 2 tablespoons butter
>
> 1 to 2 yellow onions, coarsely chopped
>
> 3 to 4 garlic cloves, minced
>
> 2 tablespoons Worcestershire sauce
>
> 1 tablespoon cider vinegar
>
> 2 teaspoons coarse sea salt

1¼ teaspoons freshly ground pepper
1½ pounds ground beef chuck
½ pound ground pork
⅔ cup pitted and diced dried prunes
2 large eggs
¼ cup chopped fresh flat-leaf parsley

Preheat the oven to 350°F.

Put the bread crumbs in a large bowl and stir in the milk. Set aside for a few minutes to allow the bread crumbs to soften.

In a skillet over medium heat, melt the butter. Add the onions and garlic and sauté until barely softened, about 3 minutes. Quickly stir in the Worcestershire sauce, vinegar, salt, and pepper. Transfer the onion mixture to the bowl with the moist bread crumbs and stir until blended.

Add the ground beef, ground pork, and diced prunes to the onion-bread crumb mixture, then add the eggs and parsley. Using clean hands, gently but thoroughly mix the ingredients until evenly distributed (you don't want to mix too vigorously or the meatloaf will be tough).

Press the mixture into a standard 5-by-9-inch loaf pan and set in a larger baking dish (to catch any overflow of the juices). Bake until the meatloaf is firm, about 1¼ hours. Depending on the fat content of the meats, the meatloaf may exude a lot of juice while it is cooking. If desired, use a turkey baster to remove the excess juice.

Remove the meatloaf from the oven and let stand for 10 to 15 minutes. Unmold and slice the meatloaf, if desired, or cut slices directly from the pan. Serve hot.

CHAPTER THREE

Oregon Vineyards Multiply

By the mid-1980s, there were four thousand acres of wine grapes planted and fifty Oregon wineries. Very few had tried national distribution, so Oregon wines were still relatively unknown in other parts of the country. We started national sales with a well-known Burgundy importer, Robert Haas, who confessed, when we first met him in the late 1970s, that he hadn't yet tasted a domestic Pinot Noir he liked. We watched his face as he tasted ours, and when he started nodding as he swirled it in his mouth, we smiled with relief. Bob Haas's firm, Vineyard Brands, placed our wine across the country, in boutique wine stores and expensive restaurants. We were thrilled. But we quickly learned that an Oregon wine had no cachet in Manhattan, Boston, Washington, DC, or Chicago. It sat on the shelves.

When we were speaking to people about our wine, Bill and I routinely had to pull out a map of the United States to point out Oregon as the state north of California. On one trip, Bill was on a panel with Bernard Portet, the iconic winemaker for Clos Du Val, one of Napa's star wineries. Bernard was considered one of the best winemakers of the time. While Bill and Bernard were waiting for the panel to begin, Bill leaned over to Bernard. "I understand why I'm here," he said. "No one has ever heard of Sokol Blosser or Oregon. But why are you here? Everyone knows you." Bernard's reply showed wisdom we were just learning. "I'm here precisely because of people like you," he replied. "People will forget me as soon as a hot new winery comes along." We had assumed that once Sokol Blosser wine was known and enjoyed, sales would continue on their own and we wouldn't have to pound the pavement quite so hard. Bernard's comment was a lesson we would learn again and again over the years—there was no finish line. We had to continually keep up our presence in the market. Sales and marketing would always be a challenge.

In September 1985, a special promotion set up by the Oregon Wine Advisory Board (WAB) became one of the Oregon industry's defining moments. Oregon's WAB had been created by the legislature in 1984, at the urging of Oregon winegrowers, to do wine marketing and wine-grape research. Its funding came from the industry, in the form of a small per-gallon tax on bottled wine and a per-ton tax on Oregon grapes. The WAB policy-making board, selected by the Director of the Oregon Department of Agriculture, was composed of vineyard and winery people from the major wine areas in the state. Bill was one of the first board members.

The board gave the responsibility for wine-grape research to Oregon State University's Food Science and Horticulture Departments, creating a focus on grapes and wine that had, until then, been negligible at the university. Members of WAB directed the marketing side themselves, hiring outside public-relations people to help. One of the first ploys of their new public-relations consultant, Fred Delkin, was to set up a special tasting of Oregon Pinot Noir in New York City. This was the first time the Oregon wineries had collaborated to promote themselves on a national scale.

Fred had convinced the International Wine Center in New York City to host a taste-off between French Burgundy and Oregon Pinot Noir of the 1983 vintage. About ten of the best Burgundies and fifteen of the finest Oregon Pinot Noirs were selected for tasting. Invitations went out to the top sommeliers, wine retailers, and wine writers in the New York area. It would be a blind tasting, and that idea was seductive to people who prided themselves on their discriminating palates. Attendees were asked to taste, indicate whether they thought each wine was from Burgundy or Oregon, and then rank their top five favorites.

Shortly before Bill went off to New York for the tasting, in September 1985, he and I walked through the vineyard wondering whether we should even bother to harvest our Pinot Noir. Selling Pinot Noir was such a struggle. Priced at $7.95 a bottle, we figured we had a three-year supply at the current rate of sales. We decided to wait until he returned to revisit our options.

A betting person would have put their money on a French sweep. And they would have lost. To the astonishment of the tasters, when the wines were revealed, the top five favorites were all from Oregon. Both of the top two had been made with grapes at Sokol Blosser, one by us and the other by another winery just starting, Yamhill Valley Vineyards. The tasters had the grace to admit that they simply could not distinguish the French Burgundy from the Oregon Pinot Noir. This was before social media, but the buzz of the results could be heard from coast to coast. There was no question about going ahead with the harvest.

The winery phone started ringing. Wine-tasting groups all over the country wanted to re-create the New York City tasting to prove to themselves that Oregon's showing in New York wasn't a fluke. It wasn't. Groups in Chicago, Washington DC, Detroit, Dallas, Atlanta, St. Louis, Seattle, and San Francisco ordered wine, held tastings, and reported similar results. We sold out of our three-year supply of Pinot Noir in three months.

After the lauded 1983 vintage, the wine world eagerly awaited the next year's wine. Unfortunately, Oregon's 1984 vintage, because of the monster rain during harvest, was a disaster. Many concluded that the success of Oregon's 1983 vintage was just a lucky one-time shot. But when the stellar 1985 vintage appeared, Oregon's fragile reputation started rebuilding. The 1985 vintage ranks as one of Oregon's greatest. I still dream about Sokol Blosser's 1985 Red Hills Pinot Noir, though it is long gone and I haven't tasted it in years. It combined, in a magnificent way, two qualities I love in a Pinot Noir, earthiness and elegance.

———

BY 1985, THE WINE industry had become prominent enough locally that community groups and chambers of commerce were looking for ways to use it to promote their interests. As the largest town in the area, with the most active civic groups, McMinnville acted first and the International Pinot Noir Celebration (IPNC) was born. Preliminary financing came from a group of prominent local businessmen—the past presidents of the McMinnville Chamber of Commerce—who saw the event as an economic development project to promote their city. The newly formed McMinnville Downtown Association wanted to help because it saw opportunity to promote the historic downtown. The local wineries were willing to be involved because the event positioned them well. Even the State of Oregon got involved by providing an economic development grant to promote the Oregon wine industry and help the local economy. The genius of the project was in how well the event, which focused on a single wine, was thought through and positioned by the IPNC founding board members.

The founding board decided that only principals—owners or winemakers—from the best Pinot Noir wineries all over the world, but especially from Burgundy, California, and Oregon, would be invited to show their wines. Most wine/food events at the time were held at resorts and fancy hotels. Ours would be held among the old oaks on the beautiful, serene campus of Linfield College in McMinnville. It would be a celebration, with camaraderie, not a competition, a key issue with the French who still fumed over the New York tasting. Well-known chefs would be invited to create fabulous meals to go with Pinot Noir. The program would include tastings and seminars—enough education to make serious wine drinkers happy but not so much as to dampen the mood—as well as four- and five-course luncheons and dinners. Attendees would be an equal mix of wine-loving consumers and members of the wine trade. The event would be limited to 350 attendees and 100 winery principals, so that attendees could enjoy quality time with the winery owners and winemakers.

We knew the concept was good. But before offering it to the public, we had to convince the right wineries from California and Burgundy to participate. We put together an honorary board so we could list their names, which were well-known, instead of ours, which weren't, on our stationery. People like English wine writer Serena Sutcliffe, Oregon Governor Neil Goldschmidt, and prominent Burgundian wine figure Robert Drouhin agreed to lend their names. Then the local winemakers who had contacts in California and abroad prevailed on their cohorts to participate. The original idea was to make the event truly international by rotating the venue among Oregon, France, and California. But after the first few years, both the California and the Burgundian participants told us we should keep it in Oregon. They told us they weren't up to the organizational challenge it presented.

As the planning progressed in 1986 and got more complex, I realized the IPNC would sink under the weight of its vision if it didn't have a point person. I offered to organize the event if the organization would pay me. The board agreed, and the McMinnville Chamber of Commerce offered me working space in its unused basement. During that first summer, I'd bring seven-year-old Alison with me to help stuff envelopes in the cool of the empty basement while I methodically answered the phone, processed registrations, recruited volunteers, and worried about finances.

I couldn't have done it alone and the International Pinot Noir Celebration was really run by volunteers for almost ten years. McMinnville's most prominent citizens stepped up and pitched in anonymously. Watching the attendees' water glasses filled by McMinnville's mayor, bank president, fire chief, and county sheriff never failed to make me smile. IPNC's first board chairman was the head of the local Hewlett-Packard plant, and his Hewlett-Packard engineers devised the intricate logistics for moving the correct allotment of the two hundred cases of wine to various campus destinations for tastings, workshops, and meals.

The event grew into its name, and after a few years, we no longer needed an honorary board to give us credibility. The IPNC played a crucial role for the industry by bringing the right people to Oregon wine country and positioning Oregon as a mecca for Pinot Noir lovers. Over the years, the board of directors considered doubling the event, moving it to another venue, or duplicating it and taking it on the road. None of these things happened. It remained a low-key event on a college campus in McMinnville, Oregon, where attendees rubbed elbows with winemakers and the food and wine were otherworldly.

Bill was one of the founding members of the IPNC board. After being the director for several years, I remained on the board for a time. Twenty-five years after its debut, the annual IPNC weekend was still selling out and my son, Alex, was its president. Was this polished young man welcoming the international crowd and opening the event the same little boy I found taking his nap in the sandbox after playing with his Tonka trucks until he could no longer keep his eyes open? Shivers of passing time spun down my spine.

One of the key players in developing the IPNC concept and directing its emphasis toward food as well as wine was Nick Peirano, whose local restaurant played an important role in my life from the time it opened. Nick's Italian Café served as an oasis for Bill and me, while also educating our palates by introducing us to authentic Northern Italian cuisine. Nick's, as it came to be known, opened in McMinnville in 1977, the same year Sokol Blosser Winery produced its first vintage. Started by two friends, Nick Peirano and John West, it was ahead of its time and an oddity in McMinnville, where the 1977 restaurant roster included Oriental Gardens, the Blue Moon tavern, Tommy's Coffee Shop, and the counter at Thrifty Drug. The fast-food giants hadn't yet discovered the area, but there were no white-tablecloth restaurants either. Nick and John took over an old coffee shop, Café Dinette, but didn't have the funds to do more than paint the interior. So we sat in worn turquoise plastic booths or at the counter on low backless bar stools and ate exquisite food. I remember how excited we were for Nick's when they were able to replace the turquoise plastic with more upscale brown Naugahyde.

Going to Nick's Italian Café for dinner became the prize Bill and I awarded ourselves for surviving another month. Always just the two of us, we considered Nick's the oasis in our hectic lives. From the moment we opened the door and were enveloped in the scent of roasted garlic and fresh bread, to the last luscious mouthful of chocolate-hazelnut torte, Nick's was a familiar and well-loved ritual. Besides the entertainment of working our way through the prix fixe menu of five courses, dinner at Nick's was our chance to talk about things that mattered, to lay out strategies for the winery, to talk about the kids, and just to be together. We made more than a few key decisions over dinner at Nick's.

Over the years, Nick's played a significant role in our culinary education. Julia Child had introduced us to gourmet cooking, and we had been to several fancy restaurants around the country. But the "farm-to-table" food scene hadn't yet developed. It was a revelation to dine in a restaurant that served splendid meals using just-picked produce and premium ingredients, without being expensive or pretentious. The waitstaff and sous chefs, competent and friendly, were local people we knew on a first name basis.

The Italian restaurants of that time specialized in spaghetti and meatballs, always in a tomato sauce. The spaghetti came from a box—nobody in our region took the time and expense to make their own pasta—the Parmesan cheese from a can. In contrast, Nick's signature minestrone soup with basil pesto and hand-grated Parmesan, and his house-made hazelnut-mushroom lasagna, or cheese ravioli, enlivened our sensibilities with their extraordinary flavors. Nick's was on the cutting edge of an upscale eating trend, and we had the good fortune to ride the wave with him. What synchronicity that the rise of delicious, high-quality restaurant food and wine intertwined as Nick's and the Oregon wine industry gained fame together. Nick's Italian Café became known throughout the country as the place to eat in Oregon wine country.

One night we made what turned out to be an irrevocable decision—we took the kids with us to Nick's. They had been begging us for some time to take them with us. Nik was fourteen, Alex eleven, and Alison five. They were on their best behavior all evening. They'd never been to a dinner with so many courses. Alison, when she got so tired and full she couldn't stay awake, quietly climbed down, lay under the table, and went to sleep like a little puppy. Bill and I looked at each other across the table and knew we had come to the end of one era and the beginning of another—our children's foray into the wonderful world of fine food. From then on, Nick's became a whole family event.

———

IN THOSE DAYS, BUSINESS, family, and social life were so jumbled as to be inseparable. Wine even seeped into our escapist reading. Bill and I both liked mysteries and eagerly awaited every new mystery by Bostonian Robert B. Parker (not to be confused with Robert M. Parker, of *The Wine Advocate*). Food and wine figured prominently with his protagonist, Spencer, his girlfriend, Susan, and best friend, Hawk. Sometimes recipes were included and wines mentioned. Bill admired Spencer's epicurean taste until the book he was reading declared that the best Pinot Noir came from California. Not willing to let this go unanswered, Bill wrote to Parker suggesting that, while Spencer normally had an impeccable palate, somehow he went wrong on Pinot Noir, as the best Pinot Noir really came from Oregon. Parker invited Bill to send him a few bottles which he quickly did. No word back. Then *A Catskill Eagle* came out in 1985 in which our winery is mentioned by name and the character Hawk echoes Bill's statement that Oregon produces the best Pinot Noir.

This would have been enough for us, but there was more. Eight years later, Parker mentioned Sokol Blosser Pinot Noir again, in his book *Paper Doll*. It was a poignant reference made by the hero, isolated in a small jail cell, thinking about things he loved, including Sokol Blosser Pinot Noir. That same year, Robert M. Parker, the famous wine critic and publisher of *The Wine Advocate*, awarded Sokol Blosser Pinot Noir an outstanding score, finishing his review with "Bravo!" This synchronicity was too good to let pass. I sent around an announcement with the headline "Published Parkers Praise Sokol Blosser Pinot Noir" and quoted segments from both.

———

OUR HOME AND VINEYARD were considered to be in rural Dayton, but we were actually right in between the small farming town of Dayton, which had been bypassed by a major state highway, and the small farming town of Dundee, which still had a major state highway running through it. Both were quiet little communities until the wine industry reinvented them as wine country destinations.

Dundee's hillsides, which sloped down to the highway, had been dotted with prune plums, hazelnuts, walnuts, and cherries. They were converted rather swiftly into wine grapes. The old prune and nut dryer that had dominated the town's main street became Argyle Winery. The Nite Hawk truck stop morphed first into Pinot Pete's wine deli, then Tina's, one of little Dundee's three white-tablecloth restaurants catering to winery visitors. Finding itself strategically located in the center of the growing wine industry, Dundee became, as an Associated Press writer christened it, "the epicenter of the Oregon wine industry."

By that time, the earliest winery hangout had closed, but it deserves a mention because of its role in our lives. In the early 1980s, Alice's Restaurant, a small concrete block building serving breakfast and lunch, became the place for meetings or a welcome respite from work. We'd pull into Alice's, which shared a parking lot with the tiny Dundee Post Office in the middle of Dundee, and park our dusty vineyard pickup along with all the other dust covered vehicles. We could tell, from all the cars and trucks, that the restaurant was hopping and Bubbles the waitress was hustling out Alice's breakfast burritos and signature salsa hash brown potatoes, or one of her special hamburgers with hand-cut french fries.

I don't know what possessed Alice to start her restaurant, since she said what she really wanted to do all her life was become an airline stewardess, but she created a much-needed niche in the local wine community—a friendly, casual place to meet. Her decision to specialize in hamburgers named for the small towns in Yamhill County provided the right local touch and, if the menu wasn't cutting edge, it was satisfying. We relaxed over an Amity Amigo hamburger with green chiles, salsa, and cheese, or the Monmouth Mouthful, a double cheeseburger with bacon and a fried egg, or the basic Dundee Dandy, which came with just lettuce, tomato, and pickle. In total, ten local towns had burgers named after them. I know if Alice's were still in Dundee, her menu would have been updated. She might be featuring a Vintner's Vegetarian burger, and the Amity Amigo might be black bean rather than beef based.

By the end of the decade, Alice decided she was finally ready to pursue her childhood dream and closed the restaurant to start flight attendant training. We were sorry to see Alice's close, and appreciated that she had provided a springboard for Dundee's culinary future. The founders of both Tina's and Red Hills Provincial worked for Alice before starting their own upscale eateries.

Dick and Nancy Ponzi notched Dundee's culinary scene higher in 1999 when they built a small complex in the center of town to house both a wine tasting room and a restaurant, the Dundee Bistro. Jody and Michelle Kropf opened the Red Hills Market in 2011, modeled on the popular Oakville Grocery in Napa. Both places became wine industry meeting spots, as well as dining destinations for hungry tourists. Dundee got its first hotel in 2011, the Inn at Red Hills, at the west end of Dundee. No longer sleepy, Dundee's main street flourished with the wine industry.

As the main route from Portland to the Oregon central coast, truck and tourist traffic through Dundee got worse with every good wine write-up. Attempts to move traffic off the main street with a bypass around the town were in the works for forty years before a solution was finally approved, funded, and built to open in 2017.

Dayton, on the other hand, located on the flat along the Yamhill River, remained undiscovered except for its famous restaurant, the Joel Palmer House. Jack and Heidi Czarnecki came to Oregon in the 1990s with the dream of combining their mushroom hunting and culinary skills with fine dining and local wines. They opened their restaurant in a historic house, built by Joel Palmer, one of Oregon's prominent pioneers of the mid-nineteenth century. Palmer had traveled on the Oregon Trail in 1845, was active in frontier government, and was notable in my mind for being one of the few who treated the Native Americans fairly. I read a biography of him and was so impressed that in honor of the Oregon Trail Sesquicentennial in 1993, I made a special Pinot Noir bottling with Joel Palmer's picture on the label. Palmer's great-great-grandson heard about it and bought our whole production.

Dayton's renaissance began when its native son, Bill Stoller, became its patron. The son of one of the local turkey-growing brothers, Bill eschewed the turkey business, moved away, and found success building a temporary personnel business. He subsequently came back to his roots to start a vineyard and bought out his uncle's turkey farm, right across from the rented house in which Bill and I lived when we first started. The hillsides, rich with years of turkey manure, made Stoller vineyards green and lush.

Nearby Dayton was blessed with a historic and picturesque town square, full of potential but neither funds nor leadership to lift itself out of its run-down state until Bill bought up the buildings around the square and started redevelopment.

Soon, the idea of a wine country inn surfaced in the chamber of commerce, which argued that wine tourists to our area would enjoy staying in a luxury inn nestled among the vineyards, taking their meals in a gourmet restaurant, while surrounded by the vineyards' natural beauty. As early as the 1980s, Tony Meeker, Yamhill County's representative in the Oregon Senate, procured funds for a feasibility study. The conclusion was that there was not enough demand or traffic to wine country for a luxury inn to succeed.

The idea resurfaced after the turn of the century with a proposal by Portland developers to build a luxury inn in the Dundee Hills. In order to proceed, promoters of an inn would have to get a variance from the existing laws, which protected farmland from development. David Lett's son, Jason, continued his father's fight to preserve farmland for agriculture and fought the proposal. Sokol Blosser joined him.

The idea of an inn appealed to us, but we felt it needed to be within the urban growth boundary, not on potential vineyard land. The Dundee Hills had become the Côte D'Or of Oregon wine country. We argued that the highest and best use of hillside land was vineyards, not urban amenities, saying: "Do you want to kill the goose that laid the golden egg? Once you start urbanizing farmland, there's no going back. That's why we have land use laws."

While we were fighting the inn proposed for the Dundee Hills, the Austin family in Newberg, known for their philanthropy, proposed a housing development, anchored by a luxury wine country inn, to be located just outside of Newberg, but within its urban growth boundary. The inn was Joan Austin's dream, a gift to the place that had given rise to her successful business, A-dec Dental Equipment. I spoke out in favor of this project, knowing that whatever the Austins did would be done well. The upscale Allison Inn & Spa opened its doors in 2009 to rave reviews and bookings beyond expectations. It quickly became the pride of Yamhill County.

....

Nick's Minestrone

This soup from Nick's Italian Café became legendary in Oregon wine country in the 1970s, and has been featured in national food magazines over the years. Joan Drabkin, who worked with Nick in the restaurant kitchen in the early years and was the first Culinary Director of the International Pinot Noir Celebration (IPNC), took Nick's family recipe and tailored it for the home cook. The most important component of this soup is the long-simmered broth, which takes a full day to develop its deep flavor. You'll need to plan ahead. It makes a good weekend project for a summer cool day. Pinot Noir, of course, is the right wine with this delicious soup.

Makes 12 servings

For the broth
    4 carrots, diced
    4 celery stalks, diced
    2 green bell peppers, diced
    2 yellow onions, diced
    1 cup flat-leaf parsley leaves, finely chopped

6 garlic cloves, minced

1-pound chunk of salt pork

One 14-ounce can diced tomatoes

½ cup tomato paste

¼ cup beef stock base

4 tablespoons dried basil, crushed

1 tablespoon freshly ground black pepper

1 tablespoon dried rosemary, crushed

1 tablespoon dried oregano, crushed

For the pesto

2 cups fresh basil leaves (or half basil leaves, half flat-leaf parsley leaves)

6 to 8 cloves garlic

1 cup mixed freshly grated Parmesan and pecorino Romano cheese

3 tablespoons olive oil

Kosher salt

1 pound carrots, sliced

1 pound fresh or frozen green beans, chopped

12 ounces shelled fresh or frozen green peas

Freshly grated Parmesan or pecorino Romano cheese for passing
at the table (optional)

To make the broth, in a large pot, combine the diced carrots, celery, bell peppers, onions, parsley, garlic, salt pork, and 3 quarts water. Set over high heat and bring the liquid just to a boil, then reduce the heat to medium-low, cover, and simmer until the soup has a deep flavor and rich auburn color, about 6 hours.

Remove the salt pork from the broth and transfer it to a food processor; keep the broth at a simmer. Process the salt pork until finely chopped. Place a fine mesh sieve over the broth pot and pour in the chopped salt pork. Using a large metal spoon, push the salt pork through the strainer into the liquid. Using the spoon, repeatedly skim the liquid until all the fat has been removed from the surface. Discard the fat. Add the tomatoes, tomato paste, beef stock base, basil, pepper, rosemary, and oregano to the broth and bring the liquid back to a simmer. Simmer, covered, over low heat, until the vegetables have almost disintegrated, at least 2 more hours. (If you're not finishing the soup right away, let the broth cool completely, then transfer it to a storage container and refrigerate or freeze until you're ready to serve.)

To make the pesto, in a food processor, combine the basil and garlic and process until finely chopped. Add the cheeses and process briefly just to combine. With the machine running, add the olive oil, 1 tablespoon at a time, until it forms a thick paste. Stir in salt to taste. Transfer the pesto to a bowl, cover, and refrigerate until serving time, up to 1 day in advance.

When you are ready to serve the soup, if you've made the broth ahead of time, pour it into a clean pot. Bring the broth just to a boil over high heat. Reduce the heat to low so that the liquid just simmers. Add the sliced carrots, green beans, and peas and simmer until the vegetables are soft, about 30 more minutes.

Ladle the soup into bowls and garnish each bowl with about 2 tablespoons of the pesto. Pass extra cheese at the table, if desired.

CHAPTER FOUR

Vision, Heartache, Love

The Christmas holidays of 1990 found us in Seaside, on the Oregon Coast, in a large rented house with the extended family. We were ten—Bill's parents, his sister Taffy, his Aunt Dottie, my mother, Bill and me, and our three kids—plus our dog, Bagel. We bought the last tree in the local Christmas tree lot and decorated it with colorful paper cutouts. We played charades and Trivial Pursuit, gorged on local Dungeness crab accompanied by Sokol Blosser Riesling for Christmas dinner, and shopped the post-Christmas sales. When we weren't with the family, Bill and I took Bagel and walked on the beach. We were in a serious, ongoing discussion about the challenges facing us and the winery and what we should do.

The general recession of the late 1980s, with its deadly combination of skyrocketing interest rates and sluggish wine sales, took Sokol Blosser Winery to a crisis point. Strapped for cash, we cut back, using our tasting room staff to process the grapes. Along with the winery's financial distress, Bill's and my personal standard of living had slipped over the past ten years. Every year we had tightened our belts a little more. The pinch was getting unbearable.

"One of us needs to get a real job," I told Bill. In December 1990, it had been ten years since Bill had taken over as president. "We can't go on like this," I continued, feeling I had finally put into words what I'd been feeling for way too long.

"You could go back to teaching high school social studies," Bill suggested. I stopped walking and looked at him, trying to decide if that was a quip or if he was serious. It wasn't just the ocean wind that made him squint. Bill was drained, beaten down from confronting one obstacle after another for the past decade. A pang of guilt swept over me. I should do more; I should be the one to get another job.

"Yes, I guess I could," I said, but going back to teaching was a terrible thought. I had been a teacher and had only to renew my teaching certificate to begin working again, but my heart felt heavy just thinking about creating lesson plans, grading illegible papers, and trying to keep control of a roomful of high school students whose hormones were on fast-forward while their brains were on hold.

Then I recognized something else that lurked in a corner of my heart. After being the decision maker for the vineyard for ten years, I realized that I liked working for myself and I loved the vineyard. It wasn't less work. Being the boss made me work harder, feeling I had to set an example. But I chafed at the thought of working for someone else. Also, annoying as it was, I recognized that Bill would command a much higher salary in the marketplace than I could. It made more sense for him to get an outside job.

"Would you consider going back to planning?" I asked. He raised his eyebrows at my suggestion; I thought I saw a flicker of hope in his expression.

"Yes," he said, sounding surprised at his answer. We had been standing alone on the windswept beach, facing each other during those three minutes of conversation. A moment of silence hung between us as we each let our words sink in. Then, as if a lightbulb went off, the conversation suddenly took a 180-degree turn and the solution fell into place, a surprise neither of us could have predicted.

A week later, on January 2, 1991, Bill announced, at a hastily called meeting with our partners, that I would take over as president of Sokol Blosser Winery. The decision was sudden, although Bill's leaving wasn't unexpected. They knew how burned out he was. The surprise was my taking over, and our partners turned to me with new eyes, curious and wary. They knew me as a vineyard manager; winery president implied a shift in focus and priorities. What won them over was that I was willing to work for half Bill's salary, far less than if they had hired an experienced person. Equally important was that Bill and I owned half of the business and if we were willing to put the winery's future in my hands, they would go along. They would keep me on a short leash.

In this way, I got a job for which I would never otherwise have been hired. My degree was for teaching, not business, an MAT not an MBA. Hiring me may not have been the best business decision, but it was my chance and I grabbed it. I don't know what made me think I could run a business, especially one as troubled as ours. But finally passionate about our enterprise, I found myself eager to jump into the mess I had inherited. As a woman, my position as president of Sokol Blosser was virtually unique at the time.

Women traditionally took on support roles in the wine industry, as in most agricultural and processing enterprises in the late twentieth century. This doesn't diminish the hard work and importance to the development of the Oregon wine industry of women like Nancy Ponzi, Diana Lett, Ginny Adelsheim, Pat Campbell, or Kina Erath. Each one worked tirelessly and had significant input at their respective vineyards and wineries. But they were not the first-string players, not the decision makers.

Wives were the bench players, husbands the starters. The bench players were critical to winning the game, but the focus was on the guys. While the early pioneers were talked about as couples, the media photographed and interviewed the husbands. The wives appeared in family photos and not much was said about who they were. It was a sign of the times. Gender roles were just starting to evolve.

But behind the scenes, they were enterprising, talented, and hardworking. Kina Erath devoted herself to working tirelessly in the vineyard while raising her two boys. Diana Lett used her writing and marketing skills to promote Eyrie Winery. Ginny Adelsheim, a professional artist, created a series of drawings for the Adelsheim Vineyard labels, as well as the winery's terra cotta ornamentation. Nancy Ponzi started teaching yoga, wine appreciation, and culinary classes before moving full-time into marketing Ponzi wines and serving on wine industry boards. Years later, Bill admitted the founders looked at themselves as a men's club. Proving the point, Dick Erath entitled his memoir, *The Boys Up North*. That the wives were invisible was typical for the era, before the women's movement changed the playing field. I resented it and relished the challenge of becoming president, thankful to be given the chance to be a female decision maker in a mostly male industry. My three older brothers had taught me to be at ease with men and I considered it a test, as a woman, to succeed in the male-dominated wine world.

There was no transition period. After a brief respite, Bill went back to work in Portland at CH2M HILL, the large engineering-planning firm he had left ten years earlier to work full-time at the winery. They were glad to have him back and referred to his decade away as his sabbatical. Reenergized, Bill soon rose to become head of the firm's Portland office.

On January 3, as I sat in the former president's chair and looked around Bill's former office, I realized I now had power, but little knowledge. I didn't know where anything was and spent my first days looking through drawers and file cabinets to see what was there. Bill had handed me the key, then disappeared. He may have been waiting for me to call for advice, but I never did.

As I moved up from bench player to starter, a dormant entrepreneurial drive I didn't know I had surfaced from deep inside, spurring me on. Petrified but exhilarated, I took over the presidency of Sokol Blosser Winery at age forty-six, slowly growing into my role. Now, I look back with wonderment. This was something I never imagined doing. Not that I didn't have wild dreams, but running a vineyard and winery was never in the mix. I was not a farm girl, a wine geek, or a businessperson.

From the moment I took the president's chair, I saw problems that needed immediate attention in every part of the operation. They reminded me of the boulders that bubbled up in the vineyard soil unexpectedly and had to be moved to prevent equipment problems. Yet they worked beautifully for landscaping. That tired cliché "Turn lemons into lemonade" was my mantra as I confronted operational boulders and looked for ways to make them work for us. In 1987, our vineyard friends who owned Hyland Vineyards and Durant Vineyards had bought out my father's and brothers' shares of the winery. This was a huge relief for Bill and me. We entered our partnership with great optimism for the future. But what had started with such promise began to disintegrate after several years. As 50-percent owners, they had the right to provide 50 percent of the grapes for each harvest, and to take part in setting the price for those grapes. That price could be, and often was, higher than the general market. Their interest in winery ownership was to send any profit back to the vineyards; ours was to invest in the winery and build the brand. Our interests had ceased to be aligned.

For two years we sent profits back to our partner vineyards through an elaborate bottle-pricing formula, but then we had years without profits. Our outside accountant made us realize that we had given away our profits in the good years but weren't getting comparable concessions from the vineyards in the bad years. The tough years without profit fueled conflict among us as, I am sure, did lack of faith in my management. By late 1991, Hyland was looking for someone to buy its shares, and my relations with the Durant and Hyland owners could best be described as civilized but hostile. I know that Bill, commuting to Portland, was glad to be removed from the turmoil.

At that time, Alex and Alison were riding to Portland with Bill to attend a private school, so Bill suggested we move to the city. I could commute to the vineyard. When Bill first floated this idea, I was horrified at the thought of moving away from the vineyard, even though it did make sense since three of the four of us still at home had to be in Portland all day. Since I no longer worked in the vineyard itself, and had meetings in Portland more and more often, it was a logical move. Once settled in an apartment in the heart of downtown Portland, I quickly realized the advantages. Two blocks from Nordstrom's and near our favorite downtown restaurants, our apartment overlooked the city's Park Blocks, which were full of big old trees, grass, and flowerbeds. We got used to hearing sirens and street sweepers at night instead of coyotes and crickets. I didn't even mind the forty-five-minute commute. In many ways, it was a relief to get physically away from work.

During this difficult time, while I was learning to manage the winery and the estate vineyards, cope with poor sales and excess inventory, refinance debt, and deal with the supplier-owner problem, I relied on our outside accountant, Jack Irvine, to help me think things through. More than once, I called him in total frustration, angry with myself for not knowing what to do. He kept telling me to think of how the pearl in an oyster grows—by friction against a grain of sand within the shell. He told me to think of myself as the potential pearl and Hyland and Durant as the grains of sand, and that in years to come I would value that friction for the toughness it gave me.

I sure needed that toughness, if only to cover my insecurity. I wished I could toss off numbers with the aplomb of an MBA, but my eyes glazed over discussing ratios. Whenever I was asked for a number, I had to look it up. At more than one board meeting I was close to tears as the partners treated my lack of financial savvy with sarcasm and disdain. Bill stayed silent, letting me fend for myself. I imagined myself donning a football helmet before board meetings, and I'd call Jack and tell him I needed my chinstrap tightened and a pep talk. At each new meeting, I was a little better prepared, but I still went into every one feeling alone and vulnerable.

While difficulties with our partners took up a good deal of emotional time, my daily priorities were to motivate my staff, get sales moving, and generate some cash. I knew I couldn't turn the tide alone and took the five key people in production, sales, and accounting off for a two-day retreat to explain our plight and plan our strategy. They had not understood how deep a financial hole we were in, and I could see both concern and determination on their faces when I asked them to help. Each contributed to the plan, and its impact was immediately apparent as employee morale lifted and cash from the sale of excess inventory started flowing in.

The second priority was to refinance the winery's debt. The bank we were with surprised us by calling our loan. We were baffled since we had never missed a payment, then found out the bank was positioning itself for sale by divesting its loan portfolio. While I looked for a new bank, Jack Irvine negotiated a write-down of our existing bank loan to make us look more financially appealing to a potential new bank partner. I contacted the Portland banks that worked with other wineries, but never got past the receptionist. When I mentioned our predicament to Andy Sichler, who headed the local McMinnville branch of KeyBank, he invited me in to talk. At that time, KeyBank had no wineries or vineyards in its loan portfolio—the field was considered too risky. I wrote up a straightforward overview of the winery, explaining the difficult position we were in, the reasons for it, and my plan for climbing out. Andy convinced KeyBank to refinance us. I was determined they wouldn't regret their decision and Andy told me later he never doubted I would do what I said. KeyBank's faith in me kept me loyal to them for years, even after Andy retired.

The next priority was to increase national sales. While we had distributed nationally since 1981, three-fourths of our sales were still in Oregon, and we had been concentrating on moving wine wholesale through our distributor and retail in our tasting room. I handled national sales myself, dealing directly with our distributors in the different markets. While I had distribution in many good markets, we had a big hole in New York City, which was traditionally the most important wine market in the country. I set out to find a distributor who would care about my small, faraway Oregon winery. Friends pointed me in the direction of Lauber Imports, run by Ed Lauber and his son, Mark. I began the courtship process by telephoning Mark to test his possible interest. I sent wine samples, and then flew to New York to meet with Mark and Ed. We hit it off, and in the late summer of 1991, Lauber Imports took on its first Oregon winery. Bill flew to New York with me, and we spent that hot, humid weekend strolling in Central Park and eating at restaurants we hoped would soon sell our wine.

Of the many distributors I worked with over the years, only a few seemed sufficiently well-run to garner my respect. Measured against almost any standard, Lauber Imports landed at the top. Every April, Lauber hosted two "Grand Annual" tastings for the wine trade, a modest one in New Jersey and a huge one in New York, on the fourteenth floor of the glitzy Times Square Marriott Marquis. Owners, winemakers, and national sales managers flew in from all over the world for these events. We stood elbow to elbow at long tables for five hours, pouring wine for hundreds of wine buyers and wine writers. Behind us, at eye level, neon models sauntered across giant billboards advertising sportswear, martinis, and music.

Through Lauber, I made wine-industry friends from Argentina, France, Italy, California, and New York. Because we were together year after year, the wineries in the Lauber portfolio felt like an extended family. We looked forward to seeing one another at least once a year, and I always went out of my way, wherever I was, to order one of the

Lauber family of wines in a restaurant; others told me they did the same. Only Lauber, among all the distributors I got to know, elicited a "family" feeling among the wineries in its portfolio. Years later as Ed retired, Lauber sold to the country's largest distributor network. I was glad to have been with them in their early years.

I met some of my favorite people in the wine business through Ed and his wife, Marsha Palanci, who were well loved in the industry. I often stayed with them at their apartment on the Upper East Side. No matter the season or the weather, Ed's booming voice woke me in time for their six o'clock, three-mile walk or run. Weekdays our jaunts went along the East River, stopping for coffee and bagels at a corner coffee shop on the way back. On weekends, we'd make our way through Central Park to a small pastry shop on the Upper West Side, near the cathedral of St. John the Divine. Ed and Marsha made New York my favorite market, and I tried to go there at least twice a year. Since I traveled by myself it meant a lot to have friends, especially on weekends.

I also tried out large-scale events, such as the Aspen Food and Wine Festival, the Telluride Wine Festival, the Santa Fe Chile and Wine Festival, and the New Orleans Food and Wine Experience. Even with the added visibility of being on a panel, my wine got lost in the sea of wineries. For most of the 1990s, I participated in the annual Albany (New York) Wine Festival, held at the Desmond Hotel at the end of January. Ed Lauber usually drove me up, and I never left the hotel— usually because we were snowed in. Every year, before signing up, I questioned whether I was in my right mind, going to Upstate New York in midwinter. One year, on my way to the festival, I met a woman from another Oregon winery in the Portland airport and, of course, we asked each other's destination. I said, "Albany, New York." She said, "Maui." I forced a smile, thinking, "What's wrong with this picture?"

From a business perspective, I actually looked forward to the Albany weekend. I could see all the Upstate New York retailers and restaurant wine buyers who attended and, after the crush of customers during the tastings, I could relax with the small group of regulars who came from other wineries. We compared notes on distributor difficulties and shared industry gossip. More than once I heard news about my home turf in Oregon by traveling to New York. It was also my chance to keep up with happenings in the heart of the domestic wine industry, Napa and Sonoma, where most of the wineries attending were located.

Before or after Albany, I tried to include a stop at the Culinary Institute of America (CIA) in Hyde Park, New York, to teach a wine class, do a tasting for the students, and host a winery dinner for the public in one of their five student-run restaurants. I wanted that opportunity to talk about Oregon Pinot Noir in general, and Sokol Blosser in particular, to people I knew would someday be among the top chefs and restaurateurs of the nation. I always invited the students to visit Sokol Blosser and, over the years, a number appeared. From humble beginnings in a former monastery, the CIA had developed a campus full of corporate-named buildings and an applicant waiting list.

The CIA might have had the clout to go after donations in the millions, but most fundraising was done on a much smaller scale. I must have had donation requests from charities in nearly every town, village, suburb, and city in the country that had a wine auction for a good cause. Only one outside of Oregon commanded my regular attendance—the High Museum Art and Wine Auction in Atlanta every March. The weather was so unpredictable that one year I had to buy a winter coat to combat the snow flurries and another year I sweltered in ninety-degree heat. But hot or cold, I wanted to be there because the auction and the events surrounding it were beautifully run and it was clear that the organizers truly appreciated the attending wineries. Activities started two days before the live auction, with a tasting for the wine trade that gave wineries the opportunity to meet Atlanta's restaurant and retail wine buyers. Dinners for art patrons in private homes, at which the wineries could display their wines to some of Atlanta's well-heeled consumers, were another feature. But these were just the warm-up. The real festivities started with a black-tie gala on Friday evening, with a viewing of Saturday's auction items and a silent auction.

The live-auction activities took place Saturday afternoon under the big top— a series of huge white tents, complete with flooring and chandeliers and decorated with colored lighting and extravagant floral displays. When I first heard the auction was to be in a tent, I was dubious, but this event redefined the word *tent* for me. Auction day started at 10:00 AM with two hours of wine and food tasting, with Atlanta's top restaurants participating. Just after noon, conversation was stopped by the arrival, seemingly out of nowhere, of the "Marching Abominables," a zany band of thirty instrument-toting adults of all sizes and shapes, flamboyantly dressed in ruffled crinolines, spandex, and tie-dye. They sashayed around the tables and led the way into the auction tent, putting the crowd in just the right mood for an afternoon of intense bidding for art, lavish wine trips, and unique wine items. The auction raised big money for the High Museum.

Deciding what to contribute to this auction was always difficult. It had to be something really special. One year I had a local glass artist create a stained-glass lid for a large wooden box packed with six bottles of our best Pinot Noir. Another year, I commissioned a replica of a traditional Northwestern Native American bentwood box, with black and red animal totem figures silk-screened along the sides and ends— again packed with six bottles of our very best wine.

There was free time between wine tastings, and it was in Atlanta that Laurie Puzo, Education Director at Domaine Chandon, taught me the art of "aerobic shopping." We whizzed through the sale racks in the stores at the Lenox Square mall with the energy and speed of Olympic sprinters. Too busy to shop most of the time, it was a rare opportunity and I went home with a bulging suitcase.

About the time I was negotiating with Lauber Imports, I took a hard look at myself in the mirror and decided that, as president of a winery with a national market, I needed to look more professional. The 1980s had witnessed my Mother Earth phase—I plaited my long hair in French braids every morning, perfect for working in the vineyard. I had cut it short in the late '80s and was now concerned about the encroaching gray. Other women advised me that while it was okay, even distinguished, for men to have gray hair, women with gray hair just looked old. I wanted to look chic, not matronly, so off I went to get my dark brown hair frosted to cover the gray. With each frosting, my hair got blonder and blonder, until finally I let go and went totally blonde. I saw my counterparts everywhere, making me wonder if every professional woman in my generation went through a blonde phase.

Thirteen-year-old Alison suggested I engage a Nordstrom personal shopper to help me look presidential. She offered to come along and help. I sat in a large dressing room full of mirrors as the personal shopper swept in and out with different looks. I gamely tried the outfits on, discarding immediately the ones I thought either too trendy or too plain, lingering over others, trying to decide if they captured the stylish, professional look I was after. With Alison's approval, I came away with a new wardrobe, loving my new silver-gray silk pants suit that flowed and draped elegantly and pink wool blazer that seemed to brighten the world. I was ready to hit the road, meet wine buyers, schmooze with wine writers, and sell Sokol Blosser wine.

I soon learned that meeting the chefs, sommeliers, wine buyers, and wine media was just the beginning. They couldn't buy directly from me. I could get them interested, but the actual sale had to go through a wholesale distributor. Distributors control a winery's access to the market they cover. Get two winery salespeople together and they will inevitably start discussing the pros and cons of various distributors. The distributors usually have a few effective sales reps and many who don't much care and will sell whatever is easiest, usually based on incentives, ratings, or cost. Big wineries offered perks like cell phones, TVs, gas

In Atlanta, doing an in-store tasting at Harry's Market. I was so thrilled to have my wine prominently displayed, I needed a photo of it. I'm standing in front of stacked cases of the whole line of Sokol Blosser wine. As you can see, this was during my "blonde phase," in 1997.

barbecues, or trips to Europe or California or Australia as motivators. My goal was always to find and cultivate the few who would remember to talk about Sokol Blosser.

Our national sales grew slowly but steadily during the 1990s, as Oregon wine became known and I spent more time on the road. I traveled as much as I felt I could and still run the winery. My guiding principle was this: If I was traveling more than I wanted but less than I thought I should, I had reached the right equilibrium. Nik and Alex were off on their own. Alison was still at home, but she had started to distance herself from me—payback for my teenage years when I considered my parents a cross I had to bear. The mothers of her schoolmates were younger than I and didn't work outside the home, so I was embarrassingly different. She allowed me to pick her up after a school party but gave strict instructions not to come in but to wait outside.

We were oddly distant, yet close. I so badly wanted my daughter to have the relationship with me that I didn't have with my mother, but during that time, I almost gave up. Then, when she was sixteen, she started dating a young man who convinced her to look at her mother not as a dingbat, but as a woman running a successful business. She started to see me through different lenses and we grew closer. During her senior year of high school, when she was studying in France and felt lonely, we wrote each other almost every day, via a brand-new medium of communication called e-mail.

Alison loved to travel, and I took her with me when I could. One summer while still in high school, she accompanied me to the Telluride Wine Festival. We spent time with my friends who were there too, Laurie Puzo from Domaine Chandon and Eugenia Keegan, president of Bouchaine. I admired and loved to be with those women. More experienced and connected, they mentored me, introducing me to people they thought I should know. It was support and encouragement I needed in the male-dominated wine world. I wanted Alison to learn from successful professional women, and they generously obliged. Eugenia even invited Alison to visit her for a weekend in Napa. After working as my assistant one summer during college, and then after doing marketing and public relations at other companies, Alison came to help me at Sokol Blosser. We were just trying it out. One day she said to me, "Mom, I want to go back to school and get my MBA. I don't want to go to night school. I want to take two years off and go full-time. I'm going to apply to the University of

Washington. Okay?" I hated to lose such a good assistant but sent her off in 2002 with my blessing, hoping she would want to come back to the winery.

To keep her interest, I invited her to go with me to the tenth anniversary of the High Museum Auction in Atlanta, to give her a taste of the more glamorous side of the wine business. It coincided with her spring break at the University of Washington and she was happy to put her books away, leave her little apartment, and come with me. The auction's theme was "Women of Wine" and I was one of ten women being honored. After attending the auction alone for so long, it felt good to have Alison's company. On the first night, I took her to Canoe, a favorite restaurant where Kevin Good, the manager and wine buyer, had become a friend. We had a fabulous five-course meal, sipping a different wine with each course. We relaxed, chatting with Kevin, and with Sonoma winemaker Merry Edwards and her husband who were seated nearby, and eating until we couldn't fit in another bite. When I asked for the bill, Kevin said our dinner was his treat. What a grand, and rare, indulgence. Alison's eyes grew large, and I could see she was filing this away as she contemplated the future.

We also had an active retail business at our winery tasting room, and we considered ways to increase the number of winery visitors. Could we lure them out with music? I had envisioned music at Sokol Blosser since we started planning the winery, but the idea got buried over the years. I pictured a small orchestra playing Mozart while the audience sat on a grassy hillside, surrounded by vineyards, overlooking the valley. Concertgoers would spread red-checkered tablecloths for their gourmet picnic dinners, open bottles of Sokol Blosser wine, enjoy the music floating across the lawn, and leave with good memories of the evening and the winery. My mother, who had grown up in Chicago in a musical family and was an accomplished musician herself, had told me about summer concerts in the early 1900s at nearby Ravinia. The wealthy families would settle themselves on blankets while their servants took out

Three generations of Sokol Blosser women: Alison, age fifteen, sporting her teenage braces; my mother, Phyllis Sokol, a spritely eighty-nine; and me, age fifty. I had to travel to Chicago for a wine event and decided to take Alison for the experience, and my mother to see her old haunts as she was born and raised there. 1994

candelabra and set up the family picnic. Servants and candelabra were not in my picture, but affluent wine lovers, eating, drinking, and listening to music certainly were.

My "music under the stars" dream resurfaced when a promoter who had produced successful soft-rock concerts at the Portland Zoo and other venues approached us. All we had to offer was space—a grassy hillside we could turn into an amphitheater. We had no stage, no electricity or water in the potential amphitheater area, and no good parking. And the county ordinance regulating large public gatherings was demanding. Nicknamed the Woodstock ordinance, it had been passed to prevent the kind of festival that had gotten out of hand in Woodstock, New York, in the late 1960s. The ordinance had lain dormant on the books for almost twenty years, until we came along and called it into play. It required applying to the county for the desired date, detailing the purpose and the logistics, and then procuring the approval of the local fire department, the county sanitarian, and the county sheriff.

We knew that Robert Mondavi and Wente in California and Chateau Ste. Michelle Winery in Washington had summer concerts of popular music, but no winery in Oregon had tried it. Gary Mortensen, my vice president, was a music buff and offered to take the lead in organizing it, so we dived in. For eight consecutive years, 1992 through 1999, we had a summer music festival.

Reality forced me to give up the idea of Mozart, or anything classical, because it would not draw enough audience. We looked for popular performers who had big names but were no longer the hottest box-office draws, and thus were affordable. Harry Belafonte, Johnny Mathis, George Benson, Los Lobos, Tower of Power, Ray Charles, John Denver, the Neville Brothers, Little Feat, Joan Baez, The Manhattan Transfer, Al Jarreau, Tony Bennett, Nanci Griffith, Rickie Lee Jones, Steven Stills, and Peter, Paul and Mary all came to Dundee, Oregon, to perform at Sokol Blosser. We called the series Sokol Blosser Live, although a friend dubbed it "Sokol Blosser, Are They Still Alive?" when she heard the golden oldies we were featuring.

The first year, with the difficulties of applying to the county, setting up a stage, and booking performers, we produced only one concert. On an unusually warm, mellow night in mid-September, Los Lobos performed before a sellout crowd. The audience sat on the grassy hillside eating dinners catered by McCormick & Schmick's, drinking Sokol Blosser wine, and swaying to the Latino-influenced beat. The evening was just as magical as I had imagined, only slightly marred by the parking-area congestion after the show.

The promoter came up with only two shows the second year, so we engaged a larger production company, and from then on we did five shows a season. The production company went to a lot of expense to expand the stage, set up the canopy and lighting, and bring in the amplification and sound system, so they wanted as many concerts as possible to recoup the costs. Because the concerts drained our staff time and energy, I didn't want one every weekend. Five was our compromise.

When we started the concerts, I hadn't thought it would be too hard on the staff. After all, the producer was taking care of production, traffic control, parking, and even the food vendor. Gary handled all the details with the producer and was the point person during concerts. My role at the performances was to be with our guests and to go on stage during intermission to welcome people, thank our sponsors, and honor the charity of the evening. But when the food vendor was understaffed and people had to stand in line for an hour to get food, or the performers took too long doing their sound check and people had to wait in the hot sun beyond the advertised entry time, or there were long lines for the portable toilets, or the traffic out of Portland was so bad that concertgoers arrived angry and late, they blamed Sokol Blosser and our staff had to deal with the many phone calls for information as well as the complaints from irritated attendees.

It became clear that people faulted Sokol Blosser for whatever went wrong, regardless of whether we were responsible or not. Food, weather, traffic, long lines—Sokol Blosser took the heat. I was a nervous wreck during the concerts, trying to watch the food line and security personnel and worrying about what could go wrong while smiling and trying to be a gracious host. I attended all thirty-six concerts over the eight years, and I don't remember hearing the music at most of them.

Three concerts stand out in my mind—John Denver, Johnny Mathis, and Ray Charles—each for a different reason. John Denver's performance was one of his last, and the only one of our concerts that was signed for deaf audience members while he sang. During the entire performance, two signers at the side of the stage quietly alternated as he sang. They swayed silently to the music, their faces animated as they communicated with their hands. They were so compelling, the audience stopped focusing solely on John Denver, and the signers became part of the performance.

Johnny Mathis had been at the top of the charts when I entered high school, and I couldn't believe he was still performing. In the weeks before the concert, I was astonished by the number of phone calls from friends, and friends of friends, begging to meet him. No other performer had sparked this much interest. I arranged what the producer called a meet-and-greet, so just before Mr. Mathis performed, I led a group of animated women, full of anticipation at meeting their idol, down behind the stage to his trailer. When we entered, he welcomed us, shook hands and gave each woman a signed picture. I stood back, trying not to look as shocked as I felt. Was this handsome man, radiating health and fitness, the same one I had listened to almost forty years earlier? How could he look so good? There was a full moon that night, and as the mostly female audience sat on blankets and lawn chairs listening to Johnny Mathis croon "Chances Are," their dreamy smiles betrayed old romantic memories.

On the other hand, I cringe and apologize when people tell me they attended the Ray Charles concert. We always monitored the weather, so we knew it was going to rain. We predicted attendance would be light. I should have known Oregonians don't stay home when it's wet; we had a full house as the rain settled in for the night. The only tented areas were for the concert sponsors, so most of the audience sat in the open amphitheater, under tarps and raincoats if they were lucky. Those without rain gear just sat in the rain. I couldn't believe so many people stayed. The electrical system shorted out after the opening act, which delayed Ray Charles's appearance. And the wooden stage was too wet and slick for much dancing.

When people tried to leave, they found our gentle grass hillside parking area had turned to mud. Cars slid all over. Worst were the four-wheel-drive vehicles, because their owners assumed they could do anything. Alex ran down to the equipment shed to get the tractor and spent hours pulling cars over to the gravel driveway. His hands became so muddy and slippery that his five-month-old wedding ring slipped off. He never found it, though he combed the property with a metal detector.

Years later, a young woman named Brooke Anthony, who came to work in our accounting office, offered a more heartwarming view of the Ray Charles concert. She told me that she had been backstage with her mother and grandmother that evening, helping the local caterer feed the band. When the concert started, her grandma called her and her mother onto a wing of the stage. She remembered the three generations swaying to Ray Charles's beat and looking out through the dark rain at a sea of tarps also swaying back and forth.

For most of the 1990s, our summer concerts brought us cash and publicity. Then their success started to have a negative side. People would ask, "Aren't you the winery that does those great concerts?" This hit me hard. I wanted to be known for great wine, not great concerts. Did we have to choose? It took a crisis to end the run.

In 1999, we decided to produce the concerts ourselves. We had watched three different production companies over the years; we knew what we had to do, and we thought we could do it better. The only danger was that we would be taking on the financial risk, which had previously been carried by the production companies. There was a surfeit of concerts that summer in Portland, and our lineup of performers wasn't a strong enough draw. As a result, we never sold enough tickets. Our concert series lost so much money it put the winery at risk. The combination of financial disaster and the toll on staff made me realize we couldn't continue. Concert fans were disappointed, but I was greatly relieved. I made plans to plant most of the concert parking area.

———

WHEN I BECAME PRESIDENT of the winery, my immediate goal was to get us out of a financial hole. I was so focused on generating cash to keep the business alive, I didn't see what was happening in the wine world around me. When I finally looked up, I saw that Sokol Blosser was being left behind. It took several years of trying to understand what was happening and deciding what to do.

During the 1980s and the early '90s, there had been so few Oregon wineries that those of us with a national presence had the limelight. Then, as Oregon wines gained prestige, more and more vineyards and wineries appeared. The first international investment in Oregon was in made in 1986 by an Australian winemaker and entrepreneur, Brian Croser. He created the Dundee Wine Company, which produced wine as Argyle Winery. Brian and his winemaker, Rollin Soles, wanted to produce Champagne-style sparkling wine from the abundant Pinot Noir and Chardonnay in the area. Their first year, before their facility was ready, Rollin made their wine at Sokol Blosser's facility. Despite the fact that their winery was housed on Dundee's main drag, the Australian presence in Oregon did not make a big splash.

It took old-world investment for the wine world to sit up and take notice. In 1987, Robert Drouhin, the prominent French négotiant and head of Maison Joseph Drouhin in Burgundy, bought a hundred acres close to Sokol Blosser in the Dundee Hills. Robert's daughter, Véronique, had finished her enological studies in France and came to be the winemaker—not moving to Oregon, but visiting at key times during the year to supervise the winemaking. Dave Adelsheim and David Lett had helped Robert find the site, and it was all kept very quiet until August 1987, when Governor Neil Goldschmidt made a public announcement.

Drouhin made a statement we repeated whenever we had the chance: "There are only two places in the world I would plant Pinot Noir—Burgundy and Oregon." This proclamation from a well-respected Frenchman affirmed what we had been saying for the previous seventeen years. Our proclamations had fallen on skeptical ears, but when Robert Drouhin spoke with his money, people listened.

Robert started out buying grapes from local vineyards, including Sokol Blosser, and when he released his first wine, a 1988 Pinot Noir, he invited the local winegrowers to a reception in his cellar. We stood in the barrel room of his new winery, taking in the aroma of new French oak and wine. He poured his first Pinot Noir for us and said he was deliberately pricing it high to make a statement. Top Cabernet Sauvignon wines sold for fifty dollars or more, he said. Top Pinot Noir should be able to command thirty dollars a bottle. This was twice as much as the rest of us priced our wine and we were awed and thrilled. We needed to make more money on our Pinot Noir, and if anyone could make it happen, it was Robert Drouhin. We cheered him loudly. "Go, Robert!" someone shouted.

Domaine Drouhin Oregon ushered in a steady stream of new vineyards and wineries spilling up and down the Willamette Valley in the 1990s. King Estate, WillaKenzie Estate, Archery Summit, Lemelson Vineyards, and Domaine Serene were all new operations that indicated significant investment—architecturally striking buildings, technologically advanced equipment, exquisite catering kitchens, beautiful landscaping, and highly credentialed winemakers. Because the influx was a stream, not a flood, and because it was a while before each of the new properties had wine on the market, the results of all this new investment took time to manifest. The changes in the industry crept up on us. During the late 1970s and early 1980s, we knew all the newcomers. They came and talked to us and often worked a harvest at Sokol Blosser. The whole Willamette Valley wine industry still fit in any of our living rooms. Slowly, as the incoming stream grew, the personal contact lessened, and new names seemed to appear out of nowhere.

We had ringside seats watching the launch of Domaine Drouhin Oregon in 1988 and Archery Summit in 1992. All we had to do was look across our vineyard. We had such a good view that the owners of Archery Summit came to Sokol Blosser to observe the progress of their construction, and we got to know them. We used to joke that a coin-operated telescope aimed at these two wineries to take advantage of all the tourist interest would have helped Sokol Blosser pay off its loans. Early photos of our vineyard showed the wheat fields that became those vineyards. We blew up the pictures and put them, along with other old family pictures, in our tasting room. Sokol Blosser had history. Did anyone care besides us? The public was only mildly interested. The wine press and consumers were interested in what was new, not what was old.

Besides being one of the wine pioneers, what made Sokol Blosser special? Where was our niche? Our winery building, so modern in 1977, was out of date compared to the new wineries that boasted the latest technology. And our John Storrs-designed tasting room looked small and shabby compared to the newer, larger, and more hip ones. We didn't have a French winemaker, owner, or investor. Once at the forefront of the Oregon wine industry, Sokol Blosser had fallen to the middle of the pack. In the early '90s, my radar picked up little of this, though I watched as other older wineries, like Adelsheim Vineyard, took in investors and built beautiful new facilities. I was too busy getting Sokol Blosser out of its financial hole, producing concerts at the winery, and figuring out how to buy out our vineyard partners, a dilemma much on my mind.

We had tried to find other investors who would buy out our partners, then had looked at taking in additional investors. At one point, we had been so frustrated that we started to put together a deal to sell the whole winery. Fortunately, that fell through. Resolution came when our friends at KeyBank told me how I could raise the money to buy out our partners. One of the results of the growth of the wine industry was that our vineyard, which Bill and I owned separately from the winery, had become valuable enough that we could borrow against it. It was our good fortune to have located in what had become the highest-value wine real estate in Oregon.

In the end, both Hyland and Durant owners indicated they would be willing to sell us their shares. The idea of wholly owning what

I'd always considered "our" winery made me giddy. When it became a real possibility, I stepped back to let Bill be our spokesman. He was willing, although not eager, for us to be sole owner and bear all the risk. I wanted it so much I knew I would be a lousy negotiator. I stayed behind the scenes, cheering Bill on.

The final transaction stays etched in my memory. On October 26, 1996, at 10:00 am, Bill and I walked through the front door of a local title company and signed the stack of legal papers that gave us full ownership of Sokol Blosser Winery. Twenty years after starting the winery with my father and brothers, we were finally able to claim it as ours alone. As I signed my name for the last time, giving Bill and me title to Sokol Blosser Winery, I felt an albatross drop from my neck. The buyout took its toll on our balance sheet, but from that day forward we would be accountable only to ourselves. The destiny of the winery would be ours to choose.

Free to move forward, I looked around and then began to realize how far behind we were. Sokol Blosser was producing thirty thousand cases of wine annually. About half of it was "value-priced" Riesling, Pinot Noir, and Chardonnay that sold primarily in Oregon under our second label, SB Select. The rest was sold under our premium Sokol Blosser label. Starting a second "value" label had become a two-edged sword. By providing cash flow during tough times, it had kept us in business. On the other hand, our presence in the market with an inexpensive line devalued our image as a high-end winery. Distributors found it easier to sell the inexpensive wine and ignored the higher end bottles, so as the second-tier sales increased, the sales of our higher-end of wines slowed. We needed to decide which path we wanted to follow.

I wanted to grow superb grapes and create top quality wine, not simply move X number of boxes, so for me the decision to compete on quality, rather than price and volume, was simple. Implementing it was not. I spent the next year grappling with the right vision for Sokol Blosser. Questions with no easy answers ran through my head: If we eliminated our SB Select second label, how would we generate cash flow to take its place? No longer beholden to our vineyard partners, we had more freedom to decide what wines we wanted to make. We still had land to plant; was it time to reevaluate what we should be growing? If we decided to do anything different, how would we manage the transition? After the huge loan to buy out our partners, could we afford more debt to do anything else? The right path was not clear to me, and I spent hours poring over financial projections for different possibilities.

Since I knew our packaging needed a new look whatever path I chose, I decided to start with redoing our label, which was now twenty years old. What had once seemed elegant now appeared stodgy. We went to Sandstrom Design, touted to us as the most creative in Portland, and they fulfilled our expectations. Sally Morrow, the designer who worked with us, gave us just the look we were after—stylish without being stiff, simple without being plain. The label debuted in the summer of 1997 and won immediate praise from both consumers and the wine industry.

To get publicity and national visibility for our new image, I hired Marsha Palanci, whose public relations firm, Cornerstone Communications, was in Manhattan. Marsha came up with the perfect publicity plan. Television stations shied away from promoting wine directly on their local morning talk shows, but cooking segments were the rage, sandwiched between weather and traffic updates. If I could give a cooking demonstration, it would be natural to pair a Sokol Blosser wine with the dish. Marsha could place my cooking segments in every market I visited. It was genius—free publicity and lots of visibility for Sokol Blosser, everywhere in the United States.

Marsha knew I had studied teaching and was relatively at ease speaking to groups, but suggested a quick course in "media training" to hone my TV presentation skills. She picked Lou Ekus, whose office was a two-hundred-year-old converted gristmill in western Massachusetts, and whose client list included such luminaries as cookbook author and radio show host Lynne Rossetto Kasper and Chef Emeril Lagasse.

Marsha talked me into it, reassuring me she would go along for support. I decided it might be interesting; I'd at least learn something.

My first assignment was to choose recipes to demonstrate that would go with my wine. The first inkling that Marsha's grand plan might not work was when I realized I had no repertoire of recipes from which to choose. Food was a critical part of my life and business and I had a wonderful library of cookbooks, but I seldom had time to use them. Ignoring my doubts, I consulted a cookbook by Marie Simmons, a friend Marsha had introduced me to, chose several of her recipes I thought looked good, and tried them out.

Some friendships are meant to be and I think Susan's and mine is one, because over the years our paths kept crossing in the most positive way.

In the early 1990s, I was moving in the fast track in food media in NYC. It was during this time I met Susan at a small get-together of friends at Marsha Palanci's Manhattan apartment. I was bemoaning the fact I was about to leave my ideal life and a great career to drive across the country to be with my husband, John, who had just accepted a job to work in San Francisco. I viewed the move with trepidation.

A few years later, when I attended the International Pinot Noir Celebration (IPNC) as a media guest, John and I sat with Susan and Bill Blosser at one of the meals, and connected immediately. Susan and I kept in touch for a number of years as I enjoyed creating recipes to pair with the wines Susan selected for Sokol Blosser's wine club.

This was the kind of work I embraced. My recipes included a range of flavors from Braised Duck with Winter Squash, Mushrooms, and Pears, to Goat Cheese "Fondue" with Crisped Fried Shallots and Bacon, to Hot Smoked Salmon, Potato and Egg Salad. All matched with marvelous Sokol Blosser wines.

When John retired, we moved to Eugene, Oregon. We joined Susan and Russ as they hosted an annual summer harvest dinner, either at the winery or their home. Several couples would bring fresh ingredients from their garden or the farmers market and we would cook together.

Over the years the menu evolved and we embraced the cuisine of the Northwest, constantly marveling at the fact we had landed in such a beautiful place where farmers markets thrive, our backyard chickens keep us supplied with eggs, our tomatoes are prolific, and our fig trees keep giving. Thank you, Susan, for your inspiration and friendship. We love being your friends, neighbors, and wine aficionados.

Marie Simmons,
James Beard Award-Winning Cookbook Author

The cold, rainy February day matched my dour mood as Marsha and I flew to Hartford, Connecticut, rented a car, and made our way along the back roads of western Massachusetts to Lou's house. The two-day training involved videotaping me in Lou's demonstration kitchen, with him acting as host; watching and critiquing the tape; and then doing it all again. And again. And again. The goal was for me to be able to teach the recipe and create the dish in the few minutes allotted while keeping up friendly banter with the host. It felt like that old game of trying to rub your head while patting your stomach.

I anticipated that the process would be painfully embarrassing and it was. I learned not to "up talk," that is, raise my voice at the end of a sentence—a common female foible. I learned how to reduce my overall message to a few key points and then "bridge" from whatever question the host asked back to those points. I learned to connect with the audience through the host, who was the reason they were watching the show. And I learned how important it was to be high-energy—exaggerated by a factor of two, to compensate for the deadening medium of television. By the end of the two days I was able to make the recipes, smile, and talk at the same time. Lou gave me a video of my final performance.

I had spent a lot of money on this piece of education and Marsha was ready for me to make use of it and start a media tour. Before that could happen I had to go back to the winery where I immediately became embroiled in day-to-day business. Thoughts of a media tour got pushed to the back burner, but something about it bothered me. It finally hit me that Marsha's ingenious plan had a fatal flaw—me. I couldn't in good conscience put myself in the public eye as a cooking teacher. I did do a few sessions with a local Portland TV station, and decided it just wasn't me. Feeling guilty and shamefaced at disappointing her, I told Marsha I couldn't do it. The video from my media training stayed untouched on a shelf. I've never had the courage to watch it.

Another of Marsha's inspirations, which I wholeheartedly endorsed, was Sokol Blosser's competition to define the character of Oregon Pinot Noir. The project was another public-relations dream because it had several opportunities for media attention. Marsha put out a press release to the wine media to announce the contest, and then six months later another one to announce the winner, followed by a big press luncheon in Manhattan. The challenge included questions and prompts like: "If Pinot Noir were a person, who would it be? Choose a famous person, living or dead, who you think best personifies Oregon Pinot Noir. Write a short essay describing your nominee. . . ."

A wide variety of people, both male and female, were nominated as typifying Pinot Noir. Words like charming, sophisticated, elegant, graceful, and subtle kept reappearing in the essays. But the differences were what made it interesting. Colette was nominated for her sensuality, evocative quality, and tendency to be a tease; Maya Angelou because she was poetic, intense, lively, complex, and visionary. Two first ladies, Jacqueline Kennedy Onassis and Hillary Rodham Clinton, were candidates. Two actresses, Katharine Hepburn and Catherine Deneuve, were cited for their beauty, elegance, and complexity. The male entries ran the gamut from Lee Iacocca, for his ability to take a difficult situation and make it golden, to Fred Astaire, for his sophistication and ability to dance across the floor like Pinot Noir across the palate; to David Bowie, for his otherworldly transcendence and nonconformity; and to Clint Eastwood, for his multifaceted talent. None of these nominees won.

I had asked two friends with impeccable wine and literary credentials to be the judges: Steven Koblik, wine lover and erudite president of Reed College, and Heidi Yorkshire, author and wine columnist for the Portland-based *Oregonian*. They unanimously chose the entry proposing Cary Grant as the epitome of Pinot Noir. The winner, wine writer Steve Heimoff, wrote that Cary Grant best characterized Oregon Pinot Noir because "his personality was romantic, urbane, charming, seductive, and sophisticated. He had lots of style and finesse. He possessed youthful charm, yet he aged well. He was graceful, elegant, and debonair. His voice and mannerisms were silky smooth. His style was seamless. All the parts came together in harmony." He may have been describing Cary Grant, but this was the best-ever description of Pinot Noir.

Each person who entered the contest received a bottle of Sokol Blosser Pinot Noir with a note thanking them for participating. Steve spent a week in Oregon wine country as our guest, including attendance at the International Pinot Noir Celebration in McMinnville. The media lunch Marsha arranged at a restaurant in Manhattan was so well attended that we had to squeeze into the room. Guests were welcomed by a huge poster board of Cary Grant looking his most elegant and seductive, and each received a gift video of his movie *To Catch a Thief.* I loved everything about this project.

One of the best parts of working with Marsha was meeting her friends, other professional women connected to wine and food. They were mainly writers, but in different arenas—some specialized in cookbooks, others wrote only for wine publications, still others wrote for lifestyle media. Most lived and worked in New York or California. It felt good to be around other professional women in related fields and our animated discussions, always over food, ranged from analysis of

Martha Stewart's popularity to meal descriptions and anecdotes from their recent tours to Tuscany or Sicily or Greece.

I had two round-trip plane tickets between New York and Portland that had to be used, so I asked Marsha if we could use them to bring wine writers to Sokol Blosser. She made arrangements with two of her friends from New York, Nancy Wolfson and Marguerite Thomas, to come to Portland one June weekend. I had never met either woman, but I knew Nancy had been beauty editor at several women's magazines, including *Glamour,* and Marguerite was a published author who wrote regularly for wine magazines. I was especially curious to see what a beauty editor would look like and watched so carefully for two women with extensive makeup and expensive clothes that I hardly glanced at the two simply dressed women who walked over to me and introduced themselves. Nancy and Marguerite weren't that different from me. I relaxed immediately, and it felt even easier when I learned they hadn't met before they got on the airplane. By the end of the visit, the three of us felt like sisters. As their recreation director, I went far beyond showing them around the winery. We took a guided tour of Portland's Japanese Garden, went kayaking on the Willamette River, attended a baroque chamber-music concert in one of Portland's historic churches, and ate at as many Portland restaurants as we could fit in. We spent the last afternoon at my home in Portland and while they walked down trendy Northwest Twenty-Third Street to see the shops, I collapsed on the couch, exhausted.

The public-relations efforts and daily push to sell our wine kept me busy although I was still struggling to find the right identity for the winery. What did I really want? I couldn't force a vision, so I could only hope my subconscious was working on it while I kept the business running. I guess it was, because as the new year began, the fog started to lift as I came face to face with one of a winery's most important challenges—the winemaking itself.

It was January 1998, and I was in New York City. After a hectic morning calling on accounts, Jeff Davis, the Lauber sales rep I was with that day, and I were relaxing over lunch. I sensed he had something on his mind. He finally worked up his nerve to tell me that he was concerned about Sokol Blosser's wine quality. He was blunt. Lauber Imports had just taken on Domaine Drouhin Oregon, right up the hill from us. His comments went like this: Sokol Blosser was located close to Domaine Drouhin, right? So the grapes from the two vineyards would be comparable, right? Then why wasn't our wine from recent vintages as good as theirs? He looked at me anxiously, afraid he had overstepped his bounds.

I looked back silently, not because I was insulted but because a lightbulb had just gone off in my head. I realized he had just articulated something that had been simmering in the back of my brain for some time. We did have a great vineyard site. Why hadn't this translated into superlative wine quality? I remembered a friend asking me, when I said I was ready to go after the high-quality wine market, whether I had the right winemaker to take me there. I had equivocated at the time, and she hadn't pressed, but now I wondered if she had been trying to get me to face the situation.

Managing the vineyard and running the business was my passion. I was not, and never wanted to be, a winemaker. It's a profession requiring an unusual combination of skills in both art and science. Most people's talents lie in one field or the other. Like a great chef, a first-rate winemaker goes beyond the recipe, beyond chemistry and microbiology, into the realm of creativity, using informed intuition to make crucial judgments at each step. But there's a fundamental difference: a chef can re-create that great dish night after night. A winemaker makes wine only once a year. And if the wine must age, it may take years to find out its true worth. Thirty to forty vintages, or winemaking opportunities, comprise a winemaker's entire career. A profession in which the outcomes are so few, and each is so vital, requires tremendous patience, focus, skill, and passion.

In our segment of the market, there is no substitute for wine quality. It is the basis for all else. Neither excellent marketing, nor management, nor sales personnel can compensate for lack of flavor in the bottle, so the position of winemaker is all-important. As I came to the realization that I needed a new winemaker before the next harvest, I knew I faced a daunting task. There were no Oregon winemakers I wanted to pursue, but a winemaker from any other region would be used to different grapes and a different wine lifestyle. How was I going to find someone I could afford, who understood Oregon Pinot Noir? I called my friend Eugenia in Napa to see if she knew of any assistant winemakers who might be willing to move to Oregon for the challenge of making great Pinot Noir. I was disappointed when she called back to tell me she'd struck out. Suddenly I remembered that in the late 1980s, Bill had hired an enologist from Robert Mondavi Winery to consult on our barrel program. I mentioned him.

"I want someone just like Russ Rosner," I told Eugenia. "He has what we need. He is familiar with Sokol Blosser, he understands Oregon fruit, and he has top-notch training." Eugenia knew him slightly and agreed. I knew he had worked at an Oregon winery for a while, but neither of us knew what he was doing now. Eugenia picked up her local phone book, and there he was. She offered to call Russ and test his interest, and asked whether she should reveal my name. I told her to go ahead. I wasn't sure whether knowing it was Sokol Blosser would make him more, or less, interested, but I thought we might as well find out.

"You'll never guess what Russ is doing," Eugenia teased when she called back.

"What?" I could feel my pulse quickening.

"Nothing!" she almost shouted. "He isn't working and it sounds like he's trying to decide what direction to go."

"Is he interested in Sokol Blosser?" By now my pulse was racing.

"Yes," she said.

Russ Rosner became winemaker at Sokol Blosser in 1998 and led the drive toward high quality. French oak barrels were his specialty and we usually had Pinot Noir in barrels from over a dozen French barrel makers. (Photo credit: Doreen L. Wynja.)

I took a deep breath and let it out slowly.

I flew to Napa, filled with hope and trepidation, and interviewed Russ over the next two days. Bill flew down for the second interview. Russ was the same ultraserious guy I remembered. Work and fly fishing were his passions. No family or entangling relationships. He had lived in Napa, the center of quality winemaking in the United States, for the past sixteen years. Moving to Oregon was a step he would consider, but not take lightly. He had several other job options at larger operations, but I could see that working with Oregon Pinot Noir, and being the only winemaker, appealed to him.

There was so much to do at the winery; I didn't want someone whose decisions and behavior I had to monitor. If I could find someone with the skills to do the job and the integrity to do it honestly and responsibly, I was willing to give that person significant control over the whole production realm. Was Russ Rosner the right one? And if he were, how could I convince him to come work for us?

Bill and I agreed, as did Eugenia, who sat in on the interviews at her house, that Russ could be the right person for Sokol Blosser. He wasn't flashy or even outgoing, but solid, dependable, well-trained, and passionate about wine quality. If anything, we worried that he was too serious, too detail-oriented. Eugenia called some friends who had worked with him, and when her report came in favorable, we sent Russ a proposal and offered to fly him up to see the facility. He declined to visit, and then deliberated for three weeks, apparently struggling with the decision to leave Napa. I was getting increasingly nervous, knowing I had no backup plan. Finally, he called. Yes, he would start in July and move to Oregon in August. It would be a huge change for Russ and for Sokol Blosser. I fervently hoped it would work.

If I had any illusions about a new winemaker being all we needed to achieve higher quality, they were quickly dispelled. I started to see our production facility through Russ's eyes. I knew our old winery building and equipment hadn't kept up with the times, but now

I saw that it was more than just old; it was an impediment to making great wine. Russ admitted that if he had accepted our invitation to tour the facilities and seen how inadequate they were, he probably wouldn't have taken the job. He pushed us to define our commitment to quality. People talk glibly about quality, he said, but few realize how much focus and diligence it takes. If high quality was our vision, how far were we willing, and able, to go to achieve it?

From 1983 to 1993 I was one of the winemakers at the Robert Mondavi Winery in the Napa Valley. In the late '80s we embarked on a quest to make great Pinot Noir, and I became fascinated by that variety. About that time I met Susan and her husband, Bill, when I gave them a special tour and tasting. Shortly thereafter, Bill asked me if I would consider consulting for Sokol Blosser, which Mondavi graciously allowed me to do, and for a couple of years I traveled to Oregon a few times to help their winemaker with their winemaking procedures, blending, and barrel program.

Around 1990 Bill asked me if I would be interested in becoming the winemaker for Sokol Blosser; while I was tempted by the opportunity to make Pinot Noir in one of the few places in the world it was meant to be grown, I was not yet ready to leave one of the foremost wineries in the world, with its fantastic facility, equipment, and resources, for a decidedly less state-of-the-art winery.

A few years later I did leave Robert Mondavi and worked for a couple of different wineries, but didn't find my ideal situation. In 1998 I was seriously considering an offer from a winery on the East Coast, when Susan called to see if I might now be interested in becoming the winemaker for Sokol Blosser. Facing a major fork in the road—leaving California but staying on the west coast or leaving California for the East Coast—I opted for the opportunity to make great Pinot Noir at Sokol Blosser. I moved to Oregon and have never looked back. Little did I know at the time how much more than a winemaking job my decision would become.

Russ Rosner
Sokol Blosser Winemaker, 1998–2013

Russ led the charge to upgrade our winemaking quality with a new, more efficient destemmer, a larger press to allow Russ to do whole cluster pressing, longer barrel aging, and ultimately, a new climate-controlled barrel cellar.

There were further difficult decisions to be made about narrowing down our line of wines, upgrading our image and reputation, creating the right ambience in the tasting room, and the type of personnel we needed to carry out all our plans. A lot of work lay ahead, but after years of floundering, the vision was taking shape. I finally knew where I wanted to take the winery and felt focused and energized.

That spring I also thought long and hard about whether I really wanted to bring any of the kids into the business, and whether I should. I had urged them all in other directions, but Alex kept circling back. Years before, I had hired him to work in the cellar, but our partners had objected strenuously when they found out, arguing that it was too awkward for a hired winemaker to supervise an owner. Furious and embarrassed, I had to go back and tell Alex he couldn't work for us. His response was to go across the hill and take a position as vineyard foreman at nearby Archery Summit, which was just planting its vineyards. From there he had gone back to college to finish his bachelor's degree, and he was now working for a wine wholesaler in Portland.

I needed to hire someone to help with sales, and Alex had the qualities I was looking for. There were no more partners, so the decision path was open. Alex wasn't pushing to come into the business, but his warmth and interest in others had made him at ease with people from the time he could talk. I also knew that bringing Alex into the business was more emotionally loaded than just hiring a new employee. What would it be like being boss, not just mom? How would the other employees react? Would I be too soft with him—or too hard? What if it didn't work out? Everyone knows stories about family businesses in which siblings and parents end up mired in anger and hostility.

On the other hand, why shouldn't I be mentoring my son in the wine business? Wasn't that one of the benefits of a family business? What could be better than working with someone you love? I had a friend who owned a successful art gallery and had both her daughters working with her. The business was flourishing and she loved the arrangement. After agonizing for months, I asked Alex to come work with me, spurred on by the need for help in the national market and my joy at the thought of working with one of my children. Russ and Alex both started in July. My son who used to stand on a chair to do the dishes now had a desk near mine.

"Mom," he said on his first day, "what should I call you at work?"

I thought for a minute, then said, "Susan, I suppose. We need to be businesslike."

We managed to keep up the formality for a while, but gradually defaulted. At a fancy wine dinner, or when he was standing in front of a distributor's sales force trying to get attention for Sokol Blosser, Alex's references to "Mom" only reminded people that we were family.

———

Russ and Alex arrived on the scene as we debuted Evolution No. 9, a brand-new product that we had created to solve an old problem. We had been producing Müller-Thurgau wine since the first vintage, 1977, but it had always been borderline for profitability. In the fall of 1997, the head of Block Distributing in San Antonio started me thinking when he suggested, semi-seriously, that I come up with a proprietary name for our Müller-Thurgau. The wine was good, he told me, but its odd varietal name made it hard for his salespeople to sell.

I hadn't considered that before, but why not? Our Müller-Thurgau, retailing at $7.95, was so low margin that it was good only for absorbing overhead. I had to do something that would make it more profitable. Would a proprietary name do the job? I didn't think so. But how about making it a blended wine? Most white blends retailed for no more than ten dollars, but I did know one that was well-regarded and sold for a good price. It was called Conundrum, was made by a California winery, and retailed for about twenty dollars a bottle. It became our model. When I took the idea back to Gary, my imaginative vice president, he was ready to start working on it right away.

First, we had to find a name and create the package. Credit for the clever, offbeat name and label goes to the design team of David Brooks and Sally Morrow. Their genius was in creating something that was original and imaginative without crossing the line into cute, corny, or trendy. Sally had designed our new Sokol Blosser label the year before. David, a close friend of Gary's, had written copy for our brochures, ads, and invitations for years, and had declared himself the keeper of our image. But they had never worked together for us, and it became a magical collaboration.

A casual remark by a wine friend shaped a key part of the program. Wine personality Joshua Wesson had sold many cases of Müller-Thurgau for us in his Best Cellars store in Manhattan. We met for coffee in the early spring of 1998, when I was in New York. By that time, we had the concept of the blended white wine and the name Evolution No. 9. I wanted Josh's reaction, maybe even his blessing. I admired his wacky sense of humor, way with words, and keen business sense, and I was not alone; he had a large following. He lamented the passing of Müller-Thurgau as an individual wine, since he had been so successful with it at his store. But he liked our new project and, almost in passing, said, "I assume by the name that the wine will be a blend of nine different grape varieties." I hadn't linked the name with the grapes, and nine varieties seemed like a lot. "Do you think that's important?" I asked. "I think it's critical," he said.

Bingo! The decision to make the wine a blend of nine varieties, made that morning over coffee on the Upper East Side, became a keystone of the marketing program. We had been planning to blend only three or four white varieties, but it turned out to be easy to come up with nine. We had a little showcase vineyard right outside our tasting room, which had started out as a test plot of different grape varieties for an Oregon State University research project. In it we had rows of Muscat, Müller-Thurgau, Sylvaner, Pinot Blanc, Gewürztraminer, Chardonnay, Riesling, and Pinot Gris. With the addition of Semillon, we had our nine varieties.

My Texas broker at the time suggested that we highlight the new wine's affinity for what he called "cuisines of heat." Müller-Thurgau went so well with spicy foods, the new wine should, too. Restaurants were moving to lighter menus, with recipes that contained the complex flavors of cilantro, mint, lemongrass, ginger, cumin, hot chilies, or wasabi. These flavors did not match well with heavily oaked Chardonnays and tannin-laden Cabernet Sauvignons, but paired beautifully with Evolution No. 9.

When the wine came onto the market, in the early summer of 1998, our distributors were dubious. This wine was unlike anything they had seen and they weren't sure the public would respond. The label had an attitude, with its big "No. 9" on the front, and there was a little booklet dangling from a key chain on the neck of the bottle. One of our best distributors, in Northern California, told me he didn't think it would sell because it wasn't serious enough. It's true that we wanted the packaging to be the antithesis of the traditionally snobby wine label and deliberately chose not to put either a vintage date or an appellation designating origin of the grapes on the label. But the wine itself we took very seriously.

Some understood the label immediately. Liner & Elsen, a wine store in Portland run by Bob Liner and Matt Elsen, wrote it up in their monthly newsletter, saying,

"The "hottest" new white wine from the Oregon wine country doesn't come from some new trendy startup winery. It's not made by some visiting celebrity French winemaker either. It's not a slick marketing trick conjured up by some transplanted Californian who flew up here from Chateau Bigbucks in Snapanoma. No, the wine that's all the rage is "Evolution No. 9"—it's the tastiest new wine on the shelf and it comes from none other than the winery at the top of the long and winding road, the venerable Sokol Blosser Winery. The packaging is terrific, and the wine . . . well, "Nothing like it has ever been." 9 varietals come together. Pour it backwards and walk across the street barefoot. Drink some. Huge, tropical fruit bouquet (the Walrus was Paul), off-dry, lush, koo-koo kachoo, crisp finish. May it serve you well. Yeah, yeah, yeah. . . ."

Our California distributor watched as opinion leaders in the influential San Francisco Bay Area embraced Evolution No. 9. Leaders in the gay and lesbian community in San Francisco bought it enthusiastically, partly because Vivien Gay, a friend of ours and a leader in that community, talked it up. But there's also no substitute for luck, and that came when Gene Burns, a radio personality whose Saturday morning program on San Francisco's KGO had a huge audience, invited me to be on his show. He had tasted our new wine at a local restaurant, on the recommendation of the server, and had loved it so much that he wanted me to talk about it on his program. If I had ever had any doubts about the power of the media, they were erased by the deluge of inquiries and sales after Gene's show. Not only did Bay Area stores soon sell out of Evolution No. 9, but the winery had to keep one person on the phone all that day, taking orders.

Evolution No. 9 was a bold new concept for us and, in fact, for

Oregon. It started slowly, but when it found its niche in the market, sales rose steadily. Production started in 1998 at 2,700 cases and increased twelve-fold in five years. Conceived as the solution to an ongoing problem, it became a home run in its own right. The combination of an engaging name, an ingenious label, and great flavor made it a winner in every sense. This little wine even received fan mail and had its own website where people could tell us their stories. How did we get so lucky? We didn't do any of the things big corporations do in developing new products, mainly because we didn't have the money. Sokol Blosser's research-and-development department consisted of Gary, my vice president, and me. How happy, how serendipitous, how desperately needed was this success. Sales of Evolution provided the cash flow we needed to revitalize Sokol Blosser.

Only a threatened lawsuit alleging copyright infringement by an East Coast brewing company dampened our high spirits. The attorneys I consulted were eager to go to court, certain that Sokol Blosser had an excellent chance of winning, but I resisted, fearing the emotional and financial drain of a lawsuit. Negotiating without attorneys was, I am convinced, the reason we resolved the issue amicably. We ultimately agreed to restrict the sales to certain markets and modify the label.

We asked Sally Morrow and David Brooks to "evolve" the label and the name, and they more than met the challenge. They came up with the "Chill. Pour. Sip. Chill" slogan, which we trademarked along with the now shortened name, "Evolution." The transition to the new package was seamless, but the original name seemed engraved in people's minds. I continued to see Evolution listed on wine lists or in reviews as Evolution No. 9.

———

MY VISION WAS STARTING to take shape and 1998 saw the business start to come together. At the same time, my personal life began to fall apart. Judging from appearances, my marriage to Bill was a success.

We had built a business together and had three great kids. The problem was inside me. Years of suppressed feelings finally wanted out. A psychologist I went to had told me I was a "pleaser." I'd never heard the term before, but I understood it immediately. I spent my childhood trying to please my parents, and my marriage, up to that point, trying to please my husband, always thinking that for each of them to love me, I had to make them happy. Seeking praise, acceptance, and love, I hid my own feelings. As I focused on pleasing, my emotional life became so confused I lost track of what I really wanted. The sad part was that trying to please everyone else didn't work. I always felt that nothing I did was ever quite enough. The strain of trying to be the person I thought Bill wanted me to be kept me in a state of perpetual self-criticism. I never saw the paradox of wanting to be loved for who I was while I was trying to be someone else.

Being the decision maker, first at the vineyard and then at the winery, forced me to identify what I wanted on a business level. After I learned to do that, I felt like two people. At work, I was at ease, competent, and decisive. I liked that person. My success running the winery gave me confidence I'd never had before, and I relished the feeling that I was doing something well. But at home, I was still a pleaser, quashing my feelings to be the person I thought Bill wanted. As that person, I became depressed. Despite the many winery crises, I laughed and smiled more at work than I did at home. In time, I decided I didn't want to be two different people. I needed to put the pieces together and couldn't do it within our existing marriage.

In the late fall and winter of 1998, my relationship with Bill unraveled despite frank conversation and working with a counselor. I moved from being angry and feeling like the victim to understanding that, by putting myself in the position of pleaser, I was also the perpetrator. Perhaps Bill had allowed and even encouraged that role, but I could have modified our relationship significantly if I had been true to myself, instead of trying so hard to be the person I thought he wanted me to be. Now, with so much negative history, marriage had started to feel like a cage. I was fifty-four years old and knew that if I left, I would probably never find anyone else—men my age wanted someone younger—and would most likely be alone for the rest of my life. Being of the generation of women who were taught to feel incomplete without a man, that was tough to accept. But when being alone began to seem preferable to staying married, the decision was made.

The kids were shocked when we told them. Since they were all married, with homes of their own, I thought they would take it in stride. That was a major miscalculation. They knew Bill and I had gone through tough times in the past, but since neither of us had confided our personal problems to them, my leaving caught them by surprise. They took our stability for granted, and I had just exploded their view of reality. Their sympathy interlaced with their distress that I had broken up the family.

They kept asking me why, and while I wanted to explain how I felt, I was uncomfortable saying anything negative about Bill. He was an engaged and loving father. I thought of when Alex was too young to drive but belonged to a bicycle racing team, how Bill got up early to drive him to the team's ride every Saturday morning, then waited to drive him back home, an hour each way. I thought of how Bill taught Nik to drive the tractor and how he read to each of the children from the time they were little. They said they wanted answers but my sense was they didn't want to hear what I would say. So I never really explained my decision.

In the waning days of December of 1998, filled with fear at being on my own and sadness at admitting failure after so many years, I moved out. But deep inside, a small spark of anticipation flickered. I had never lived alone, moving from my parents' home into the marital home right after college. I found a little apartment overlooking the Park Blocks in downtown Portland, where my cat, YumYum, and I set up housekeeping. I deliberately left with little more than my clothes, a few books, and two treasures—the samovar my great-grandmother had brought with her from Russia in the 1880s and a large wooden loon carved by Native American artist Amanda Crowe, a present from my brother Ronnie. I wanted a fresh start.

What a difficult and melancholy job it was, to walk away from almost thirty-three years of marriage. I was afraid I would wake up one day and realize I'd made a terrible mistake. Each morning before getting out of bed, I gingerly probed my emotional state to reassure myself that I was still okay with my decision. I had sown chaos by breaking up the family. My children's agony showed me how inextricably connected we were. Preoccupied with my own unhappiness, I hadn't considered how my leaving their father would shatter their world, threaten their sense of security, and untangle the threads that held us together, even though they were adults and had left home. I also underestimated the strength of my own ties to the family unit. Christmas and the other family rituals I'd taken for granted were never the same. Leaving Bill generated a tough emotional tradeoff. In my attempt to find myself, I had destroyed the family element that was one of my core values. A deep sadness over that unraveling will always be with me.

I called my mother, whom I considered the model of an independent woman, to tell her I was leaving Bill and waited for her to congratulate me on this huge move I was making. She was silent for a moment before responding. "You left Bill? Why would you do that? He was a good husband, wasn't he?" Her short exclamations burst through the phone lines. "You won't be invited to parties as a single woman," she went on. She seemed to be scolding me, implying that unless Bill were physically abusing me, why wouldn't I stay with him, for my own good?

In her commanding way, she demanded details—what had he done? Since my leaving seemed sudden to her, I'm sure she thought there was a triggering event that made me angry enough to leave. She asked if I had, for example, caught him in bed with another woman. I was hurt, then angry, and immediately withdrew from the conversation. I didn't bother to tell her I was trying to put the pieces of myself together.

Confiding would only give her ammunition to chastise me with.

When I didn't call her for the next two weeks, she telephoned Alison to ask what was wrong. Mother had no idea how much she had upset me and continued to ask me periodically about my decision. I always changed the subject. She died wondering why I left Bill when he was such a good husband. It took me years after her death to wish I had confided in her, woman to woman, and gone beyond our instinctual and stereotypical mother-daughter confrontation.

Telling people that Bill and I were no longer together proved awkward. Business associates always asked how Bill was. If I said we had separated, everyone immediately assumed that Bill had left me and said how sorry they were. That facile assumption annoyed me, but correcting them by blurting out that I had left him didn't seem right either. It took two years to finally be able to tell people matter-of-factly and not be embarrassed.

In my childhood, divorce was considered failure and was usually filled with anger and recrimination. When Bill and I filed the final paperwork to make the divorce official, we acknowledged to each other that we had done a good job of raising the kids and building a business, but had not been successful with each other personally. We knew we shared bonds that neither of us would ever have with anyone else, and that we would always be joined on some level. We went to the courthouse together to file for divorce, so that neither of us would have to suffer the indignity of being subpoenaed. If any divorce could be called good, ours was.

Even though our split was amicable for the circumstances, I was not prepared for the huge financial blow that divorce would inflict. In Oregon, a couple's possessions in divorce are considered to be owned fifty-fifty, regardless of pre-divorce ownership. My status as majority owner of both the vineyards and the winery thus vanished with the dissolution of the marriage. I had come to identify with the winery and had put so much energy and emotion into it, I wanted to own it all. To do that, I would have to trade virtually everything else just to get back a majority share. Having control to be able to move the winery forward with my vision was my top priority, so the decision was not hard. Bill was willing to let me buy him out, and it took us about two weeks to agree on the disposition of our interests. We turned the process over to the attorneys—his, mine, and the winery's—who then took almost eighteen months to work out the details and put them in writing.

Part of the divorce settlement involved a formal name change. When I married Bill, I moved from being Susan Sokol to Susan Blosser. There was never a thought of keeping my own name, which was a good thing because it was illegal at the time. In Oregon, at least, it was not until 1973 that the state legislature, in the last days of the session, passed a bill allowing a woman to keep her own name when she married. That the bill passed by only two votes shows how slowly the old mind-set died. When I became president of the winery, I started using Sokol Blosser as my last name, proud that I could claim both, having been born a Sokol and married a Blosser. When we divorced, I made Sokol Blosser my legal last name.

For months I was exhilarated by the thought of owning the winery myself. But time had a mellowing effect. I began to see that while buying Bill out might have satisfied me emotionally, it was not the best strategy for the business. Bill's experience was valuable and we needed his talents on the winery board. Alex worked with Jack Irvine to come up with a plan in which he, Nik, and Alison would defer income from their share of the vineyard to create retirement income for Bill and me. The money was the same for Bill whether he stayed in or got out, and when he decided to stay in, I found myself glad he remained involved. As the winery board evolved, Bill and I, as the old guard, usually found ourselves on the same side.

I look back on 1998 as a time of tumult and upheaval on all fronts, business and personal. Over the course of the twelve months, I hired a new winemaker, brought my son into the business, launched a new, very successful wine, and left my husband of thirty-three years. I had started to discover myself, the person underneath the "pleaser." It was no coincidence that this was also the year I stopped dyeing my hair blonde and let it return to its natural color, by then mostly gray.

———

WHEN I LEFT BILL, my business life might have been in full flower, but my personal life came to a standstill. I had no interest in meeting single men or replacing my marriage with another relationship. Between travel and hosting winery guests, I had a small social life. Marsha Palanci came to visit the winery in January, right after I had moved out, and I surprised her at the airport with the news that she would be staying in my new apartment. She was my first visitor, and in my tender emotional state, I was glad to be with a friend.

I couldn't imagine dating, and matchmaking of any kind, through friends or the Internet, sounded abhorrent. I spent time with female friends, or, if I wanted company for an event or a movie, I asked Russ to go with me. I knew he hadn't met many people in the area and probably wouldn't on his own. I appointed myself his local travel guide, and together we visited Portland's museums and famous gardens.

When I hired Russ, I saw him as introverted, cautious, and focused—qualities that drew me to him as a winemaker. When we worked together, I appreciated his willingness to answer my tentatively posed questions about winemaking that previous winemakers, and even Bill, had treated with condescension. With Russ at the helm, I felt welcome in the cellar for the first time. He seemed content to go home and be alone, but I pursued him; he was one of the few people I enjoyed being with. I had discovered that his sharp mind and remote exterior protected a warm heart and hid a riotous sense of humor. There was a lot more to Russ than he let people see, and I found myself wanting to know him better. We started spending more and more time together, apart from work.

Who can fathom the human heart? Just when I had come to terms with never having another relationship, one happened. Right or wrong, once Russ and I each overcame our doubts, we let ourselves go, and entered a heady affair that consumed us both. I worried that I was on the rebound from Bill, but I rationalized that I had been grieving my failed relationship with Bill for years, and that the actual break had been cathartic. A lifetime of pent-up feelings came pouring out. We became inseparable; I didn't want to do anything he wasn't part of. When I traveled alone for business, I wrote him poems, puerile and passionate. He was my other half and I plunged on, knowing I was breaking every rule in the book by having an affair with my winemaker.

We were circumspect at work and at industry events, but when it became clear to me that Russ and I had a relationship that went far beyond employer-employee and was not just temporary, I knew I had to tell the family, especially Bill. I was nervous when I called Bill and arranged to meet him for a drink in Portland. I expected him to berate me for being stupid enough to get involved with an employee, and I steeled myself for the onslaught. Instead, he said, "I'm happy for you," and acted like he meant it. It helped that he was in a new relationship as well, and he told me about her. I couldn't believe it had gone so well; I breathed a big sigh of relief.

The reaction of my children, on the other hand, caught me by surprise. All three, when I told them, acted shocked and dumbfounded. "What do you think you're doing?" Alison cried. Bill, from whom I was separated but not yet officially divorced at the time, had accepted the news better than our kids, who, with varying degrees of hysteria, scolded me as if they were the parents and I the child. I called Eugenia, who knew about my new relationship. "Eugenia, my kids don't approve of me," I told her.

"What are you doing about it?" she asked.

"I'm avoiding them," I confessed.

I had to pull the phone away from my ear, she hooted so loudly.

When she got over laughing at the role reversal, she advised me to deal with it and talk to them. I felt fragile emotionally, but I finally sat down with them and asked them to give me the same freedom to make mistakes that I had given them when they were falling in love. I reminded them how I had supported their decisions. They thought back. "Oh, yeah," they said. "You did." I also told them I knew the dangers of starting a relationship with Russ, and I would not let it hurt the winery. My friend Heidi Yorkshire, who couldn't believe how happy I looked, told them, "Look how in love your mother is. Let her be. Be happy for her."

Russ and I just wanted to be alone and go out to eat where no one would know us. It wasn't easy as, after selling wine to Portland restaurants for so many years, it was hard for me to go anyplace without knowing someone and feeling like I was being watched. We found the perfect spot, right in downtown Portland, just a walk from my apartment, where we could dine anonymously. Our dinners at India House became a regular event where we would feast on tandoori chicken, and bowls of bhindi masala, saag paneer, baingan bharta, aloo gobi, all accompanied with freshly baked naan. Nestled in a booth in the darkened restaurant, where most of the other diners were Indian or Pakistani, we felt liberated from our gossiping industry.

We took turns paying for dinner and one night, when it was my turn, the server noticed my name on the credit card and asked if I was with the winery. I couldn't deny it and he immediately brought the owner of the restaurant over to meet me. We were such good customers, the owner told us, he wanted to carry our wine. Our cover was blown and we were no longer incognito, but the upshot was that Evolution wine found a new home and the owner put a "Reserved" sign on our favorite table when he knew we were coming. India House became the top seller in Portland of our white Evolution blend.

When we were able to dine at India House, we routinely ordered all our favorite dishes, which was way too much for one meal. Our table for four would be covered with dishes of vegetables, plates of naan, basmati rice, sizzling platters of tandoori, and a bottle of chilled Evolution wine—all for just the two of us. We would look at the bounty before us and smile at each other with the pleasure of beginning our feast, knowing that we would take home enough to feed us during the week.

On my next trip to New York, Marsha Palanci and I had dinner with wine writer Marguerite Thomas, a wine industry friend whom I hadn't seen for more than a year. I told them what had been happening, and especially how surprised I was that my adult kids were having so much difficulty with all the changes, including my new relationship. Marguerite understood and told a similar story. Her husband had died several years before; she was now in a new relationship and her grown kids were acting like disapproving parents. We commiserated. Did we have to give up someone we loved because our kids, who had left home and had their own lives, objected? We had to live our own lives, too. There we were, two middle-aged women talking about our boyfriends like two teenage girls. Except we were in an elegant midtown Manhattan restaurant instead of at a drive-in, talking over architecturally arranged vegetables and Asian noodles instead of burgers and fries, and drinking Evolution wine instead of milkshakes.

By the end of the year, Russ and I, and my cat, YumYum, were settled into a house Russ and I had bought together, about twenty minutes from the winery. Our relationship went against all common sense, all rules for business success, and all conventions of employer-employee interaction. I was never at ease working side-by-side with Bill, yet I loved working with Russ. His passion and drive for quality was my gyroscope at work. I never anticipated, and could not have imagined when I hired him, that Russ would be part of not only the winery's renaissance, but also mine.

....

Saag Paneer

Here is one of the tastes I love from India House, the restaurant in Portland where Russ and I used to go regularly. This recipe was adapted from *Whole World Vegetarian* (Houghton Mifflin, May 2016) by Marie Simmons. Ghee is a type of clarified butter used in Indian cooking. You can find it in upscale supermarkets or health food stores. Paneer is a type of fresh, cow's milk cheese popular in India. Look for it in similar outlets. You can adjust the amount of chile in the dish to your taste—add a bit more if you like it spicy. Serve with hot cooked rice or warmed naan (an Indian-style flatbread). The wine to drink? Evolution White, of course.

Makes 4 servings

> 1 pound fresh spinach leaves, tough stems trimmed, washed, drained,
>   and coarsely chopped
> 5 tablespoons prepared ghee, clarified butter,
>   or coconut oil
> 10 ounces paneer, cut into ½-inch chunks
> 1 cup finely chopped yellow onion
> 2 to 3 teaspoons full-bodied Madras curry powder
> ½ teaspoon ground turmeric
> ½ teaspoon coarse sea salt, or to taste
> 2 teaspoons finely chopped fresh green or red chile,
>   plus more to taste, if desired
> 1 garlic clove, minced
> 1 to 2 teaspoons finely chopped fresh peeled ginger
> 1 cup unsweetened full-fat coconut milk
> ½ cup drained, finely chopped fresh or canned tomato
> 2 tablespoons coarsely chopped fresh cilantro (optional)

Put the spinach in a steamer basket set over a pan of boiling water. Cover the pan and let the spinach steam until it is wilted and tender, about 5 minutes. Transfer the spinach to a large strainer or colander and press with the back of a spoon to remove as much water as possible. Set the spinach aside.

In a large skillet over medium-high heat, warm 3 tablespoons of the ghee until it's until hot enough to sizzle a piece of the paneer. Add the paneer chunks in a single layer and cook, turning with tongs, until they are lightly browned on all sides, 2 to 3 minutes per side. Transfer the browned paneer to a plate.

Add the remaining 2 tablespoons of the ghee to the skillet and place over medium heat. Add the onion and cook, stirring, until golden, about 10 minutes. Stir in the curry powder, turmeric, and salt and cook for about 1 minute. Stir in the chile, garlic, and ginger.

Add the steamed spinach, coconut milk, and tomato to the pan and warm until the liquid gently simmers. Reduce the heat to low and cook, uncovered, stirring occasionally, until the flavors are well integrated, about 5 minutes. Gently stir in the browned paneer and serve right away. Sprinkle servings with cilantro, if desired.

CHAPTER FIVE

Embracing Sustainability

The late 1990s also saw the term *sustainability* come into the lexicon. My lens on farming and business evolved as I learned more about what sustainability could mean. I had grown up thinking the world of business was Machiavellian—the ends justify the means, so do whatever it takes to succeed—and it didn't feel right. My notion of the corporate tycoon was modeled on the nineteenth-century robber barons I had studied in American history—pillage the land, take advantage of workers to build your fortune, and then give a little back so you can go down in history as a great philanthropist.

When I took over the winery, I didn't want to play that way. For me, the lure of business was the challenge to succeed in something I was passionate about, but the journey was just as important as the destination, a perspective I didn't believe to be widely shared by conventional business leaders. I wanted to do well and do good at the same time. So I kept my head down and quietly moved my business forward. Then, in the early 1990s, a business friend asked if I would be interested in joining with him and other Portland businesses to start an Oregon chapter of Business for Social Responsibility (BSR). The national BSR organization, just gaining ground, had been founded by well-respected companies including Stride Rite, Gap, Levi Strauss & Co., and Ben & Jerry's. It emphasized concern not just for profit, but also for people and the environment—the "triple bottom line." This was the first time I had heard that phrase and it touched something deep inside me. Discovering values-driven cohorts in the business world gave me the confidence to lift my head up and be public about my approach to business. I began keeping notes on what I was learning, which years later turned into a book of short essays about running a values-driven business, being true to yourself, and still being successful.

I became one of the founding members of the Portland Chapter of Business for Social Responsibility. In addition to being on the policy-making board of directors of the new organization, a few of us met monthly just to talk about our companies. We were a small group, including the owner of an international children's clothing company, the principal of an accounting firm, the founder of a lighting and vintage hardware manufacturer, an architect, and a chef and restaurant owner. We called our informal group "Business with Soul," and met regularly, sharing the challenges of trying to define and implement sustainability in the workplace. I was the only winery person, and enjoyed my new friends in diverse fields.

Shortly after joining BSR, my approach to farming changed in a way that was so fundamental that it affected my whole worldview. Reading books by poet and environmentalist Wendell Berry and by food policy journalist and professor Michael Pollan compelled me to reexamine my view of farming. When we started the vineyard in the 1970s, we farmed like the other grape growers and local farmers, using chemicals to combat pests and disease, and synthetic fertilizer to make the vines grow. Using synthetic chemicals was the norm. We considered ourselves environmentalists, so we used the chemicals sparingly, but we accepted that they were necessary. When we sprayed diazinon or malathion to get rid of the cherry fruit fly, we were thinking only about our crop, not about the ecosystem. When arsenic sprays and DDT were banned in the 1950s, our friend and neighbor Ted Wirfs hated that his chemical arsenal had been compromised. "Haven't had a good crop of peaches since," he would lament. Ted considered himself a good farmer and believed that using chemicals to keep crops clean was part of being a "steward of the land." This notion was one of the chemical companies' favorite phrases.

In the 1970s, farmers didn't consider that the chemicals killed more than just the pests they were aimed at. But in fact, many killed everything they touched. In conventional farming, the soil was considered a growing medium, so if chemicals destroyed the soil's microbial life and made it unable to nourish plants, the solution was to replenish with synthetic fertilizer. The human mind, adept at embracing opposing beliefs without seeing a conflict, allowed farmers who considered themselves stewards of the land to have no problem in using toxic chemicals that sterilized the soil and damaged the ecosystem.

The underlying assumption was that the farmer's job was to tame, or at least control, nature. Chemicals that worked well when they were introduced proved to be temporary fixes since the pests they aimed to control developed resistance to those same chemicals. As smart as we humans think we are, the "lesser" forms of life—weeds and insects—seem to outsmart us every time. The interdependence of all living things, the perilous consequences of chemical agriculture, and the need to work with rather than against nature began to hit home.

As I farmed the vineyard, I learned that working with nature meant building up the soil to be able to provide nutrition to plants naturally, instead of chemically—like the difference between normal digestion and intravenous feeding—and encouraging a diverse array of species to coexist, thus establishing a balanced ecosystem. Instead of using chemicals to eliminate bugs and disease, we had to learn to create a competitive environment in which no bug or disease could dominate. This approach, called sustainable agriculture, or agroecology, allowed farmers and environmentalists to be on the same side, and that made sense to me. Affirmation of our sustainable farming appeared when the Pacific Rivers Council, headquartered in Portland, created a Salmon-Safe designation to bestow on farms that produced their crops without harming salmon. This environmental marketing program was developed with the belief that if people had a choice, they would choose products that helped protect salmon. In the vineyard, it meant limiting toxic chemicals and erosion that would end up in streams and rivers. Sokol Blosser became the first Salmon-Safe winery and the Pacific Rivers Council announced the program in the spring of 1996, at a press conference with TV coverage, at Sokol Blosser. The task of educating the public began that day with the news media, who were full of questions about how farming on our hillsides and protecting salmon were related.

The following year, Ted Casteel from Bethel Heights Vineyard and Al MacDonald from Seven Springs Vineyard formalized a sustainability program imported from Europe that they called LIVE (Low Impact Viticulture & Enology). Oregon's LIVE program was one of many sustainable programs in the United States, but was the only one with international recognition through the International Office of Biological Control, a prestigious European certifier. The program encouraged farmers to see the vineyard as a whole system, established guidelines for sustainable vineyard practices, and offered ecological options that encouraged biodiversity and reduced use of synthetic inputs. This way of looking at farming was so different from what the growers were used to, it took time to grasp. But when growers understood that vineyards would be healthier and longer-lived, they signed on, and the LIVE program garnered enough support to become institutionalized in Oregon. Salmon-Safe and LIVE later worked together for joint certification.

After a three-year transition period, the first vineyards earned LIVE certification in 1999. Sokol Blosser was among that group. Once a review panel ensured that the wines weren't flawed, wineries could display the LIVE symbol on their label. Bethel Heights was the first winery to do this. The problem was that no one understood what LIVE meant. Marketing sustainability was not yet in vogue.

I didn't believe that the Salmon-Safe or LIVE designations would help us market our wines unless we supported them with mega advertising and promotion. None of us had the dollars for that kind of campaign. What interested me more was finding out how sustainability really played out on the ground, in my own vineyard. Once I understood the importance of LIVE's central concept, biodiversity, I looked for ways to implement it at Sokol Blosser. Since we grew only one crop, wine grapes, we needed to take elaborate measures to create enough biodiversity to provide the necessary competition. A monoculture is an open invitation to predators of that one crop.

In my cover crop experiments in the 1980s, I had searched for a single species that would do the job. Now I saw the value of planting a combination of species that would do triple duty by increasing microbial life in the soil, attracting beneficial insects with their flowers, and adding organic matter to the soil. To enhance the soil ecosystem, called the soil food web, I wanted compost—rich, sweet-smelling, and full of earthworms and microbial life. First I bought it, and then we started making it ourselves, using our own grape pomace (the grape stems and skins left after pressing), horse and cow manure, and straw. We let the cover crop mixes we planted in the fall grow high in the spring before we mowed and worked them in to build up the humus content of the soil.

The large trees on the perimeter of our vineyard, which I'd previously regarded only as roosts for grape-eating birds, I now saw as wildlife habitat for the hawks, owls, raccoons, deer, and coyotes that were important players in our vineyard ecosystem. We joined the

Prescott Western Bluebird Recovery Project and put up nesting boxes sized for the bluebirds. They and the swallows formed our insect patrol. In a few years, we had a small flock of bluebirds that were monitored and banded each season. Coming up the winery road every morning, we would see them sitting on vineyard wires. The flash of brilliant blue was always a thrill. When I helped with the banding, the baby bluebird whose tiny body pulsated in my hand symbolized the miracle of all the diverse life in our vineyard ecosystem.

Walking in the vineyard turned into a nature walk. I watched dragonflies traveling around the grape canopy and heard the background hum of bees. I would come across one of our six feral cats (spayed and neutered by Portland's Feral Cat Coalition) sitting perfectly still, watching the fresh dirt of an active gopher mound, ready to pounce. I dubbed them our Rodent Patrol and they took their job seriously. Right above me, swallows soared and dived to grab small insects out of the air. Higher up a hawk circled, probably eyeing a mouse. A majestic great blue heron might fly over. I felt a vibrancy in the vineyard I hadn't felt since the early years. Biodiversity had given it new life and energy.

The LIVE program did not mandate organic practices, but for me organic farming was the next step. Why use any synthetic chemicals that would kill the ecosystem we were trying to encourage? Federal standards had recently been put in place, and organic was, by the turn of the century, a legal term. Farms and products could not legally claim to be organic unless they were certified. Going after organic certification would mean I could no longer use the synthetic products we had traditionally used to kill mildew and rot. I would have to give up Roundup, the best chemical we had for killing unwanted growth under the vines. While I was deciding whether to go through the mountain of paperwork that organic certification entailed, I joined a group of colleagues who were studying biodynamics, another farming approach coming into vogue. We hired a biodynamic horticulturist to come up from California once a month to instruct us.

The fervor I felt for the environment—what we had done to it and what we needed to do to resuscitate it—was much on my mind. The problem was far bigger than my vineyard, but I had contributed to the earth's damage, and I could contribute to its renewal. I was on a mission to change, and change quickly.

Common Growing Terms

Agroecology *is the application of ecological principles to farming, with the goal of creating sustainable food systems.*

Biodiversity *is the variety of living things.*

Biodynamic *agriculture is based on organic agriculture but includes esoteric cosmic concepts defined by Rudolf Steiner (1861–1925).*

Ecology *is the study of interactions among living things in their environment, called an ecosystem.*

Monoculture *is growing only one crop.*

Organic *has been a legal term since the federal National Organic Program rules came out in 2000, which set the standards for organic production. Organic farming promotes recycling of resources, ecological balance, and biodiversity.*

Sustainability *is the ability to continue a behavior indefinitely. Environmental sustainability is the rate at which renewable resources, pollution creation, and nonrenewable resource depletion can be continued. Planetary health relies on the capacity for self-renewal.*

I joined a small group of winegrowers who began to study the founder of biodynamics, an early twentieth-century Austrian named Rudolf Steiner, whose vision was to revitalize the earth by connecting natural science and mysticism. Steiner took organic principles to a paranormal level, invoking not only the cosmos, but also otherworldly dimensions. Organic farming operated on the assumption that the earth was a complex biological system. Biodynamics envisioned the earth as part of a living cosmos, dependent on planetary movement. I couldn't decide if Steiner was a nut or if he had hit on a truth worth understanding. Our instructor talked at length about invisible energetic forces that converted non-matter into matter inside the vine. He told us that biodynamic preparations enlivened the soil like yeast enlivens dough.

We were hesitant, having come together to find practical farming solutions and new ways to protect our vines from disease and destructive insects, to indulge in mystical theory. It was all I could manage to coordinate labor, weather, and equipment readiness to accomplish farming procedures. Was it really necessary to take into account the phase of the moon and the stations of the planets for everything we did? Our instructor emphasized the importance of spraying plant essences during the growing season, such as chamomile flowers, dandelion leaves, yarrow, nettle, and valerian. "Don't drench the vines like with other sprays, just aim a gentle mist into the air, and let the energy float down onto the vines." Plant essences were not available in the chemical aisles at our local farm stores. We had to plan ahead and mail order them. You had to be a believer to go to all that bother. The reason we went to the trouble of learning something so difficult to understand and so foreign to our thinking was that the best vineyards in France, the mother lode of wine, had embraced biodynamics.

For two years, in 2002 and 2003, I experimented, setting aside two vineyard blocks to farm biodynamically. This took ignoring Luis's, my vineyard manager, and Alex's incredulity. I procured the plant essence sprays, and asked Luis to follow the proper application ritual. This involved lashing together pruned grape canes to make a stick broom— the kind a black-garbed witch with a pointy hat would fly on. Protocol for the broom was to stir the spray formulations, going in alternating directions to create a vortex, for thirty to sixty minutes, depending on the spray. I also asked the crew to construct a compost pile, with grape pomace, cow manure, and straw, a giant, thirty-foot-long, six-foot high lasagna, which I then inoculated with special biodynamic preparations. Luis did it all without complaining, although I imagined he rolled his eyes behind my back and used choice words explaining these unusual procedures to his crew.

I followed the prescribed procedures, but wanted to understand them better so I could make decisions myself instead of relying on outside advice. The second year of our experimentation, Philippe, a French biodynamic viticulturist consulted for me once a month. I hoped he would explain how he decided what was needed and give me insight into the biodynamic program.

On one spring visit, as the vineyard glistened in the cool morning air, Alex and Luis accompanied Philippe and me as we walked through our biodynamic blocks. The new grape shoots, with their tiny green leaves and miniature clusters, shimmered with morning dew. Eager to learn, I felt like a puppy scampering through the vineyard, trying to keep up with my lanky consultant. Philippe stopped periodically to stare intently at the vines, the three of us halting in our tracks behind him. He barked a command for my next vineyard procedure. What was he seeing? What did the vine look like through a biodynamic lens? I asked. Philippe peered down at me with that condescending look the French are so good at. "I'm looking," he said, with splendid pomposity, "at the quality of light," and strode on down the row. He clearly wasn't about to share his enlightenment. Alex and Luis and I looked at each other and shrugged our shoulders.

As we continued, stepping over gopher mounds on our walk, I asked what he recommended we do about the gophers that were wreaking havoc in the vineyard, creating dirt mounds, disrupting the ground cover, even killing vines. He told us to catch some, cut off their heads, and put them on stakes around the vineyard. I'll never forget the look Alex and Luis gave each other, a combination of disbelief and disgust. That was the last season Philippe consulted for us.

Several years later, when Alex took over the vineyards as part of a major transition for the winery, he chose to concentrate on organic farming rather than biodynamic. He told me he'd had it with vineyard consultants. "Mom," he said, "our years on this land and our understanding of our vines are worth more than the crackpots who have come in and given us bad advice. Our common sense is better than their so-called expertise. Just because they call themselves experts doesn't mean they are." I understood his decision and agreed with his view of consultants, but connecting spirituality with farming fascinated me. By seeing the farm as a living cosmic system, every part intertwined, from the planets, to the farmer, down to the microbes and rocks in the soil, biodynamics expanded my understanding of universal interdependence and the idea of cosmic energy flow, a theme I would keep running into.

Our experience with Philippe made me consider organic certification more seriously. I sent for the application from the United States Department of Agriculture (USDA), just to see what was required. The leap between claiming to farm organically and actually being certified was huge. Besides extensive recordkeeping, we had to take into account possible contamination from neighboring farms. Plus, the big thing was that it eliminated irrevocably the possibility of using synthetic chemicals. There was no safety net. We had to farm proactively to avoid potential problems.

After dallying around and filling out the cumbersome forms, which required five years of records and extensive explanations of every farm input, I put forth a final burst of energy and determination, completed it all, and sent in the inches-thick application. I felt it was a major achievement just to apply. After a lengthy review and inspection, we entered our three-year transition to full organic certification. Sixty vineyards were in the LIVE program by then, but certified organic vineyards were few. When we received our full certification, in 2005, several small Oregon vineyards (two to ten acres) were certified, but only seven (out of three hundred) Oregon wineries with vineyards had made the USDA organic list. They were Bergström Vineyards, Brick House Vineyards, Cooper Mountain Vineyards, Evesham Wood Vineyard, King Estate Winery, Lemelson Vineyards, and Sokol Blosser.

But farming was only one piece of sustainability. I had learned, to paraphrase John Muir, that when you tug on one piece of nature, you find it's connected to everything else. This was driven home when Russ and I went to a sustainability workshop, in 1999, that focused on The Natural Step program. The name made it sound like an orthopedic shoe company, but the concept ignited a small fire in my brain. Based on accepted scientific principles, it addressed humans' relationship with the physical universe and offered a framework of system conditions under which all human action should take place. Those system conditions focused on rectifying the systematic degradation of the environment that occurs when we use natural resources (petroleum, coal) faster than they can be created, turn these resources into products that don't decompose (plastics), and create waste that has nowhere to go in our closed planetary system.

Considered in this broader light, our degree of unsustainability horrified and humbled me. I looked at how many nonrenewable resources we used. How naive I had been, all the while thinking of myself as an environmentalist. My business, indeed my whole life, our whole culture, fed on unsustainable practices. Eliminating synthetic chemicals and fertilizers and farming organically was just a small start. Sustainability was a much bigger concept.

My new lens of understanding brought to light issues in every part of our operation. Black plastic sheeting under our new plantings for weed suppression and water retention eliminated herbicide use but it also used a nonrecyclable petroleum product. The tin capsules and metallic labels we used in our packaging looked upscale and classy but were not the most sustainable options. We stocked our tasting room with bleached paper products and ran reams virgin paper for the copiers and printers. We did it without thinking; it was the way things were done. I began the long, slow process of educating myself and my employees and scrutinizing everything we did. Sustainability across the operation became our new mantra.

We soon had the chance to put our new principles to work on a major project: building a new wine cellar. It was time to face the issue of barrel storage for Pinot Noir, which we had put off because of the huge capital outlay we knew it would entail. Our winery building that housed the barrels was too hot in summer, too cold in winter, and never humid enough to prevent excessive evaporation through the French oak barrels. And because we intended to double our Pinot Noir production, we would need room for more barrels as soon as our new plantings started producing.

After considering the different options, we concluded that the most efficient solution would be a new building adjacent to the winery. We had no budget for architectural flourishes, but decided we would try to follow the precepts of The Natural Step and build it sustainably. Bill suggested we look at the US Green Building Council's new LEED certification program, which set strict guidelines for sustainable building. We had started with an architect who had winery but no "green" experience. We decided to switch to a firm that specialized in sustainable building, SERA Architects, and Russ worked closely with them for the next year to be sure that the new cellar was not only sustainable but would be perfect for aging Pinot Noir.

The simple structure that resulted belied the amount of thought behind it and its complex underpinnings. Dug into the hillside, the cellar had a low profile and a rounded top covered with three feet of soil that was quickly rampant with wildflowers of every color, adding to the biodiversity of the vineyard. In its 5,200 square feet of silent, humid darkness, the barrels could age at a constant fifty-five to sixty degrees Fahrenheit year-round without any air-conditioning. For meeting its strict siting, energy, water, materials, and waste criteria, the US Green Building Council awarded us their esteemed LEED Silver 2.0 certification.

In 2002, Sokol Blosser became the first winery in the country to achieve this distinction. The LEED certification meant a lot to me. Sustainable construction was so far out of the mainstream at that time that it took substantial extra effort to make it happen. I made sure the large silver plaque we received got installed on a post positioned prominently at the entrance to the new cellar.

I can't remember a time when I wasn't fanatical about conservation. I was raised with a strong emphasis on an awareness of how we as a species were using, and using up, our natural resources. I was searching out foods produced without potentially harmful chemicals and going to great lengths to find ways to recycle long before organic, green, and sustainable were part of the general lexicon. So I was thrilled that Susan and the Sokol Blosser family were interested in pursuing those things also. In 2000 we remodeled our original tasting room, and when I told the contractor we wanted it to be done sustainably he thought I meant we wanted it to last a long time. We had to teach him about formaldehyde-free particle board, FSC (Forest Stewardship Council) wood, and low or no VOC paints, products that were not widely in use, hard to find, and much more expensive than conventional products.

When we built our underground barrel cellar in 2005 we used that same contractor and, although we still had to be the ones to ask for the most sustainable options for every aspect of the building, he was now much more knowledgeable and the materials were much more available, although still more expensive. That contractor now advertises his company as specialists in sustainable building, a field with considerable demand.

It was the same when dealing with the vendors for our packaging supplies. The representatives for the companies from which we purchased our bottles, corks, labels, and cases were always surprised and stumped when I asked for various sustainable choices, like lighter weight bottles or label paper made with 100 percent recycled content or even from

The first winery building to achieve the US Green Building Council's rigorous LEED certification, our new barrel cellar combined old-fashioned root cellar with modern technology, giving Sokol Blosser Pinot Noir perfect aging conditions. With its native grasses on top and lavender, Russian sage, yarrow, and other beneficial insect-attriting plants at each end, it also became part of the winery's biodiversity program. 2002. (Photo credit: Doreen L. Wynja.)

alternative "tree-free" sources, like bamboo or kenaf. I constantly felt as if I was the first to ask these questions and, appropriately for an Oregon winery, like we were salmon swimming upstream.

Russ Rosner
Sokol Blosser Winemaker, 1998–2013

The building had caused a lot of talk in the industry, so we held an open house. Oregon's governor, Ted Kulongoski, who had made sustainability a priority in his new administration, came and spoke, as did Secretary of State Bill Bradbury, the head of Oregon's Sustainability Task Force. The governor, well briefed in diplomacy, stood against a backdrop of French oak barrels full of Pinot Noir, on a platform made that morning of wine pallets, and began by telling the gathering, "Twenty-five years ago, Bill and Susan put wine in a bottle, and Oregon has been better off since." His speech delighted the guests, and the Sokol Blosser family wore big smiles. Christine Ervin, the president of the US Green Building Council, told the gathering that while more than eight hundred had registered their intent, only thirty-seven projects in the United States had achieved LEED certification.

I had met with her the preceding year to discuss the certification requirements and consider the obstacles; I had left our meeting discouraged but not totally flattened. At our open house, she told me that when we did decide to take on the challenge, she had thought to herself, "If anyone can make this happen, it's Susan." She'd had faith in me I hadn't had in myself.

While Sokol Blosser was the first winery and the first agricultural project to achieve LEED certification, sustainable building, while rare, was not new. Notable wineries in California, such as Fetzer and Sanford, had followed sustainable principles in their buildings. Sokol Blosser brought the concept to Oregon and newer wineries took on the challenge. Stoller Family Estate built its winery in 2006 and bested Sokol Blosser by achieving LEED Gold. I was glad to speak at the formal opening of Stoller's new building and applaud Bill Stoller for one-upping me by achieving LEED Gold. Driving up to his winery, I couldn't help reflecting that the fields that once assailed my senses with the smell and gobble of huge flocks of turkeys now flourished serenely with acres of wine grapes.

My drive toward sustainability at the vineyards and winery reflected heartfelt values shared by my family, especially Bill and Nik, as well as Russ, whose uncompromising sustainability ethic kept us moving in the right direction. After Bill turned over the winery presidency to me, his planning career focused on issues of sustainability, and talking with him about his work was my introduction to the subject. Nik's career had a similar focus. He and a friend had started an environmental publishing company, producing coupon books for sustainable products, starting in Portland and eventually adding books for Seattle, Minneapolis-St. Paul, Denver, Boulder, and the San Francisco Bay Area.

....

Zucchini Ribbon Salad with Oregon Pink Shrimp, Lemon, Olive Oil, and Herbs

For many years, Russ and I supported the Monterey Bay Aquarium's spring event called "Cooking for Solutions." The event's dual mission was to raise funds for the aquarium as well as educate the media and the public on sustainable seafood and healthy oceans. We became advocates of the aquarium's Seafood Watch program and made a point of supporting restaurants that used seafood that was sustainably harvested. Tiny Oregon pink shrimp—sustainably fished, abundant, versatile, and delicious—fit the program's criteria. Cooked and ready to eat, I buy them by the pound, divide them into serving size portions, and freeze them for future use. If you don't live in Oregon, look for bay shrimp, preferably from local waters and sourced sustainably. When my garden is overflowing with zucchini, I use the tiny shrimp in this light summer salad. You can use green, yellow, or striped zucchini for this as long as they are less than 8 inches long and up to 2 inches in diameter—any larger and the zucchini seeds become challenging to work with. Sokol Blosser Rosé of Pinot Noir is the perfect companion.

Makes 4 servings

> 3 fresh young zucchini, each 6 to 8 inches long, ends trimmed
> ¼ cup thinly sliced green onion tops
> 2 tablespoons finely chopped fresh dill
> 2 tablespoons finely chopped fresh mint

2 tablespoons finely chopped fresh flat-leaf parsley

¼ cup good-quality extra-virgin olive oil

2 teaspoons finely grated fresh lemon zest

2 tablespoons fresh lemon juice, plus more if needed

1 small garlic clove, grated

½ teaspoon coarse sea salt, plus more if needed

⅓ cup chopped pitted green olives (optional)

½ pound cooked Oregon pink shrimp or bay shrimp, rinsed and patted dry

Using a vegetable peeler, shave the zucchini lengthwise into long, paper-thin strips roughly ⅓ to ½ inch wide. Turn the zucchini as you go and press firmly to form even, ribbon-like strips. (Don't worry if you are unable to shave the seedy cores; discard them or reserve for another use.) Alternatively, you can use a spiralizer to make long, spaghetti-like zucchini tendrils. You should have about 4 cups of zucchini strips.

In a large bowl, combine the zucchini strips and green onions. Add the dill, mint, and parsley and toss lightly.

In a small bowl, whisk together the olive oil, lemon zest, lemon juice, garlic, and salt until blended. Add the lemon juice mixture to the zucchini-green onion mixture and toss to coat. Taste and add a bit more lemon juice and salt to taste, if needed. (Tip: if you are adding olives, they will contribute additional saltiness.)

Divide the zucchini mixture among serving plates, top with the olives (if using) and shrimp, and serve right away.

CHAPTER SIX

Passing the Baton

If the 1970s were about establishing our vineyard and winery, the 1980s about survival, and the '90s about getting the vision, the first part of the twenty-first century saw the ascendency of the second generation. Like everything previous, the road was bumpy and uncertain. Bill and I were no longer husband and wife, but we were together in our commitment to family. That commitment, felt by our three children as well, held us together through times that could easily have split us apart.

After Bill and I formally divorced, and the five of us (Bill, the three kids, and me) got together for a winery board meeting, I casually floated the idea of selling the winery. I was flexing my owner's muscle and thinking about all the options. Shocked looks from my kids told me how strongly all three felt about Sokol Blosser Winery.

Nik, Alex, and Alison were not only unanimous, they were vehement about keeping the winery in the family. They grew up with the vineyard and winery as part of their lives, but Bill and I never talked to them about joining us. It was a hard life. I had assumed that seeing their parents' struggle would have made them want to leave, but that wasn't the case.

Our oldest son, Nik, said he didn't want to give up such an important part of his childhood. He had good memories of driving the tractor, picking cherries when we still had orchards and selling them to winery visitors, building a giant tree house, and generally roaming the vineyard. Nik demonstrated his own entrepreneurial gene when he started his own business in Portland, Celilo Group Media, a media company to expand the market for sustainable products. But his emotional ties to the vineyard and winery hadn't waned. His heart was at the vineyard even if he lived in Portland.

Alex, the middle child, had gone off to college in San Antonio, Texas, without any specific goals, ready to follow whatever caught his fancy. Within a year, he realized that the vineyard was in his blood. He missed it enough that he transferred to Oregon State University, then left school to work, first at a neighboring vineyard and then for a Portland wine distributor. In 1998, I talked him into coming to work for me to help with sales. At the time, I was fully engaged in instituting my vision of Sokol Blosser's renaissance and thinking only of the immediate future; I needed his help. Alex was then twenty-four, adept at setting up grocery store Snapple displays, and just learning the wine business. After joining me, he finished college and attended night school at Portland State University to get his MBA. Alex and his wife built a house at the base of the vineyard so their twin boys could grow up as Alex did, close to the earth, among the vines. He definitely didn't want to sell.

Our youngest child and only daughter, Alison, six years younger than Alex, had spent her last year of high school studying in France, then decided to stay home, attend Portland State University, and get married. She worked part-time for me while she was in school. Her organizational prowess and capacity for thinking ahead made her a valuable assistant. I discovered she liked to try out my chair when I wasn't there. Once, I returned and found her sitting at my desk. She swiveled around when I came in, stopping with surprise when she saw me. Eying her as I put my briefcase down, I wondered if she was thinking about her future. As she slowly relinquished my seat, I asked, "What role do you see for yourself at the winery?" She didn't hesitate.

"Your position," she said with a playful grin. We both laughed at the thought. She was barely twenty.

After graduation, she worked for me for a while, then decided she too needed an MBA and went off to the University of Washington for two years, renting an apartment, and commuting back to Portland on weekends, toting her cat in a carrier next to her. She didn't want to sell the winery.

As the majority stockowner, I could have pushed for another option, but the idea of selling didn't appeal to me either. I was just floating different options as they occurred to me. Positioned at the helm, and in full ownership control, I was ready to lead the family business forward into the future. I didn't know how short that future would be.

In January 2004, as another gray Oregon winter day began, I answered my office phone to hear a voice on the other end ask me if I would be available to receive an honorary doctorate at the University of Portland's graduation weekend in May. An honorary doctorate? Was this a practical joke? When the university spokesman, Brian Doyle, finally convinced me that this was no crank call, I had to ask, "Why me?"

"We've been watching you," Brian said. "You exemplify qualities we admire and want to promote, especially entrepreneurship within the context of sustainability and community service." Being watched without knowing it made me uneasy, but I was thrilled with the recognition. Fixated on what I wanted to accomplish, it never occurred to me that anyone, especially outside of the wine industry, might be watching. Yet, being a university professor had once been a dream of mine; getting an honorary doctorate would be sweet.

"I would be deeply honored," I said, hoping to sound dignified, worthy of such an honor. Then I hung up the phone and twirled around in my office chair. It was all I could do to keep from jumping up and shouting "Yippee!"

Graduation weekend, as I donned my long black robe with its turquoise satin collar, I stopped thinking about the challenges ahead and allowed myself a rare moment of achievement. Russ was making our wines better than ever. We were riding a wave of success with our proprietary blend Evolution; our full acreage was finally planted and the vineyard nearing organic certification. Sokol Blosser was a leader in sustainable practices, both in the vineyard and winery, especially as the first winery to achieve the US Green Building Council's hard-to-get LEED certification with our new barrel cellar. Customers across the United States and in key global markets, including Japan and Canada, could buy Sokol Blosser wine in the best stores and restaurants. Pinot Noir had new cachet and ours was considered one of the best. I had almost completed my first book, *At Home in the Vineyard*, telling the story of our winery, the creation and growth of the Oregon wine industry, and my personal journey from liberal arts major with no skills to business executive.

I had climbed the mountain I'd set out to climb, and the surprise honorary doctorate symbolized my success. I knew I was in my prime. But with reflexes from decades of running a business, I was already asking what's next. We couldn't just coast. A business needs a vision to drive it, and the winery needed a new one. Then it hit me: maybe it shouldn't be mine. Maybe it should come from the next generation.

Over the previous year, some seemingly unrelated incidents had lodged in the back of my mind. Together, they formed a pattern pointing to the need for change. For one thing, fatigue hovered over me. The exhilaration of triumphing over challenges had evolved into weariness. After wanting so fiercely to own and run the winery, and giving up so much to achieve it, I found myself reluctant to take on projects that previously I would have tackled eagerly. A little voice in my head whispered that my reluctance could hold the business back. I tried not to listen. My sense of duty kept me going. But the little voice remained.

On a sales trip to Texas, riding with one of our distributor's sales people, I had a sudden image of how I must look to this young person taking me around. Glancing sideways at the hip young man driving, I wondered how he would recount his day to his spouse. I guessed that he might describe me as the old lady he was assigned to spend the day with. He had numerous wines in his portfolio to sell. I had only a few hours to make him a fan of mine. Someone closer to his age, who could relate as a peer, would have a better chance of connecting. Maybe I was getting too old to be doing this.

Financially, the business was getting more complex and competitive. Was I the right person to be taking Sokol Blosser to the next stage? Having grown the winery from twenty thousand cases to over sixty thousand, had I reached my level of incompetence, to use a phrase from the Peter Principle? When the wine industry was in its infancy, I had been able to manage, even do well. Maybe it was time for someone with more sophisticated skills to take the company forward.

Midway through the year, I drove into Portland to have lunch with Nik. I had cleared my schedule and looked forward to having time alone with my thoughtful and strategic son. He was so busy I didn't get to see him enough; I valued his ideas and opinions. In his mid-thirties, with a receding hairline, three kids of his own, and a fledgling business, we talked easily and openly. I smiled to myself as I pulled up to his office to pick him up, remembering the Mother's Day card he sent me when his first child was almost a year old. "Mom," it said, "I had no idea. Love, Nik."

I happened to mention how tired I was. I meant it as a casual comment but Nik looked at me and said, with obvious caring, "I know. I've been wondering when you would start talking about leaving." I had no idea I'd been so transparent. I'd always assumed I would run the winery the rest of my life, that I was the only one who could. But Nik's remark made the seemingly unrelated incidents in the back of my mind coalesce. It was time to confront my weariness, my lack of a new vision, my age, and my skill set and determine what was in the best interest of the business.

A wild thought flashed through my mind: I should give up the presidency. It was the next thought that astonished me. I could imagine doing it.

I had served as chair of the board for several years, but it wasn't always clear what my role was. One day Mom and I had planned to have lunch. Over a year previous to this she had completed her ambitious ten-year plan that involved replanting all the vineyards and building a new barrel cellar. The family had been waiting for her next visionary plan, but none had been forthcoming. In fact, for the past year she just hadn't seemed motivated like before, and while we gave her space and time to refind that spark, it wasn't appearing. At this lunch she commented on her lack of enthusiasm—the first time she'd done so, although the rest of the family had begun discreetly discussing with each other the change in her. I reacted, "Yeah, I was wondering if you saw this, too," and that comment seemed to kindle the awareness of her own lack of drive that she hadn't fully acknowledged yet. That lunch was the beginning of the transition. And I guess both my patience and that comment were my job as chair.

Nik Blosser
Chairman of the Board, Sokol Blosser Winery

Nik's comments made me realize that I needed to plan for the future. Could my children be the answer? My first step was to call Pat Frishkoff, the prominent family business specialist who had founded Oregon State University's Family Business Program, for advice on whether, and how, to implement a transition to the next generation. When she met with Alex, Alison, and me, she was full of warnings. It was October 2004. Alex had been full-time at the winery for five years. Alison had just started. Pat told them that their challenge was to earn the respect of the staff whom I had hired and who looked to me, all of whom were older than Alex and Alison. My challenge, she told me bluntly, was to avoid sabotaging my kids during the transition. One of my mother's favorite sayings popped into my head· "The road to hell is paved with good intentions." It would run as a loop in the back of my mind for the next three years.

The end result of our meeting was that Alex and Alison had become my exit strategy. I felt no threat to my position; surrendering control was, at this point, a theoretical, cerebral concept. I could imagine them in the very vague future waiting for their chance, eager to take my place. But that seemed distant since now, they were still young pups.

A steep learning curve lay ahead and they knew it. Running a vineyard and winery, despite its aura of glamour, was hard work, an all-consuming, high-stakes enterprise. Our whole family depended on its success. I wanted Alex and Alison to experience the weight of the business. To accomplish that, I needed to give them enough responsibility so they would feel, all the way to their core, that the business rested on their shoulders.

During 2005, the whole next year, they each concentrated on parts of my work, Alex on sales and Alison on marketing. To see the big picture, I tried to include them in everything I did. They took in their new experiences with gusto, showing up for work each day with smiles, ready for the next challenge. I loved their spirit. Although premature, the big question in the back of their minds was who would be president. Both wanted it. When the time came, I would have to make a recommendation, and our family board would choose. I tried not to think about that.

Alex was older and had been with the winery longer. He starred as a people person, a natural salesman, compassionate and creative. As the second son, he distinguished himself from Nik, his brainy older brother, first with his quirky sense of humor and imagination, and later as a successful bicycle racer. His ability to connect with people had surfaced at an early age. When Grandma Betty, Bill's mother, came to see us, she always asked each of the kids about themselves. When he was five, Alex turned it around. "How was your day, Grandma?" Alex's warmth and charisma made him a presence in a room. I admired his easy banter, watching him engage people with a charm that was authentic and natural, and observations that ranged from amusing to hilarious.

On the other hand, his impulsiveness gave him a history of what I called "ready, fire, aim." In his enthusiasm, he took on more than he could handle, routinely double booking himself. I worried what he might let fall through the cracks.

Alison, like me, was more introverted. Tall, slim, and pretty, her drive and ambition weren't immediately obvious. She possessed a flair for organizing that surfaced in toddlerhood when she kept her toys sorted in brown shopping bags. As an adult, her color-coded calendar displayed her outstanding time management. After interning at a Portland public relations firm known for creative marketing, she worked at Nordstrom, where she learned first-rate customer service. Fluent with spreadsheets, she would be a well-organized and strategic administrator. But her fire flamed under a cool exterior, and her knack for taking command often veered toward the authoritarian.

When my senior staff took the Myers-Briggs personality tests, I burst out laughing at Alex and Alison's results. My two children were exact opposites on every score. I cringed at the thought of having to choose between them. Each was capable. Possible unpleasant scenarios, caused by the repercussions of choosing between siblings, ran through my mind. Pat could see that we were getting hung up with this dilemma. When we met with her, she diffused the situation.

"Stop talking about it and let it ride," she said. "Concentrate on the business at hand." She had enough clout that we let the subject drop. "Give them time to see who rises to the top," she told me later.

During the remainder of 2005 the board watched to see who would emerge as the obvious choice. Neither did. In January 2006, when the family board met at Alison's house to make the final decision, Pat joined us. "I have a proposal," Alex announced.

"Alison will be the next president and I will be her executive vice president." Nik, Bill, and I sat, stunned. None of us had foreseen this. I knew Alex wanted the presidency as much as Alison and wondered what made him retreat. I watched as Nik and Bill responded.

"How did you arrive at this solution? Are you backing down to avoid a family fight?" Nik asked.

Bill chimed in before Alex had a chance to answer. "Alex, don't suppress yourself to avoid controversy. That won't work in the long run."

Alison stayed silent as Alex straightened up in his chair with a determined look. "I admit the indecision wore me down," he said. "I know either of us could be president. But only one of us would make a good executive vice president. Alison couldn't accept it, but I could. So I'm willing to do it." Alison looked sheepish, and an uncomfortable silence ensued. Pat, who had been watching our interaction, spoke up.

"You don't have to choose," she said. "What's wrong with having copresidents? It's unusual. It's not easy. But it's been done successfully. You have many advantages if you can share the leadership."

She turned to Alison and asked her to consider what she would do if she were president, then became pregnant and wanted to take time off to be with her new baby.

"If you and Alex shared the leadership," Pat continued, "and were essentially interchangeable, that would be possible."

"I hadn't thought of that," Alison responded, with a pensive look that said Pat's comment had hit home, although she had no way of knowing how prophetic Pat's comment would be. Alison had no children. Early in her marriage, she had announced that she didn't want to have kids. Her brothers couldn't believe she was serious. She had teased them, saying that after seeing how much trouble their kids were, she decided she didn't want any. But Pat predicted it. When the time came for Alison to start running the winery, she was four months pregnant.

Pat looked at Alex and said, "If there's shared leadership, not only do you have someone to talk to at your level, but you have the possibility of a life outside the winery." The muscles in Alex's face relaxed and his dimples reappeared as Pat's words sunk in. With a copresidency, he would have more time with his twin boys, teaching them to throw a baseball, ride bikes, go backpacking. "That might work," he admitted.

Bill, Nik, and I looked at each other. Our board hadn't seriously considered a copresidency, but we knew that together they could be stronger than either one would be alone. We had often remarked that if we could fuse them into one, they would be an incredible force.

"Okay," said Alex, with the twinkly smile we knew meant something lighthearted was coming. "I'll agree if Alison promises to share the secret stash of gummy bears and red licorice she keeps in her desk drawer—the one she thinks no one knows about."

"Well, I'll agree too if Alex promises to replenish the ones he's already taken from it," Alison quickly rejoined.

"I'll be around to keep you both in line," Nik finished, wielding his stern, older brother voice.

Tension dissolved and, when the laughter stopped, we discussed the risks of a copresidency. After looking at it every which way, we agreed it would be the best solution. The challenge was how to ensure success with this unusual leadership plan. One safety net was to get them started with a business coach of their own. Our financial advisor, Jack, had been urging me to hire the woman who had helped him and his company. I had put off spending the money, but now it was time. We gave Marsia Gunter, their new coach, the charge of molding brother and sister into a dynamic duo, getting the future copresidents in the habit of respecting and communicating with each other, discussing issues rationally, and dealing with disagreement before something big arose.

The family had cleared a major hurdle with an elegant solution. I couldn't help being envious. The old saying about being lonely at the top was true. I had often wished for a peer to share the inner workings of the business. I was always aware of my singular position. Knowledge is power and I had to be careful how much I confided in my staff. At any time, they could leave and take my confidences with them. It had taken a little over a year to settle the presidential dilemma. Alex and Alison could now look forward to running the winery and vineyard together.

Over the first half of 2006, they met often with their new coach, working to articulate their vision for the business and create a plan for the final piece of the transition. They crafted a page of promises made to each other about communicating and dealing with issues. I stayed out of the process, concentrating on the day-to-day challenges. In July, they presented a detailed plan that had them taking over, under my tutelage, in January 2007 for a practice year. With the start of 2008, I would step back and they would formally take over as copresidents. The board approved their proposal. I had no idea how hard the practice year would prove to be.

———

To describe the final year of the transition simply as arduous doesn't do justice to the complex, puzzling, awkward, and emotional roller-coaster ride that 2007 became. Dubbed the "practice year," I was to be president in name only. Alex and Alison would take over all daily operations. I immediately felt the quandary: I wanted them to take the reins and make decisions, but as titular president, I was responsible. What if I thought they were making a mistake?

It was hard not to tell them what to do, especially when they hesitated over easy decisions, so it didn't take me long to stumble. I seesawed from total withdrawal to taking over. Alex and Alison never knew which way I would go, but then, neither did I. I had envisioned my children coming to me with situations that I, as the wise elder, would respond to with key questions to help them work their way to solutions, but I was no Socrates.

Alex proposed an executive committee of the key managers, with the idea of making decisions by consensus. I went along, willing to try Alex's approach, although my mode of operation had been to make decisions alone, after asking for input. Five of us would meet weekly at a set time and he would lead the meetings. We implemented his plan, nicknaming it Ex-Com.

At the first meeting, the others came into the office Alex and I shared and took seats around the small table. Alex explained that on Ex-Com we would discuss issues, so each department knew what the others were doing, and make administrative decisions together. I smiled my assent when the others looked to me. We then went around the table, each person reporting on what they were doing and bringing up issues for discussion and decisions. I intended to let the others make policy decisions but, following precedent, they soon turned to me for advice. I wish I could say I smiled sagely and asked what they would suggest doing, but that didn't happen. Before I could stop myself, I gave advice, like I was used to doing. Then, when I stopped to take a breath, I realized I'd broken my resolve not to intervene. My mother's refrain about the road to hell rang loudly in my ears.

That was just the start. Alex didn't show his frustration, but if I were him, I would have been livid. The trouble was that I had seen most of the problems before and knew what needed to be done. I intended to transfer an educated, intuitive ability to make decisions to those who didn't have my experience, but my exasperation and impatience at their fumbling usually triumphed.

We had endless discussions, for example, about whether we should move to colorful printed cases for our wines or continue to follow our custom of simply putting a wine label on the case to identify it. There were countervailing arguments for each alternative from marketing, financial, and environmental angles. The committee couldn't decide what to do. With no resolution in sight, impatience trumped my resolve. My speaking up hijacked the meeting, ending the discussion without giving the team the chance to work it out themselves. A wide piece of duct tape over my mouth might have helped, although I'm fairly sure I could have talked through it.

One morning, Alex came into our joint office, grinning like a cat that had just caught a mouse. He sat down and looked at me earnestly with his dimpled smile.

"Mom, I thought of what your new title should be." I hadn't been thinking ahead to what my title would be when it was no longer president, but clearly Alex and Alison had. I looked at him inquisitively.

"Founder!" he said enthusiastically. Indicative of my state of mind, my immediate reaction was cynical and negative. Perfect, I thought—vague and meaningless, but important sounding. I didn't say that to him. It was a sweet gesture on his part.

"Good thinking, Alex," I lied. "Founder sounds fine. Thank you."

Alison had followed him in.

"Mom, we want you to write your new job description," she said. "Tell us what you want to do."

Another sweet gesture that only provoked gloom. I interpreted the question as asking what relatively unimportant activity I would be satisfied doing.

With no idea how to approach writing my job description, I called Pat for advice. She responded she'd be interested in what I came up with. "Since transferring control is rare, you're charting new ground," she told me. "Family businesses don't usually address this. The retiring founder just does whatever he or she wants." That sounded fine for the founder but what about the good of the business? If the parents didn't plan for the future, the business headed toward chaos. Yet, a job description presented a challenge.

Here was a position no company would hire. This situation would surface only in a family business when a parent who had built and run the company wanted to stay on in some capacity while the kids took the reins. I wondered if I was trying to do the impossible by giving up control and sticking around. Perhaps my years as president and my penchant for decision making would prevent me from taking any other role. If I had known exactly what I wanted to do as founder, it would have helped, but since I couldn't envision myself in any role other than president, I was clueless how to proceed.

Maybe I could find a role as mentor, cheerleader, or keeper of the vision; something that would be an asset to the company and not just a drag on the payroll. With that in mind, I crafted a list of possibilities and sent it off to Pat to get her opinion. With characteristic bluntness, she wrote back, using words like "vague," "meddling," "second-guess." Apparently, my job description had omitted some important items. "Who would you report to?" she asked. "Who decides where you would travel, what events you would participate in, and what community programs you would support?"

Whoa! I could feel my heart pound at the thought of having to ask my children for permission to do some peripheral thing in the business I had built, controlled, and dominated for over twenty years. Alex and Alison would listen to my requests, but when I stepped back, they would be the decision makers, not me.

Pat asked if my being the cheerleader for the staff would make Alex and Alison be the bad cops. She pointed out that here was a way I could unintentionally sabotage my kids. My stomach knotted up reading her comments. Here I was, with the best of intentions, falling into the trap I was trying so hard to avoid. I didn't want to go back, but I was having trouble going forward. I hadn't thought about watching Alex and Alison make decisions that I didn't agree with, or going to them for approval of my activities. That would be tough. Yet, it was clear that I needed to stand back and let them take charge.

I didn't want to dampen Alex and Alison's enthusiasm, but I didn't know how to shut up. "Don't complain. Be supportive," I kept telling myself. Sometimes I wondered if I could do it. I was not turning out to be the upbeat, cheerful, encouraging person I had envisioned. Every time I saw a staff member go to Alex or Alison for advice instead of coming to me, a physical pang shot through me. Bill told me later he doubted all during the transition whether I would be able to go through with it. My family saw clearly the little cloud of gloom that floated above me.

The powerlessness of my new role had finally hit home and it baffled me. I wasn't sure if it was the loss of control that roiled my insides or no longer being important or needed. Alex and Alison needed to feel responsibility for the business at the gut level, and the only way to achieve that was to give them full control. I needed to step back. I wanted to step back. But every time I tried, I faltered. I couldn't understand why this was so hard.

Early in the year I had seen a Buddhist quote in the newspaper, which caught my attention. "In the end, only three things matter: how fully you have lived, how deeply you have loved, and how well you have learned to let go." The last phrase flashed in neon colors. Everybody knows the first two—it's what life is about. Self-help books are full of advice on learning to live to the fullest, embracing opportunity, learning to love.

The buzz is about getting more, which is what I'd done all my life, striving to accumulate knowledge, experience, expertise, influence, material well-being. Business is all about growth and expansion. Cutting back denoted failure or weakness. Deciding to give up my winery presidency may have felt right, but it went against everything I had been trained to do. I knew how to aspire to get ahead, not how to let go. 2007 taught me that transitioning out of my role as president demanded the same sort of courage and willpower that had helped me move forward. The energy just had to be focused differently. I had to learn to be president. Now I had to learn not to be president.

Part of what I had loved about running the winery was resolving situations with no right answers, requiring resourceful thinking. There was an unending supply of these over the years. Should we try to expand our export markets? If so, where? How big a discount could we offer our club members? Were brochures really an effective marketing tool? What kind of winery events would attract customers? How many cases of each wine should we make? Would hiring additional sales people pay for itself?

Transferring the problem-solving to Alex and Alison left me with just one ongoing challenge—letting go of that role. Facing difficult issues and keeping cool in a crisis had been my strengths. I thought they would help me make the transition. I was wrong. When I saw a problem, my drive to fix things trumped everything. Winter and spring of the "practice year," despite intending to be a wise elder, I ruefully concluded that meddling buttinsky would be a more fitting description.

What a peculiar position. If Alex and Alison had suddenly decided they didn't want to go through with it and wanted me to be president again, I wouldn't be happy. I didn't want my old job back. But my feet felt stuck in clay as I tried to go forward. So many times I asked myself why. On a good day I could laugh at myself, trying to let go, yet clinging to my old habits at the same time.

In February 2007, Alison and I flew to Chicago to appear at a conference for family businesses. We had been asked to participate in a panel discussion sponsored by the Family Business Center at Loyola University. The topic was transition: how family businesses pass on their ethics, values, responsibility, and power. Honored to have been invited, I also felt embarrassed at how incompetently I was handling my situation. All I could do was to speak frankly about what a hard time I was having. I was just learning what it meant to be in our special niche of family business.

We shared the panel with another family. Listening to them, two brothers who were fourth generation in their family business, it became apparent that once a family business passes to succeeding generations, it takes on a life of its own. The brothers had known they would take over the business and had been groomed for it. They talked about how they saw themselves as temporary custodians of the business. This was a significantly different mind-set from mine. As a first-generation founder, I regarded the business as personal property.

After our panel, we mingled with the conference attendees. Their comments helped me understand how unusual our "intentional transition" at Sokol Blosser was, especially for a first-generation business. One man told me that the first time he knew he would be president of his family's business was when his father announced the news at their company Christmas party. The son had been humiliated rather than thrilled; he wished to be involved in the decision, like a partner. Instead he felt treated like a child. I understood his anguish but also the father's thinking. The father looked at the business as his to give and probably thought the surprise announcement would be a wonderful present. I imagine the father anticipated bestowing the presidency on his son with pleasure and was surprised and hurt by the son's reaction.

People came up to tell me they wished their parents would face their exit instead of continuing with no planning. One woman said her parents talked vaguely about retirement, and took more vacation time every year, but couldn't bring themselves to make plans for the future of the business. Doing nothing, the path of least resistance, seemed common. Look how hard it was for me, and I wanted to do it. What propelled me forward was my conviction that the welfare of the company hinged on my surrendering control. For Alex and Alison to feel the weight of the business, they had to be the decision makers.

While more than 90 percent of the world's businesses are family owned and there are a few long-lived ones like Hoshi Ryokan, a Japanese inn (in the family since 718), or the Antinori family of Tuscany (making wine since 1385), they are the exception. Transition to the next generation seems to be the big issue. The experience at Loyola helped me understand why most family businesses don't last—succession is traumatic. Letting go tests courage, faith, and resilience.

One morning Alison came into the office I shared with Alex. We were in the process of adding office space, but I liked sharing with Alex. It was close but companionable, and we often got into productive spontaneous conversations. "Can we talk to you?" she asked. I gestured her to a seat. When she took it, Alex came over to stand behind her. They were up to something.

"Mom, we've been thinking," Alison began. She looked directly at me, her blue eyes wary but determined. Alex would have chatted a bit first, warming into it; Alison came right to the point. "Would you be willing to move out of your office so Alex and I could be together?"

My surprise at her unexpected request must have showed; she looked taken aback. My first thought was that while this may have sounded like a question, I really didn't have a choice. If I said no, I'd be sabotaging the transition. I didn't want to move, but I was stuck.

"We need to be able to talk to each other," she went on, with a calmness she couldn't have felt. "Being in the same office would help a lot." Was this a coup d'état? A vision of myself dethroned, consigned to a closet turned into an office, flashed through my mind. I could feel my face redden as I started to crumble inside. Tears welled up; I desperately hoped none would escape. I'd come to work that morning feeling upbeat. Where did this overemotional reaction come from?

The rational side of me understood their request. I tried to quash my emotions and keep tears at bay by taking a practical approach:

"Where do you want me to move?" "There's an empty desk in the big sales room where you could work," Alex assured me, revealing they had thought this through. It took backbone for them to ask their mother, the president, to vacate the office she had used for sixteen years. I was so busy fighting back the lump in my throat and the high probability of tears, I didn't appreciate their courage until later.

After blathering my consent, my computer and the contents of my desk were moved with amazing speed. Within thirty minutes, before I had time to protest, change my mind, or cry, I found myself sitting at a desk in an open office. The three others in the office smiled and welcomed me, then appeared hard at work. I sat and stared at my new desk, telling myself it was silly to feel humiliated. I should be looking at giving up my office as a generous gesture, but in my depressed state, I felt kicked out. I missed my privacy and the easy camaraderie with Alex. I did, however, have the feeling that my new office mates might be working harder than they did before I moved in next to them.

I was glad to leave on a long-anticipated sales trip to Atlanta and Toronto, taking Alison with me. We were going first to Atlanta for the High Museum Wine and Art Auction and then to Toronto for our importer's Chairman's Gala. The Atlanta auction was an event I had worked for many years, developing good friends and winery relationships. Alison would be attending alone in the future. In Toronto, I had planned a winery dinner accompanied by a reading from *At Home in the Vineyard*, my new book. Alison agreed to continue the trip with me. She didn't really see a role for herself in Toronto and told people who asked, "I'm going as Mom's baggage handler."

After a successful few days in Atlanta, we headed for Toronto where we planned to visit an old friend whose family I had lived with as an exchange student in Japan. Sachiko, who was now living in Toronto to be with her son and his family, had planned a dinner party to celebrate my book. She'd even hired a Japanese chef to cook my favorite

Japanese foods. Alison and I arrived on Sunday at midday and saw Sachiko's dinner table already set for ten, complete with name cards at each place, flowers, company china, and candles. The chef and his helper were in the kitchen; she had gone all out for this dinner.

Sachiko's family had hosted me in their home in Tokyo as an American Field Service (AFS) exchange student in 1961, when I was sixteen. When, after three months, I returned home to Milwaukee, I was so enamored of Japan—the architecture, décor, customs, food—I talked about nothing else. My brothers rolled their eyes whenever I mentioned Japan. When I made them green tea, they said it tasted just like hot water. "I bet you couldn't tell the difference blindfolded," one said. "Can so," I said. "Let's see," another challenged. So I brewed a fresh pot of tea. They tied a handkerchief around my eyes and set three cups in front of me to taste. Two tasted like water, but the third had the rich taste of the green tea I loved. "This one's the tea," I exclaimed triumphantly. As I pulled off my blindfold, they were laughing so hard they couldn't talk. "They were all hot water!" one brother managed to say, in between peals of laughter. Being the little sister was never easy.

I called Sachiko my Japanese sister and we had kept up with each other over the years. I had gone back to Tokyo twice, once with Bill on a wine trip in the early 1980s and once alone, on my way back from an International Women's Forum conference in Singapore, in 2000. On the latter trip, I was able to visit the home where I had stayed so many years before, shortly before it was torn down to make way for multiunit housing. I told my Japanese brothers and sisters how sad it made me feel to see this beautiful traditional Japanese home and garden demolished. The oldest brother of the family, who still lived in the house, explained the land it sat on was too valuable for a single-family home.

At Sachiko's home in Toronto, coming down the stairs in my silk suit for the party, just before 5:00 PM, I slipped off the bottom step, unexpectedly more narrow than the others, rolled my right ankle, and heard a crack as I landed flat on my back on the wooden floor. I looked up to see Alison, Sachiko, the chef, and his helper hovering over me. Alison ran to the kitchen for ice cubes and a plastic bag to cover my ankle, my first ever broken bone.

As I lay sprawled on the floor blocking the front door, concentrating on taking slow deep breaths to keep from fainting from the shooting pain in my foot, Sachiko's guests arrived for her party. I looked up at their inquiring faces and tried to smile. "Hello, I'm Sachi's American sister. I'm sorry to be welcoming you from down here." I hoped I didn't sound as miserable as I felt. My throbbing ankle was only half my agony: my clumsiness had just ruined Sachiko's party.

Alison didn't leave my side. When Sachiko's son, Masa, arrived, he drove us to the Emergency Department of Scarborough General, the closest hospital. My broken ankle was about to make me a card-carrying member of the Canadian health system. Four hours later, I emerged with my lower leg and ankle in a plaster cast, with strict instructions not to put any weight on that foot, and to keep it raised above my heart, an impossible request. They gave me crutches that were so large, they were useless. Back at Sachiko's, the guests had had a lovely dinner and were waiting to see me before leaving.

Alison showed me how to get upstairs to the bedroom by sitting backwards and lifting my rear from one step to the next, a technique she had learned after a high school volleyball injury. She helped me get undressed and into bed. Without her, I would have been helpless. Finally in bed, it was time to call home. I could feel myself starting to let down; no need to maintain my cheerful front. Alison called Russ to tell him what happened while I tried to compose myself. I wanted to sound matter-of-fact so I didn't worry him, but when she handed me the phone, uncontrollable sobs escaped. Russ could only listen helplessly to my blubbering.

The next morning, I sat in the backseat with my leg up while Sachiko drove us to the hotel where we would be staying for the next two nights. Our good-byes were awkward. I rarely got to see Sachi and this was not the visit we had wanted. Embarrassed, and both feeling responsible for my accident, neither of us knew what to say. After checking in at the hotel, Alison and I sat in our hotel room, discussing how to tackle our business obligations for the next two days.

"You said you were coming as my baggage handler," I told her. "That turned out to be prophetic. I can't even get my clothes out of my suitcase without you. Will you take my place at the meeting with our importer this morning? I'd like to stay here with my foot up to be ready for this afternoon." Alison's smile showed that she was pleased with the responsibility. "I can do it, Mom," she said, and off she went.

I still had to host the Sokol Blosser Winery dinner that night at one of Toronto's best restaurants, called Jamie Kennedy at the Gardiner. Every guest would receive a signed copy of my newly published book and I was to read excerpts between courses. That was not something I could delegate. I looked optimistically at my new crutches.

My first crutch management lesson came when our importer drove us to Jamie Kennedy's restaurant for lunch. Unable to attend the dinner since he was being honored as Restaurateur of the Year that evening, Jamie had invited us for lunch to see the space and have a chance to chat. Crutches tucked under my armpits, I started up the wheelchair ramp to the entrance, woefully underestimating the strength crutches demanded. Before I was halfway to the door, my shoulders and arms ached and I was panting. Once inside, the thirty-foot walk to the elevator seemed endless. Beads of sweat threatened to cascade down my flushed face. When we finally reached the dining room, I sat down and put my throbbing foot up on a chair, not caring how it looked. We put the wines we had brought for Jamie to taste on the table, set up the tasting, and ordered lunch. I looked longingly as the wine was poured, but it was the last thing I needed in my already wobbly state.

Jamie Kennedy had been a featured chef at the Monterey Bay Aquarium's Cooking for Solutions event when I first met him. He had told me he loved Pinot Noir, so when arranging our Toronto trip, I contacted him and he invited me to do a winery dinner at his new restaurant on the third floor of the Gardiner Museum. Our lunch gave me the chance to see the restaurant space and discuss the logistics of table arrangement, menu, wine pairing, and how the courses would flow.

After lunch, lurching back to the elevator, out the front door, and down the ramp again left me limp and weary. I couldn't face doing it again that evening for the dinner. In my pained state, a wheelchair sounded divine. We asked at the hotel desk. Yes, the hotel had one wheelchair; they would let us borrow it for the day. The concierge disappeared, reappearing five minutes later pushing a dusty, rickety-looking, bare bones wheelchair. It had no adjustments, but just seeing the wheels turn improved my mood immediately. It fell to Alison to roll me around. I couldn't imagine what I'd have done if I'd been alone.

When we returned to the restaurant in the evening, the dining room looked splendid. Our plan was that I'd talk about the wines and read from my book between courses. The podium I had requested, with microphone and light, stood well positioned to see the entire dining room. A podium allowed me to rest the book while I read; the microphone preserved my voice. Additional light was necessary to read in the darkened restaurant ambience. At noon, when I still thought I would be able to stand, these were important. By evening, reduced to a wheelchair, none were of use. Our last-minute revision gave Alison the chance for another first.

"Alison," I asked, "can you go up to the podium and talk to the group about the wines?" She hadn't filled in for me like this before but she knew the wines. It would be a good opportunity for her. "I can do it," she said. "After you talk about the wines, maybe you'd introduce me. Then I'll start reading." She nodded. I continued. "Are you willing to go around to the tables and talk to the guests and answer any questions?" I asked her. This would be harder. "Okay," she said, with just a slight hesitation.

The break in my ankle became the break Alison needed to push her to perform presidentially in public. Hiding any nervousness, she did a fine job talking about the wines and introducing me. I watched as she went around "working the tables," talking to the guests. Gracious and smiling, she rose to her role. This was a big step for her, and for me as well, letting her do what I had always done. Focused on my presentation, I didn't think about it at the time, but the baton was starting to switch hands.

After considering the alternatives, none of them good, I decided to read sitting at the table, from my wheelchair—no microphone, no light, and at the same level as the seated guests. I was used to engaging my audience from a podium. Tonight's unusual situation made me nervous, but my fears dissipated as I got into a rhythm. I could feel everyone's attention. There was still enough daylight coming in from the three glass walls of the restaurant, which jutted out like a peninsula, to see the print easily. Dusk ended that.

After the second course, when it was time for the next reading, the restaurant was dark, lit only by votive candles on the tables. The effect was lovely, but the only way to see the print on the page was to prop the book at my place setting and surround it with candles. My tablemates collected votives and I did the next two readings by candlelight. It felt like we were sitting around a campfire and I was telling stories.

To everyone's surprise, this unconventional presentation ended up having a special magic. Our importer reported that weeks later people were still talking about it. One of the diners, the manager of a private club, pleaded with me to come back and do a wine and book reading dinner for his members. He was even willing to let me read by candlelight. We smiled all the way back to the hotel. Everyone was happy: I with relief that I had fulfilled my obligation; Alison with pleasure at succeeding in her new role; our importer with all the wine that was sold.

After one more event, Alison and I headed home. I couldn't wait to get to an orthopedist's office to learn how long I would be laid up. The Canadian doctor who had examined me said about six weeks. The young man who put me in a cast confirmed this. Out of commission for six weeks was unacceptable. I asked if there was anything I could do to accelerate healing, like vitamins I could take, or foods I could eat. "Sardines," he said immediately. "Because they are rich in calcium to help your bones mend. Of course, I'm Portuguese," he explained. "We eat many sardines." Sardines had not been in my diet for years, but they immediately went on my mental shopping list. I was in good health; maybe, with enough sardines, I could be back in action in five weeks. Wrong. Even after I was walking again, I was in physical therapy for several months.

Losing my office no longer mattered. I couldn't get up the stairs to the offices. I tried, but didn't have the upper body strength to hoist myself up and down multiple times a day on crutches. Russ suggested I work from home and arranged for a network satellite on the winery building to be hooked to our home computer. We were about to add on and remodel the winery offices. By the time I healed, I would have my own office again.

I spent April and May working from home. My cast gave way to a large, unwieldy boot that felt like a ball and chain. Alex and Alison were negotiating to buy an additional fifteen acres of vineyard land, dubbed Blackberry Block as it was overrun with invasive Himalayan blackberries. Normally, I would have been walking all over it, examining the soil and slope. But walking on bumpy, uneven ground was out of the question for close to three months. For weeks, even navigating the grocery store with Russ was too much for me. No vineyard walks. No driving. The physical limitations made me grumpy. I wanted to be out and about.

Then the quiet serenity of my office at home, broken only by the sound of the birds and the creek outside my window, started to change my outlook. Little golden finches splashed brightly in the stream, the drops of water sparkling as they fluttered through their bath. I could work at my computer, make phone calls, go make a cup of tea, admire the spring flowers, then work some more.

At the end of May, looking up from my home computer at the little waterfall outside the office window, I realized what had happened. While I wasn't at the winery on a daily basis, my two children took charge. They relied on each other and handled the crises as well as day-to-day operations. The staff got used to me not being around and regularly looked to Alex and Alison for leadership. I started to be at peace with Alex handling the vineyard and production and Alison handling financial accounting and administration. I was grateful they were running the vineyard and winery, glad not to have to appear at an office every morning, and relieved they were dealing with the never-ending issues that made each day a challenge. The bonds had started to loosen.

I decided the universe had stepped in to finally move me off my plateau, forcing me forward with a swift, well-placed kick. All things considered, it was done in the kindest way: in a familial, caring setting, and a clean break, no displacement or surgery needed. Just enough to remove me from the frontline for almost two months. It took a physical act, but the resistance that had dragged on for so long started to release. I had no idea what the future held, but I had the sense I was creating a place for it to grow. My ankle episode, though painful, embarrassing, and inelegant, turned out to be a pivotal part of the transition.

My job description finally took shape. Alison helped me combine Pat's concerns with my indecision on how involved I wanted to be. The result was short and simple. As founder my job was to be an ambassador for the vineyards and winery, participating in projects to further the vision, mission, and goals of the business. Its vagueness appealed to me. I would have the freedom to get as involved as I chose.

It made me clearly subordinate and reporting to the copresidents. Alex and Alison would sign my employee paycheck and my expense reports. I would live with that new reality when I passed the baton. Another piece of the transition was in place.

I enjoyed telling people that, at the end of the transition, my kids would be signing my expense reimbursement checks. It always drew a chuckle. To me it symbolized a real transfer of power. Phasing out of being the "face" of the winery and letting Alex and Alison take that role was also important. Keeping the public mantle didn't seem fair, although it was common practice in family businesses. If the kids were running the business, they should represent it publicly. Alex and Alison were both first-rate winery ambassadors. The transition would be complete when their prominence eclipsed mine and I'd be introduced as their mother, rather than the other way around.

The family suggested I be chair of the board, another frequent practice for retiring CEOs. I chose not to do that. Nik, the only child not earning a living at the winery, was leading the family board and it was a perfect role, engaging him more fully in the business. Time would prove how valuable his strategic mind would be to us. As one of the new generation of young entrepreneurs, his experience with his own company provided constructive perspective.

———

My business and personal lives seemed to be taking turns in their ups and downs. While I was struggling to let go of control of the winery, Russ and I got married, he for the first time, me for the second.

Many of the winery staff admitted to being afraid of Russ, and I could see why. He cultivated a stern demeanor as a protective veneer. I could relate to that, since I also had a protective shell. As he let me into his world, Russ's playful side would appear out of nowhere. One day, as we turned into a gas station to fill up on our way home from the beach, Russ pointed to the large RV ahead of us and turned to me without warning: "God dammit, Mabel! Isn't that Fred and Babs from back home in Iowa? That's got to be him. I can't believe there's more than one guy who wears those ridiculous chartreuse pants. Jesus Christ, duck down, Mabel. We don't want him to see us."

I looked around to make sure there was no one else in the car he could be talking to, then got it and responded, "Listen, George, you just stop being so hard on folks. You aren't any fashion plate yourself. We've got another hour of driving before we get to the exhibit of the world's biggest ball of string and I want to have lots of time before it closes. Are you still hungry? We have one Twinkie left."

Once we started our version of Archie and Edith Bunker—our George and Mabel repartee—it would surface unexpectedly with verbal banter, usually when we were driving in the car, and always with "God dammit, Mabel. . . . " It spilled over into e-mails and phone messages when I was traveling. One of us would start and the other would respond in character. Call it arrogant, politically incorrect, or just plain stupid, we both found the silliness of our alternative personas a relief valve, an unexpected outlet for the wackiness each of us stored inside, hidden behind our rather staid façades.

Russ and I had already lived together for almost seven years, devoted to each other, but neither feeling the need to formalize the relationship. We talked about marriage occasionally and always agreed it wasn't necessary. When people asked why we didn't get married, I replied we liked living in sin. Since we bought a house together in 1999, then built at the vineyard in 2006, we felt we had made a significant enough commitment.

I continued to introduce Russ as our winemaker, leaving people to wonder about our relationship. "Spousal equivalent" or "boyfriend" were unappealing, so I just left it at winemaker. We would do events at the winery where we would be all business, with no hint of a personal relationship, and leave together to walk down the hill to our house, holding hands.

Then, while I was struggling through the final year of the transition, the idea of making a formal commitment suddenly seemed right. I'm not sure what triggered the switch in my thinking, but one wintry Sunday, in 2007, we sat in our living room, each with a cat on our lap, watching the juncos and finches flock to our bird feeders, and an NFL football game on TV. On impulse, I turned to Russ.

"I've been thinking about marriage," I told him. He looked at me quizzically.

"Anyone in particular?"

"How about you and me?" I said. I was smiling but he could see I was serious. His tone changed.

"Why, after all these years, are you thinking about marriage? Do we need a formal piece of paper to prove we love each other?"

"It just feels like it's time," I said. Russ stayed silent, absent-mindedly stroking the cat. Then he looked at me.

"Okay," Russ said. "I guess it is."

Although he acted like he was just going along, Russ made the first public announcement by leaning over at a formal wine industry dinner and whispering to Alison that he and I were going to get married. His announcement stopped her mid-sentence and she immediately wanted details. When Russ started telling her we were going to go in the next few weeks to a justice of the peace and it would be just us, she interrupted him. "Don't even think you can get married without us," she told him, making it clear that she and her brothers would want to be involved. "You can even go to Hawaii if you want," she said, hinting at what she thought we should do. "You just have to take us with you."

Wedding plans went on hold as I let the idea of family involvement sink in. Hawaii was out of the question, but getting married at the vineyard would certainly be appropriate for us. So we gave up our idea of running off alone and quietly getting married and decided we might as well make a public statement with family and friends.

Alex's three-year-old twins, Nikolas and Avery, stopped by my office to show off their Halloween costumes before going out for trick or treat.

An array of decisions confronted me. John Collins, an attorney friend whom I hadn't seen for years, had become a judge and agreed to perform the ceremony. I scoured *The New Yorker* website and found a 1925 cover, a drawing of an older couple entwined on a park bench, that made a perfect wedding invitation. Alison helped me search Portland to find the right outfit, a flowing Eileen Fisher ensemble.

Alex asked who I wanted to "give me away." Still fighting to be my own person, his suggestion hit a hot button. Nobody owned me and nobody was going to "give" me away. If he and Nik had thought they would escort me, I cut them off with my fierce independent stance. I had fought hard to become my own person and wanted to walk by myself. In hindsight, I regret passing up the chance to walk on the arms of my two adult sons.

An option I was willing to accept was having Alex's twin boys, Avery and Nikolas, escort me and carry the rings. I was a little concerned whether this would work as these spirited five-year-olds had three modes of getting from here to there: running, skipping, or jumping. We practiced walking slowly and deliberately, with them staying next to me, not getting ahead. "Your job is to get the three of us to Russ, all at the same time," I told them at the end of our practice. They looked at me solemnly before scampering off.

I put a lot more thought into getting married at sixty-two than I had at twenty-one. This ceremony would be our pledge to each other, a public statement, witnessed by friends and family. I wondered if marriage would change us. I had known couples who had lived together for years, then broken up after they got married.

Bill and I had a traditional Episcopal church ceremony with vows coming straight from the book. We never considered the option of writing our own vows and probably wouldn't have known what to say in any case. But now I did and here was my chance to put the partnership I wanted into words. Since I had so much trouble being myself in my relationship with Bill, I wanted to be explicit in my relationship with Russ that we were two individuals coming together, like two candles whose flames can merge to make a brighter light even though they remain separate candles. Our vows captured this:

"It is not your responsibility to make the other person happy. But the quality of your presence and partnership with the other person will have a lot to do with the happiness that abides in your home. A successful marriage is not a miraculous gift. It is rather a human achievement. Happiness through marriage has something of a mystic quality about it. There are no universal rules, but we know that life through marriage can be made radiant."

On September 9, 2007, we became husband and wife in a simple open-air morning ceremony overlooking the vineyard, attended by only immediate family, a few close friends, and employees. Bill was out of town and couldn't attend, but his mother and sister did. His mother sat next to Russ's mom. As I walked up the aisle, escorted by two serious little boys in white shirts and bow ties, I smiled at seeing the two smallish white-haired women sitting together, both unusually caring and supportive mothers-in-law.

Russ and I looked at each other as Judge Collins read our vows. Oblivious to anything but each other, both of us had misty eyes as we repeated them. The balmy morning, the picturesque vineyard, the smiling upturned faces of family and friends are engraved in my memory. Our friend Heidi had offered to sing for us. I had known Heidi for fifteen years and considered her a close friend. We regularly spent time together. Yet her offer surprised me. I knew her as a writer and journalist, had never heard her sing, and had no knowledge of her musical talent. She suggested the Beatles song "In My Life," a love song for adults, acknowledging past loves while cherishing the present. Her clear, lilting soprano floated out over the Pinot Noir vines ripening in the September sun.

The whole ceremony took a scant fifteen minutes. Afterwards, we hosted a celebratory brunch in the vineyard. Russ and I sat in the middle of a giant U-shaped table, against the backdrop of the vines. Sprays of purple, rosy, and yellow flowers, entwined with the green of our grapevines, ran down the center of the table, which overflowed with our favorite foods: platters of wild chinook salmon, roasted summer vegetables, ripe heirloom tomatoes with fresh mozzarella, watermelon-berry salad, and wine glasses of sparkling wine and Pinot Noir.

Saying our vows in front of friends and family struck something deep inside and gave me increased respect for the marriage ritual and public statement of commitment. A new phase of our lives had begun.

I couldn't have imagined singing the sweet lyrics of "In My Life," the Beatles' anthem to the triumph of love over nostalgia, in a more beautiful setting than on September 9, 2007, at the vineyard wedding of my friends Susan Sokol Blosser and Russ Rosner. The morning sun painted golden highlights on the rows of green vines, and a persistent breeze fluttered the tablecloth on the banquet table where the wedding breakfast would soon be served. Snow-capped Mount Hood punctuated the horizon to the northeast, adding eleven thousand feet of craggy majesty to the scene.

Weddings bring up memories, and this one was no exception. When I moved to Portland in 1991, the friendly community of Oregon vintners welcomed me; I was an established wine journalist, and more coverage of the industry was a plus. But my relationship with Susan grew quickly from impersonal networking to the reciprocity of true friendship. I wasn't the only one surprised when Susan's employer-employee relationship with Russ transformed into love, but by the time they decided to marry, it was clear how happy they were together, and how right this decision was.

From my spot at the microphone, I could watch Susan walk down the aisle escorted by her little grandsons, and appreciate the smiles and tears of the guests. This moment showed how gently and yet firmly Susan and Russ had woven their lives together. The wedding was the real-life expression of Lennon and McCartney's poignant song.

Heidi Yorkshire
Writer, Musician, Life-Cycle Celebrant

As we entered the last quarter of the practice year, it was clear the transition wasn't over for me yet. Just when I started to think how well I was doing, something came along to slap me on the side of the head and let me know how much farther I had to go. The word *retirement* was my next nemesis. The first public announcement of my stepping back came out in my president's letter for the winery's October wine club shipment. Our Cellar Club comprised our best and most loyal customers. I wrote in the newsletter that we would be announcing a big change after the first of the year: On January 2, 2008, I would be stepping down. Alex and Alison would take over as copresidents of the winery. I would still be around, but they would be in charge. After writing the letter in September, I forgot about it.

I had carefully avoided using the "R" word, but during the winery's Thanksgiving Open House, Cellar Club members came up to me smiling. "Congratulations. How does it feel to be retired?" they'd ask. Every time I heard "retired," I shuddered, hoping they didn't see the look of fear in my eyes. I managed to laugh and say I'd talked Alison and Alex into doing my work for me, but the involuntary cringe when I heard the "R" word told me I was still vulnerable. Little more than a month later, the practice year would be over. After three years, I hoped I would be ready.

On January 2, 2008, seventeen years to the day since I had become president of the winery, I stood up at the end of a catered luncheon to formally give up control—to "pass the baton," as Alison and Alex's business coach referred to the process, or "flip the switch," as Alex and Alison liked to say. I called it my day of reckoning.

Only one month before, I wanted to curl up in a dark closet behind my clothes so I wouldn't have to face the transfer of power I had set in motion. But I was an adult, right? So I put on the most gracious face I could muster, organized a catered lunch for the staff, sent out personal invitations, and hoped that when the time came I would rise to the occasion.

As soon as I struck my spoon against the crystal wine glass, I had everyone's attention. Employees, family, and our consultants looked up from their desserts. Outside, the rain pelted the branches of the bare bigleaf maples, but the somber weather didn't dampen the sense of anticipation inside. Today was a landmark day for the winery and for Alex and Alison. I had been aware of Alex glancing sideways at me during lunch, and of Alison smoothing invisible wrinkles in the cloth napkin in her lap. I wondered if they had as many butterflies as I did seventeen years ago.

Although they might be considered too young to take over the presidency of a multimillion-dollar business, Alison, twenty-eight, and Alex, thirty-four, and had been training for this all their lives. I thought of how Bill used to take Alison, when she was as young as five, with him to the winery in the early evening to help clean up during harvest. I had watched her walk down from our house to the winery, traipsing through the vineyard, her little hand holding tightly to her father's. Bill in his jeans, cotton shirt, and boots, Alison in pink shorts, T-shirt, and tennis shoes, moving in and out of the shadows cast by the sun setting over the hillside.

She was small enough to get inside our small wine press and hose it down. Adults could only lean in and aim the hose. Joyful at being able to do something none of the adults could do, she beamed with pride when she returned home, heedless of being soaked to the skin. That little girl had become the bright young woman sitting next to me, ready to take over.

I flashed back to ten-year-old Alex sitting at a small table at the entrance to our tasting room, welcoming guests and collecting entrance fees at our Wine Country Thanksgiving Open House. We had coached him on what to say but our sociable son scripted his own patter. "Welcome to Sokol Blosser," he said, his dimples lighting up his face as he smiled. "Would you like to buy a ticket to taste our wines?"

Who could resist? Watching from behind the bar where I was serving wine, I could see our guests melt at his earnestness. He stuck it out and, after the long three-day weekend, had welcomed enough guests to lose his voice, but also to have earned the money to buy the Space Lego set he wanted. Alex never shied from hard work. He accumulated an impressive amount of Lego bricks, which he saved for so long, that he was able to play again with them years later with his twin sons.

This day held so much meaning for me. My twenty-seven years managing the vineyard and winery had been my proving grounds. The winery and I had survived and prospered together. I felt the poignancy of giving up the position that shaped and defined my persona.

After my introduction, Bill stood up to speak. He was as slim and carefully dressed as he'd been when we first met as college students. I had a sudden image of him back then, fresh from his year in France, tall, dark, and sexy, with his prized French beret perfectly tilted on his head. His hair was now silver and his face more worn, but he still lit up when he smiled. His eyes took on warmth when he talked about his children, about how hard they had worked to help in the vineyard and the winery, and how appropriate this new opportunity would be for them and the business.

Then it was Alison's turn. Her quiet voice quavered as she started, thanking Bill and me for the privilege and important charge they had been given. Normally jovial, Alex was unexpectedly solemn, his voice trembling partway through. I was gratified to see they both clearly felt the weight of their new roles.

Several of the longtime winery staff also stood to make toasts, including Russ who, after some pleasantries, ended with a warning to the new presidents "not to screw it up." I knew he was deadly serious but he said it playfully and everyone laughed. Warm energy, full of hope for the future, filled the room. I'd been worried whether Alex's energetic five-year-old twins could sit still for the ceremony, but Avery and Nikolas were quiet and attentive. Having the third generation present reinforced the family feeling. We missed Nik, who couldn't be there.

Years before, one of our employees with a sense of humor had made Bill a wooden club with a little brass plaque inscribed "Administrative Tool." It resembled a medieval mace and had been intended as a joke, but we treated it like a royal scepter, with a place of honor in my office. I had it on the table next to me. "This is for you now," I said, as I put the Administrative Tool ceremoniously into Alex and Alison's hands. With this symbolic gift, I formally inaugurated the second generation's control. It felt like such a momentous occasion I half expected church bells to ring or someone to shout "The Queen is

The ceremonial passing of the Baton, January 2, 2008. From left to right: me, holding the "Administrative Tool," Alex, Alison, and Bill.

dead, Long Live the Queen!" My reign was over. A small quiver of excitement surged through me. We had successfully executed what, to the entire world, appeared a seamless transition.

As the party broke up and everyone went back to work, I couldn't stop smiling. The press release had gone out in an e-mail that morning. I spent the afternoon in my office answering notes from media friends who wished me well. I expected to be depressed, but the smile that emerged signaled a new emotion surging through me: liberation. This delicious sensation made me realize how much I'd held back, directing all my emotional energy toward the winery. Now, as if moving the tuner to clear the channel, the static that had filled my brain for the past thirty-eight years was gone. New sounds were coming in. My mind was free to soar. I couldn't believe what had just happened. I had let go.

....

Russ's Root Vegetable Soup

We try to eat with the seasons and, after scrambling to use all the summer vegetables from our garden, I sometimes find myself looking forward to simply buying the sturdy vegetables that flood the local farmers market in the cooler months. Low in fat and flavorful, this soup is a great way to showcase those fall and winter root vegetables. Russ created this recipe and does all the chopping, always making a big pot, as it improves significantly as it ages and the flavors meld. If you can wait, it's best to not even eat it on the first day—it will be much better on the fifth or sixth night. The amounts of the core ingredients (the rutabagas, turnips, and parsnips) can be varied according to personal taste, as long as the total of the three is about 6 to 6½ pounds. With a good crusty loaf of bread and a couple of bottles of wine, this recipe serves eight as a vegetarian main course. We like it straight from the pot, but you could garnish it with grated Parmesan cheese or chopped fresh herbs, if you like. The distinctive mushroom and truffle flavors of Sokol Blosser Pinot Noir is a perfect match for the soup's deep, earthy flavors.

Makes 8 servings

One large sweet onion, such as Vidalia, Maui, or Walla Walla
4 or 5 cloves garlic
2 pounds rutabagas
2 pounds turnips
2 pounds parsnips
1 pound garnet yams
2 large carrots
⅓ cup extra-virgin olive oil
1 quart organic vegetable broth (we use Pacific brand organic, low-sodium broths)
1 quart organic mushroom broth
1 tablespoon dried basil

¼ teaspoon granulated lemon peel

¼ teaspoon freshly ground pepper

Peel the onion, then cut it into large dice. Peel and mince the garlic. Peel the rutabagas (be sure to peel enough of the rutabaga to remove the greenish parts, which can be bitter), turnips, parsnips, yams, and carrots. Cut all the root vegetables into bite-sized chunks.

In a large (7- to 8- quart) stock pot, warm the oil over medium heat. When hot, add the onion and sauté until soft and translucent, about 5 minutes; reduce the heat if needed to prevent the onion from browning. Add the garlic and sauté until fragrant and tender, 1 to 2 minutes, taking care that it doesn't burn.

Increase the heat to medium-high and add the rutabagas. Cook, stirring frequently, for about 5 minutes. Add the remaining vegetables one at a time: next the carrots, then the yams, then the turnips, then the parsnips, allowing 4 or 5 minutes between each addition and stirring frequently.

Add the vegetable and mushroom broth, basil, lemon peel, and pepper. Raise the heat to high and bring to a boil. Reduce the heat to medium-low and simmer, partially covered, until the soup is full flavored, 1 to 2 hours. The longer the soup cooks, the better it will taste.

Ladle the soup into bowls and serve hot.

CHAPTER SEVEN

Second Generation
at the Helm

When the new copresidents took control of the winery, in 2008, the economy was booming. They had big plans for expansion and talked excitedly about producing new wines and expanding markets. Within six months the global financial services firm Lehman Brothers failed, the largest bankruptcy in United States history which, combined with a mortgage crisis and general bank overextension, caused a major recession. Alex and Alison learned in their first year how precarious business could be. As restaurant wine sales fell precipitously, sales of Sokol Blosser plummeted. The recession hit the whole wine industry hard. While the family board watched closely, the new copresidents shelved their expansion plans and hit the streets to bolster sales and keep the business alive. Bill and I looked at each other and smiled. "This is so good for them," we agreed, both of us remembering the many times we had faced threats to the winery's survival.

Working the market, the new copresidents learned a key lesson. In the extremely crowded and competitive world of premium quality wine, the most complex and challenging part of the business is marketing, selling, and building a name for the brand.

An abundance, some would say an overabundance, of fine wine exists. Row upon row of wines in retail stores, where thousands of bottles with colorful labels beckon, testifies to how crowded the market is. Just getting a place on a store's shelf is a victory. Our challenge, from the first vintage, was to make the Sokol Blosser name recognizable enough that people would seek it out. A critical step was to get wine shop owners and restaurant wine buyers on our side; first so they would stock our wine, and second so they would recommend it. Bill and I learned early on that we had to win them over one by one.

"So you're trying to grow grapes in ORE-ee-gun?" It was the late 1980s and the owner of a liquor store in New York looked at me with a combination of amusement and disbelief. His question was not unusual. I had been asked the same thing at previous accounts. "We think Oregon Pinot Noir has the potential to rival Burgundy," I told him, then followed with, "Do you have time to taste my wine?" He clearly wasn't particularly interested, but I had come all this way and my earnestness probably aroused his pity. He got out wine glasses and the wholesaler's rep accompanying me poured for the three of us. I watched the owner contemplate his first Oregon Pinot Noir, then swirl, sip, and spit. "Not sure why I should buy this when I can get a good Burgundy at the same price." He looked at me. "But send me four bottles and I'll see how it goes." Every order, however small, meant a victory for Oregon Pinot Noir.

But I couldn't personally visit every wine store and restaurant, so how could we stay visible in the market and increase sales of our wine? The ideal would be to hire our own sales team. While this made sense in Oregon, our biggest market, our national sales were too small to afford to hire our own people. The immediate answer was to hire national brokers to represent us in their portfolios. We tried two different ones between 1980 and 1991. When I became president, I decided to go it alone, hiring regional brokers in key markets. They were great people, but sales were still slower than I'd hoped.

By 1999, after I had affirmed my vision of staying in the high-end market and hired Russ to take us there, I turned my attention once more to building national sales. By that time, we had established a small presence in the national market, and my dilemma was the best way to increase our presence in the marketplace. I couldn't travel enough to expand sales myself; I needed to be at the winery to oversee operations. Alex had just come on to help but hadn't yet proved himself. I didn't feel good about calling on Bill, having just gone through our divorce. And Gary, my right-hand man and vice president, was moving on to a job in the high-tech field. When Paterno Imports, another national broker, appeared at my door offering their services, I was desperate enough to listen.

The head of the company flew in his private jet to visit me at the winery. We sat in my office, I in my turtleneck and fleece vest, at my large wood veneer desk, recently acquired on sale at an office supply store, and he and his two vice presidents in their Italian suits and shirts with monogrammed cuffs, across from me on straight-backed folding metal chairs. I listened to him talk about the clout his firm had in the marketplace, how being part of their portfolio would give us entry into places we couldn't achieve alone, how they had a whole marketing department devoted to building the brands they represented, and how they would take care of governmental compliance, which varied by state. Being with Paterno Imports, he asserted, would free me up to do other things. We could leave all our marketing and sales in their competent hands. He emphasized that he had well-known sommeliers on his staff and a chef skilled in wine and food pairing and all this would be available to promote Sokol Blosser when they invited key accounts to their headquarters, a historic estate outside of Chicago.

He suggested that he would be there for us and if Sokol Blosser hit hard times, he would help us out, even buy in. I was starting to think he was my knight in shining armor. He had enumerated all my fears and said how he would deal with them. A firm that represented some of the best wines of Europe and California believed in what Sokol Blosser could be. Despite the fact that brokers had never been the answer for us, I signed a multiyear contract in July 2000, convinced that Sokol Blosser sales were ready for liftoff.

Within a few years I realized my mistake. I had made a business decision out of fear and fantasy: fear that my small winery would be forgotten in the burgeoning wine market and fantasy that I could rely on someone else to develop our brand and increase sales. There was no magic bullet, and that reality slowly hit home. Using a third party to represent us didn't accomplish our goals. We needed to spend the money to hire our own sales team, people for whom Sokol Blosser was first priority. Since selling wine is done person to person, we needed to make friends of our wholesalers and the wholesale market. Our contract put the total responsibility for sales in the broker's hands, preventing Sokol Blosser from having direct contact with the market.

Relying on an intermediary with a large portfolio of wines impeded personal connections. It was a painful time for Sokol Blosser, but we learned an invaluable lesson. Alison and Alex, who were to bear the brunt of my decision, experienced it firsthand. I will always feel bad that I left my kids saddled with a national sales program they would not have chosen, while I learned a lesson I should have known.

The last eight years of the contract we struggled to forge relation ships within the confines of the contract. In 2015 when the contract ended, the copresidents took a calculated risk and put our own sales team in place—hiring five sales people to work with our wholesalers and take on the administrative tasks of setting pricing, monitoring sales, state by state compliance and reporting, and the oversight that comes with having remote employees. The increase in relationships and sales was immediate.

———

AFTER THE HARVEST OF 2010, Russ started talking about retiring. As a hands-on winemaker who was involved in every part of the winemaking process, he feared the winery's expanding production would push him past his capacity to oversee every detail. He didn't think it would work to just cut back to part-time. It had to be all or nothing. Russ had been at Sokol Blosser for twelve years and had significantly upgraded Sokol Blosser's wine quality. The thought of his leaving threw the family board into a quandary. The solution, right under our eyes, came as a shocker.

Fulfilling his history of doing the unexpected, Alex surprised us all with his announcement at a board meeting. "I'd like to be the winemaker," he told us, and the passion in his voice told us this was not a snap decision. Alison had known her copresident was going to make his announcement, but Bill, Nik, and I had no clue this was coming. We knew he loved working in the winery, but he had never mentioned wanting to be a winemaker.

Stunned with this new information, we looked at him in wonder. Several thoughts flashed immediately through my mind, as well as Bill's, as we discovered when we later compared notes: first, Alex had been vice president of sales before becoming copresident. He not only had experience and knew the market, but he was our star sales person. Leaving sales and moving into production not only seemed out of character but would leave us with a big hole in sales; second, Alex might have the desire, but he had little training to take on such a huge, important job; and third, his leaving sales would put Alison in charge, who had neither Alex's experience nor flair for sales. If Alex became winemaker, we were looking at a scenario in which Alex and Alison could each be moving into roles for which they had little preparation or experience.

Moved by Alex's plea, the board didn't immediately say no, but peppered him and Alison with questions: How did Alex propose to get

Russ's office served as tasting headquarters, the place where key blending decisions were made. Russ mentored Alex on the complex yet intuitive process of tasting a multitude of barrel samples and imagining which ones might complement each other. Each section of Pinot Noir dotting our hillsides was picked, vinified, and barreled separately in multiple barrel types, so we had sixty to eighty different lots to taste.

more training? What kind of support would he need to be successful? Knowing Alison didn't relish leading national sales, the board questioned whether she was agreeing just to back up her brother. She was already handling marketing, tasting room sales, and finance; what kind of support would she need to take on national sales?

Alex understood our hesitation but didn't give up a dream he had been harboring deep inside for years. A small flicker, ignited years ago, had developed into a flame, and he finally found the nerve to reveal to the family his desire for a major career change. He came back to the board with a plan: He would take online courses at University of California at Davis, hire an enologist to handle the chemistry and recordkeeping, use outside consultants as needed, and train under Russ for a transition period.

Russ thought Alex didn't have the experience to do the job and shared our concern. But when the board decided to go ahead, he did his best to get Alex ready to take over, writing out his own winemaking protocol and helping find an enologist who was a good fit. During 2012, Alex took classes and shadowed Russ, notebook in hand, every moment he wasn't dealing with sales, then worked full-time in the cellar for harvest, as he had done for years, from September through December.

The spark happened late at night, during the harvest of 1992. It was my senior year in high school, and I was working harvest at the winery with our winemaker, John Haw, and his crew. I loved the work, and loved the camaraderie. It was past midnight and I was up in John's lab telling him that I got the crush pad clean and was heading home.

"Not yet young man, you got to see how I mix the ML bacteria." He was referring to the malolactic bacteria added to start a secondary fermentation.

John was in an excited mood and his enthusiasm was stronger than my exhaustion so I stayed.

"You got to see this as you will be the winemaker someday."

What me? The winemaker? At Sokol Blosser? How could that be?

John was the first one to put that seed in my mind, and it had been growing since that night. When Russ said he wanted to retire, I'd had this winemaker tree growing in me for almost twenty years. It was a surprise to my family, but not to me. I was ready to make wine.

Alex Sokol Blosser
Copresident/Winemaker

Under Russ's mentorship, Alex managed the 2013 harvest and led the blending of the 2012 Pinot Noir barrels. Then, after spring bottling, Russ retired and, in July 2014, Alex took the title of winemaker,

Sokol Blosser's fourth since its first vintage in 1977.

The board took a chance making Alex winemaker, just like it had allowing me to become winery president in 1991. Filled with passion but short on experience, neither Alex nor I would have been hired anywhere else. But the family knew us, had faith that we could rise to the occasion, and was willing to give us the chance. This is where family business shines.

I watched Alex grow into his new role over the next few years, expanding the Evolution line, experimenting with Pinot Noir production, making his mark on the wines, and making the whole staff feel part of the process, by reaching out to them with e-mail updates. Every morning when estate fruit was harvested, he notified the whole staff of the block being picked and e-mailed a photo of the picking scene. Here is part of one of his updates to the staff, sent with some instructions and a plea for treats, just before the 2016 harvest:

> *Team,*
>
> *So harvest is soon upon us, and like I mentioned before: We want to see you, our team mates, but when it comes to suppliers or customers, or politicians, please help us by keeping them away. Guided tours are fine as long as you can keep visitors away from speeding forklifts, erratic hose sprayers, open presses, Lolin on the tractor, me pacing the crush pad, Mario dumping grapes, stinky SO_2, Doug running around, and Robin with her neon-orange fanny pack.*
>
> *We will set up a snack picnic table near the crush pit where we will be having a rotating bake sale tasting for the harvest crew. This is how it works: You bring what you think is a nice baked item for your kids' future bake sale, and we will give you honest feedback on how good it is. We are picky when it comes to baked goods, so we may need a number of plates of cookies from you before we tell you what we think of them. . . . This is us being givers. No need to thank us for this service and we only offer this free service during harvesttime.*

Nik, Alex, and Alison at the vineyard. 1984.

Thirty years later: chairman of the board Nik; copresident/CEO Alison; copresident/winemaker Alex. 2014. (Photo credit: Carolyn Wells Kramer.)

*So there you have it. Grapes are coming and it is time to make
some world-class wine!!!*
    Cheers,
    Alex

Alison's path was a little different as she was definitely not
passionate about being the head of national sales. It would mean
significant travel and handling an often challenging relationship with
our national broker. Marketing and accounting were her strengths.
Despite the reluctance that comes with moving out of one's comfort
zone, Alison decided it would be good for her to learn this side of the
business. Once the decision was made, she attacked it with her usual
determination and organization.

As Alex and Alison navigated their new roles, it became clear
that Alison needed a more definitive title to describe what she did. As
copresident/winemaker, Alex handled all production, from growing
the grapes to making the wine. His title indicated that.

Alison found herself continually having to answer questions
about what she did as copresident. As head of all sales, marketing, and
administration she was effectively the chief executive of the winery.
She and Alex agreed that her title should reflect her jobs. Alison took
the title of copresident/chief executive officer in 2014, marking one
more small notch for women in the sea of male CEOs.

THE POPULARITY OF OUR white blend, Evolution, which had built a
large following since its creation in 1998, led its fans to suggest our
wine needed a sibling, perhaps a companion red blend. I initially held
off, knowing the amount of work it would take to develop the blend,
create a name, a label design, and a marketing plan for another wine.
Evolution had only one real competitor, but a multitude of high-end
red blends already competed on wine store shelves. In 2004 I relented,

asked Russ to develop a red blend distinctly different from Pinot Noir, and asked Sally Morrow and David Brooks for their design help. They came up with the name Meditrina, which gave us such a great story that I was won over immediately.

Meditrina, the Roman goddess of wine and health (and some books say longevity as well), never appeared in any of my schoolbook studies of Roman gods and goddesses. Not like Bacchus, the Roman god of wine inebriation, whom everyone knows. Why wasn't Meditrina given equal time? This triggered my sense of feminist injustice. I set out to tell the story of Meditrina, restore her to her rightful place in history, and sell wine at the same time. My Meditrina wine developed a following, but never achieved the same acclamation as her sister, Evolution. I was never sure whether it was the extreme competition among red blends or the wine itself that held it back.

As the economy recovered from the recession of 2008, Alex and Alison went back to their plans to expand the Evolution line of wines. Evolution Big Time Red, based on Italian varietals, took the place of Meditrina, which was slowly phased out. I was sad to say good-bye to my little goddess wine, but it was Alex and Alison's decision and it made business sense.

Next came bubbles. Alison had the idea of putting bubbles into the Evolution white wine, and she and Nik thought they'd try it at Nik's house, using his Soda Stream. The wine exploded, spraying the cupboards and the floor, but they didn't give up the idea. Alex went the next step, starting the process by taking Evolution white still wine and, using the traditional Méthode Champenoise, creating a sparkling wine. Evolution Sparkling made its debut in 2012. Evolution Pinot Noir, a lower-priced alternative to our flagship Sokol Blosser wines, debuted in 2016. True to its name, Evolution had evolved. From one white blend had come the Evolution family of four wines, with plans for more simmering in Alex's brain.

....

Caribbean Evolution

This vegan entrée with a tropical twist was created by Jack Czarnecki, chef and owner of the Joel Palmer House, a restaurant not far from the winery. Chef Czarnecki created this dish to go with Sokol Blosser's first edition of Evolution White when we introduced it in New York in 1999. You can serve this colorful vegetable medley as a main course over white or brown rice, quinoa, or another grain of your choice. It also makes a tasty side dish with fish or chicken. While this dish was composed for Sokol Blosser Evolution White wine, it is also terrific with Evolution Sparkling wine.

Makes 2 main-course servings or 4 side-dish servings

¼ cup golden raisins

¼ cup natural sliced or slivered almonds

2 tablespoons soy sauce

2 teaspoons rice vinegar

1 teaspoon dark brown sugar

2 teaspoons cornstarch

¼ teaspoon cayenne pepper, or to taste

¼ pound fresh shiitake mushroom caps, or
    ½ pound cremini mushrooms, stems trimmed

1 tablespoon grapeseed or
    other neutral-flavored vegetable oil

½ cup thinly sliced green onions

4 garlic cloves, thinly sliced

½ cup pineapple chunks, cut into ½-inch pieces

½ large red bell pepper, cut into ¼-inch dice

½ cup cubed peeled green banana

2 tablespoons chopped fresh cilantro leaves and stems

Put the raisins in a heatproof bowl, cover with boiling water, and let stand until plumped, about 5 minutes. Drain the water and set the raisins aside.

Put the almonds in a dry skillet over medium-high heat and cook, stirring frequently to prevent burning, until toasted, about 2 minutes. Transfer the almonds to a plate and set aside.

In a small bowl, stir together ½ cup water, the soy sauce, vinegar, brown sugar, cornstarch, and cayenne until blended. Set aside.

Rinse the mushrooms thoroughly and pat dry. Cut the mushrooms into ½-inch slices and set aside.

Warm a skillet over medium-high heat and add the oil. When the oil is hot, add the green onions and garlic. Cook, stirring, until the vegetables are fragrant and soft, about 2 minutes. Reduce the heat to medium and add the mushrooms. Cook, stirring, until the mushrooms are tender and lightly browned, about 8 to 10 minutes, adding up to 4 tablespoons water, 1 tablespoon at a time, as needed to cook the mushrooms thoroughly without scorching.

Add the soy sauce mixture to the skillet and bring to a boil, stirring for 1 to 2 minutes until the sauce thickens.

Add the pineapple chunks, diced bell pepper, green bananas, and cilantro to the skillet and stir to blend. Divide the mixture among serving plates, top with the plumped raisins and toasted almonds, and serve right away.

CHAPTER EIGHT

Not Retirement, Reinvention

My father may have influenced my wine career, but the pivotal parent in my life was my mother. She never became actively involved in the winery business, but that was the only part of my life she didn't try to influence. I fought her attempts to control me all through my youth.

After my senior year in high school, she took me to France to attend the summer session for foreigners at the University of Grenoble. The summer of 1962, we lived in the historic part of Grenoble. We and four other Americans, all college students, stayed with Madame Michoud, a widow who used her large apartment as a *pension* for foreign students. We took meals at her long dining table, speaking French with American accents. I loved hearing the student from Nashville speak French with his southern drawl. It was a brave thing for my fifty-seven-year-old mother to do, spending a summer rooming with her teenage daughter, who made it clear what a burden it was to be with her mother.

We each attended French conversation classes. The rest of the time I did my best to distance myself. The other Americans, just a little older than I, seemed to love to be with my mother. She was so popular that two of the young women, college students in Illinois, came to visit us in Milwaukee after we returned. Their attraction baffled me since I found her mostly annoying.

On the positive side, I was continually impressed by my mother's love of life. She didn't slow down as she aged. After she moved to McMinnville in her mid-seventies, she organized a group of local women to meet for conversation and handwork which she called the "Knit Pickers"; she started a Mahjongg group and played bridge twice a week; she had weekly golf games, not cutting back from eighteen to nine holes until she was in her nineties. She followed national politics with great interest, watched TV news nightly, and never missed *Meet the Press*. She loved to talk politics and lived for political debate. Her eyes sparkled when she sparred with her conservative Republican friends every Sunday over brunch after church. I'd hear about these jousts on my Sunday visits. She stopped attending live theater, the symphony, and opera, but was never without a book to read. She traveled to visit friends and family. When one project ended, she devised another. She always had something to look forward to.

When she had turned eighty, although in good health, I knew that she was at an age when any moment could be her last. I tried to see her regularly, although I was running the winery, my life was full of demands, and I often longed to be elsewhere. We could discuss politics, literature, hobbies, food, and family. I chose my subjects carefully to avoid her judgment. That went on for twenty-two years. When she turned ninety-eight, I began to think she would live forever.

She was eighty-two when my father died, and she couldn't understand why so many of her friends who lost a husband immediately latched onto another man. "Why do they insist on finding a replacement?" she said. "They'll just end up having to take care of him."

She continued to live alone with her cat, relishing her freedom. Her window on life never narrowed. In her mid-nineties, she decided she needed a new car and told me with a mischievous grin: "The car dealer tried to talk me into buying by promising me free oil changes for life." She laughed. "He figures I'm going to die soon and he got a good deal." My brothers and I chuckled that the car dealer would soon learn the joke was on him. I called her the "energizer bunny."

She listened to classical music daily, turning up the volume over time as her hearing got worse. She had given her grand piano to my musical brother, Henry, but missed playing, so when she was almost a hundred, she rented a piano, playing every day, as much as her arthritic hands would allow. "I always start with 'The Jolly Farmer,'" she told me. I can hear her playing it now, cheerful and upbeat, her bright red nails clicking on the piano keys. Evenings, in her nightgown and robe, she sat at her computer to check her e-mail, do a daily jigsaw puzzle, and play a game of computer solitaire before bed.

She weathered a heart valve replacement and breast cancer with optimism and aplomb. Tired of cooking, she searched for compatible women who came to the house during the day and cooked her meals. She hired them based on their intelligence, how well they played Scrabble, and their cooking, in that order. She explained that she kept one woman on, even though her food wasn't very good, because she was such a good Scrabble player. Mother didn't start live-in care until she was over a hundered. Her caretakers were devoted to her.

The Christmas after she had turned a hundred, Russ and I took mother to Nik's house for a late morning brunch and gift giving. Our extended family had come together, including Bill, our children and grandchildren, aunts and uncles. We sat around the edge of Nik's large living room, the grandchildren in the middle, close to the presents. The floor was strewn with crumpled Christmas wrap and children's toys, making it impossible to move. Nik played Santa Claus. He sat next to the tree, picked up each present, and read who it was for. Most were for the grandchildren, but then he called out my name. I watched a small square package make its way from under the Christmas tree, hand to hand over to me. When I unwrapped and opened the box, I looked at mother, who was crying. Inside, nestled in velvet, were the antique gold brooch, bracelet, and ring decorated with tiny pearls and turquoise that her grandmother had brought with her from Russia. I read the note she had included in the box: "I'm passing these to you as the next matriarch of the family." Feeling the through line from my great-grandmother to me through this heirloom jewelry made me cry too.

Mother loved to have people guess her age. She looked so much younger than she was and delighted in the surprised looks when she revealed it. Surprisingly unwrinkled and with a thick head of hair, she didn't seem to me to look "old" until she was in her late nineties. When people exclaimed about her age, she'd quip "only the good die young." She acknowledged how little time she had left: "I don't even buy green bananas anymore."

Then, in the middle of the transition practice year, 2007, her health failed. Her mind was still sharp, but her heart valve developed a leak. She started having occasional episodes when her lungs filled with fluid, stressing her heart, and producing panic as she struggled to breathe. Her caretakers, now round the clock, would take her to the hospital. She'd be back home in a day or two, full of life, but she was in her 102nd year. Her body had finally succumbed and was slowly giving out, although the feisty, opinionated joking never wavered. I telephoned her when I learned she was hospitalized early in July. She recognized my voice and responded in her best cartoon character imitation, "Well, isn't this a revoltin' development!"

Staying in her own home had been a high priority. She had briefly considered moving to a retirement home after Daddy died, but decided to stay put. "I don't want to be with all those old people," she explained. She was proud to remain in her home with all the things she loved, counting the grosbeaks at her feeders and enjoying the colorful roses on her deck, her cat snuggled up next to her.

She entered the hospital suddenly again, the night of July 18, 2007. Still recovering from my broken ankle, I had a physical therapy appointment at the hospital the next morning and went to see her in the Intensive Care Unit right afterward, before starting a day full of appointments. She was sleeping, on oxygen and IVs, her face almost skeletal with hollow cheeks and sunken eyes. Could it be that my mother was finally going to die? I'd given up trying to be with her as much as I knew she wanted and, more than once, guiltily wished she would make her exit. I wondered if then I would be free from her judgmental voice that lived in my mind.

The hospital doctor, an unusually jolly man who resembled Santa Claus ("Call me Dr. D," he said) talked to me while she slept. He said she was so weak she couldn't suck water up through the straw. Her heart was failing and her lungs kept filling with fluid, making breathing difficult to the point of panic. He put her on a small dose of morphine to allay the panic and "tune her up a bit," whatever that meant. Then she could go home, probably under a hospice situation. He said it casually, but his words went right through me. We had never spoken about hospice.

Mother opened her eyes when her breakfast arrived. I fed her two tiny bites of egg, then a piece of a fresh strawberry before she closed her mouth firmly, rejecting more. Trying to feed my mother shook me to the core. I told her I loved her. She whispered she loved me, then told me to take anything I wanted from her home and closed her eyes.

A subtle change had occurred. My mother, who loved life, knew she was not going back home. I was in tears by the time I got back to the car, too distraught to face a wine industry board meeting in an hour. I could cancel that, but I couldn't cancel the speech I was scheduled to deliver that afternoon at a KeyBank for Women program. Mother, a performer herself, had taught me that the show must go on.

Back at the winery, I told Alison how upsetting seeing Grandma Phyllis had been. She comforted me with a hug and asked if I wanted her to go with me to Portland for moral support. I instinctively said, "No, I'll be fine," then admitted I would like her help. She cancelled her own appointments and drove me to Portland. Steeling myself to focus on what I had to do, I managed to forget for an hour that my mother could be dying at that very moment.

The next day, when the doctor told me the that the end was near, I instinctively felt the need to stay with my mother. I had never been this close to death before. My grandparents all died before I was born; Daddy died before my mother and I could reach his bedside. Witnessing death would be a new frontier, one I would face alone, apprehensive but riveted.

Alex appeared unexpectedly after dinner with a deck of cards, a CD player, and some classical music. "I thought Grandma would like to listen to music," he said. His thoughtfulness touched me and I was glad for his company. We put on Mozart's Requiem and played gin rummy for an hour before he went home.

The nurse who came in to check on mother told me what to expect. "Listen for changes," she told me. I stretched out on the chair bed, sleeping fitfully as the night sounds of the hospital kept intruding. Every time I woke I monitored mother's breathing. At 4:30 AM, as day broke and the sky lightened, I got up. As my mother lay motionless on the bed, I sat close to her and started talking about her parents, her Grandma Richter, her husband Gus, her friends who had died—all the people she loved who were waiting for her. I assured her that Ronnie, her attorney son, would take care of everything. Her cat would have a good home. Watching mother over the course of her last days in the hospital, I understood that we labor to die, just as we labor to be born. I'd never considered how analogous the two processes were. "We celebrate birth," the priest from her church had told me, "because we know the possibilities ahead. We don't celebrate death because we don't see the possibilities, but they are there, just in another realm, another world, another dimension. We can look back on youth; no one can look back on old age."

When mother took her last breath, I felt the energy in the room shift as her spirit rose and crossed into another dimension, leaving a lifeless body behind. It was a blessed moment. I would never think of death the same again and felt honored to have been present.

I sat with mother for a few minutes before calling the winery. Alex answered and said he would come immediately to be with me. In the silence before he arrived, I thought about how, in the last twenty years, mother had shown me how to live, growing old with grace, humor, and independence. Now she had shown me how to die, gently and serenely. The complications that made our relationship difficult—the uncomfortable critiques and unreasonable demands—were no longer important. I knew she loved me. She knew I loved her. We were bound together through many dimensions and lifetimes. The issues we had in this life were minor by comparison. The rawness of our relationship kept me from wanting her back, but her death left a surprisingly deep hole in my heart.

For several years after mother died, I thought about her less than anticipated, relieved that her judging voice inside me had receded. She'd surface at odd moments. I'd find that voice coming out of my own mouth, telling my daughter what to do. Alison closed down just as I had, then learned to tease me until I realized what I was doing and we could both laugh.

Then, suddenly, for no apparent reason, I started missing my mother. I lamented that we had not been able to get past our control issues to meet on equal footing. Thwarting her attempts to dominate me had cut her out of much of my life. Deliberately keeping our conversations superficial wasn't hard. There was still plenty to talk about as we shared a number of interests. I sought her advice on knitting patterns; We chatted about her cat; looked up the various birds that came to her feeders; discussed dieting. Family stories were a dependable fallback. An ongoing conversation was trying to decide when Daddy's Alzheimer's first started. I grew adept at changing the subject if she asked me again why I left Bill, or anything else I didn't want to share with her. She loved astrology and told me I was being secretive because I was a Scorpio.

Being a Scorpio had nothing to do with my denying my mother what she wanted to know about me. I chose not to tell her personal things fearing her judgment. Yet I yearned for that closeness. Years after she died, I started to wish I knew more about what mattered to her. Subjects we had never discussed kept occurring to me. I wondered how she felt about her mother and the grandmother who was so important to her. I wished I'd asked more details about her violin playing, her career, about aging, about facing death.

One afternoon, walking in the vineyard and thinking of all the questions I wished I'd asked, an astonishing thought hit me. I had spent years complaining that my mother wanted me to conform to her image of a good daughter instead of trying to see me as a unique individual. I pitied myself that I had been stuck with such a demanding, controlling mother. Now, years after her death, standing in the middle of a block of Pinot Noir vines, I could see a different scenario. All the while I was criticizing my mother for not valuing me as an individual, I was doing the same thing to her. I had an image in my mind of the mother I wanted her to be, one she never measured up to. I had never tried to know her as the singular individual she was. It was a humbling realization, one that brought to mind the old Pogo cartoon: "We have met the enemy and he is us."

After that thought, which hit me like a thunderbolt, an odd thing happened. When I stopped focusing on my mother's inadequacies, I started thinking about her in a new way. The more arms-length title of mother fell away; she was my mama. Happy childhood memories, suppressed for years, flooded in: putting on my best dress, patent leather shoes, and little white gloves to go to the ballet; taking the train to Chicago to visit the Museum of Science and Industry and shop at the original Marshall Field's department store; starting early in December to bake and decorate fancy Christmas cookies, wrap them in waxed paper, and store them in special Christmas tins for when my brothers would come home; playing dress up and tea party with me and my dolls.

I thought of the small blue trunk that opened to a wardrobe of doll clothes she had made for me while I was near death with a ruptured appendix just before my fifth birthday. I remember having a terrible stomachache and being rushed to the hospital. The doctor gave me a 50 percent chance of survival. Mama often told me how anxious she was, how she passed the time sewing doll clothes for me, and how penicillin, a new drug, saved me. As a child, every time she'd mention the operation, a wave of guilt swept over me. I thought she was blaming me for putting her through such an awful time. Suddenly I saw the love and understood what she must have gone through.

All the handcrafts Mama learned from her mother and grandmother, she taught me—embroidery, crochet, needlepoint, knitting. I learned to knit during the Korean War, when her church circle was knitting squares for blankets for the troops. She started me on one too so I could participate. My seven-year-old fingers clumsily pulled the yarn around one needle and over the other. Each stitch was a victory. I measured at the end of each row to see how close I was to completing my square.

One year, her church circle held their holiday bazaar at our house. It was her excuse to go overboard with Christmas decorations: large evergreen wreaths with bright red ribbons on the front door; pine greens tied with red bows across the fireplace mantle; a large, fresh tree with colored lights and shimmery ornaments; red and green candles everywhere. Fragrant smells of Christmas cookies mingled with fresh pine.

The day of the bazaar, women in stylish wool suits and little hats filled the front hall, the dining room, and the living room. I spent most of my time in the dining room, staring endlessly at the bride doll on display, with her blonde hair, fancy white handmade dress, and lacy veil. My yearning was not lost on the church ladies. At the end of the bazaar, the doll hadn't sold, and they gave it to me. This magical moment popped into my head after all those years.

It was time to reframe my past, balance my perspective, and see if, even at this late date, I could understand Mama better. I had a few clues about her musical upbringing, which had been a big part of her childhood, including her father's first question when he came home: "Has Phyllis practiced her violin today?" But I didn't know how she chose the violin, how old she was when she started playing, or what kept her going.

My older brothers remember hearing Mama play her violin in quartets at home when they were little. I don't remember seeing her play, but I do recall listening to a small homemade recording Daddy made. She was playing the "Hora Staccato," which she always referred to as "my old warhorse." In the middle of her performance, Daddy, who was holding the microphone, sneezed. My brothers and I liked to listen for the sneeze, which for us was the high point of the recording. I knew she had been first violin in the Chicago Women's Symphony, but what struck me about that was not her prowess, but that women were not allowed to play with men in the big symphony and had to form their own. I grew up loving violin music and associating the violin with my mother, but I never actually heard her perform.

After college she had formed a professional group using a stage name, "Phyllis Farel and her All Girls Band," which traveled throughout the Midwest, then New York City, playing at events ranging from auto shows to trotting races. Girl bands were trendy in the late 1920s and early '30s. She never talked to me about the other "girls" in her group or what it was like having a girls' band. I wished I'd thought to ask. A 1928 publicity photo of her and her band is all that remains. I can only look at these stylish young women in their flapper dresses and marcelled hair, posed next to their instruments, and imagine what their lives were like. Single, attractive, talented, traveling, and earning good money made for a glamorous life for young women in the 1920s. Wrapped up in my own world, I never asked her the questions I now wanted answers to.

My brother Ronnie looked at me when I met him in London five years after mother's death. It was the first time I'd seen him since then. "Do you know how much you look like Mother?" he asked. This wasn't news. Mama's friends never failed to pat my head and told me I was her "spitting image." "Am not!" I'd say to myself. But the older I get, the more I feel the bond.

Mama stares back when I look in the mirror. My deep-set eyes are her eyes. I have the same lines around my mouth. She is in me, and this both unnerves and strangely comforts me. I am fascinated by how connected I feel to her—a feeling I fought while she was alive but which now I treasure. So, when Ronnie mentioned it, I recognized the connection. "I always have," I admitted, then, thinking about her always polished appearance, added, "She was so much more glamorous."

"She lived in a more glamorous age," he replied gently. He was right. Mama came of age in the Roaring Twenties. I thought of her fashion-conscious clothes, carefully dyed and coiffed hair, flawless makeup, and bright red nails. I came of age in the 1960s, an age known for mismatched prints, jeans, and tie-dye. The closest I came to glamour were the years of my presidency when I dyed my hair blonde. When I want a good laugh, I look at pictures from my blonde phase.

Mama and I looked at the world through the eyes of our times, bookends of the twentieth century, both times of explosive change. When my mother was born, in 1905, the car and telephone were novelties, air travel nonexistent. Women couldn't vote and had little legal standing. The worlds we grew up in were miles apart. No wonder when we tried to communicate, our words went askew, heard and interpreted through our generational bias. The older I got, the more

I wanted to discuss—comparing and contrasting—our lives. I never thought I'd say it but I missed her terribly.

––––––––

WHEN I WAS PRESIDENT of Sokol Blosser Winery, I considered it the zenith of my life. I had found my place and couldn't imagine doing anything else. When I relinquished that, I needed time to sort out my life. Glad that the weight of the business had shifted off my shoulders onto Alex and Alison, I could feel the extent to which the transition, and especially the practice year, had taken its toll. I felt pummeled, physically and emotionally. It was as if the universe, trying to teach me the importance of learning to let go, was impelled to deliver the message in as many ways possible. During that final transition year, while the main storyline was letting go of my identity as president of Sokol Blosser, subplots surfaced that I hadn't expected, like redefining my relationship with my kids in changing from boss back to mom. Outside of the winery, during the same year, I witnessed the death of my mother, and remarried, finally letting go of emotions related to my marriage to Bill, which had haunted me since we separated.

The vines in the vineyard turn inward after giving up their fruit at harvest, sending all remaining energy down to their roots. We see them as dormant, but their physical appearance masks their internal activity as they prepare for the next cycle. It struck me that giving up the presidency of the winery was reaping my harvest and that, like the vines, I needed to turn inward to renew, reinvigorate, and reinvent. I eventually came to see that my work at Sokol Blosser was just part of my journey, its success giving me the credibility to move to a new stage.

I started with yoga and meditation, caught up on my reading, and found my love for gardening again. Russ built raised beds and we put in blueberry and strawberry plants, which not only supplied us all summer with fresh berries but gave us jam for the winter. Peas, beets, beans, zucchini, carrots, tomatoes, Tuscan kale, broccoli—I got to indulge myself by planting whatever I fancied. I hadn't had a large garden since the early days of the vineyard.

The big challenge was my identity. If I wasn't Susan CEO, who was I? I couldn't see myself spending my days playing golf or bridge, which I didn't care for, or even gardening and knitting, which I loved. I needed to find something that would challenge me and engage both my brain and my heart. When I came across Lao Tzu's quote, "When I let go of what I am, I become what I might be," I saw how long people had been facing this challenge. Lao Tzu lived in the sixth century BC.

Realizing that I needed a challenge made me accept that I was indeed an entrepreneur at heart. While Bill and I were building our business, I regarded that word as an insult. I thought of entrepreneurs as the robber barons of the late nineteenth century, Machiavellian risk takers seeking profit at all costs. They represented the antithesis of my triple bottom line philosophy. Then, in 2008, members of the Oregon Entrepreneurs Network nominated me for Entrepreneur of the Year. When I went to be interviewed, I questioned whether I should be there, protesting that I wasn't really an entrepreneur since money was not my motivation. They responded by making me one of their three finalists for the year.

Russ donned his tux and I my dressiest outfit and my mother's heirloom rhinestone earrings for their glamorous awards dinner. We sat in a hotel ballroom with the other 998 guests and watched the other two finalists and me interviewed on a giant screen before the winner was announced. Despite feeling I didn't belong there, I'm competitive enough to have been disappointed that the winning name was not mine. The experience, however, did make me rethink my views. Maybe an entrepreneur could be about more than money. Innovation and risk were also key components of entrepreneurship. Under that definition, I was one. Without a challenge to believe in, I am at loose ends, bored, and restless. With one, I have enormous energy and focus.

While I was considering my future, I was recruited by the Democratic Party to run for the Oregon legislature in my district. Their argument was that with my agriculture and small business experience, I fit my district. I agreed to run and spent all of 2010 preparing for the November election: raising campaign funds, educating myself on the issues, meeting voters, and strategizing with my small staff and volunteers.

As I walked the district knocking on doors, I met people who were kind and appreciative, who thanked me for running for public office, and people who were bitter, used ugly words, and blamed me for their woes. I chanced upon the woman who had taken care of Nik, almost forty years earlier, when he was a toddler in daycare at the First Presbyterian Church in McMinnville. "I've been following your career," she said, "and I'm thrilled you're running. I'm behind you 100 percent." That was a good day.

Then I would meet voters who condemned me for hiring vineyard workers they believed were "illegal aliens" and slammed the door in my face after calling me names; or people who accused me of killing babies by supporting abortion rights, or promoting drunk driving by making wine. I tried not to take it personally.

I lost the election, but the experience pointed me toward my next venture. Yamhill County, where I lived, had so much going for it. As the heart of the Oregon wine industry, it had become a wine tourism destination that, in turn, attracted top chefs and other tourism amenities. These in turn attracted manufacturers, builders, designers, and other wine industry suppliers. The wine industry had clearly made a huge impact. Yet, the poverty level was high, the overall education level low, and churches throughout the county offered free meals to help feed people. A number of local nonprofits worked hard to deal with the issues of hunger and homelessness.

My interest was cultural opportunity and I decided to use my leftover campaign funds to start a public benefit nonprofit. I christened it the Yamhill Enrichment Society (YES) with a mission "to enrich the cultural soul of Yamhill County by supporting projects in education and the arts, food and agriculture, history and community." Our tag line was "building community through innovation and collaboration." YES allowed me to combine three of my key interests—culture, economic development, and environmental concerns—but at the local rather than the state level. If I had focused during the winery management transition on what I would do, I would not have arrived at YES; founding a nonprofit was never in my thoughts.

By that time, it had been almost three years since I had left Sokol Blosser Winery. My office sat unused, my things taking up space and gathering dust. My phone line, which for years had blinked with multiple messages, sat silent and dark. Alex and Alison weren't pushing, but it was time for them to make use of space reserved for me at the winery and for me to move my base of operations to McMinnville.

The office break became final when I rented the large front room upstairs in a Victorian house that had been turned into offices. My handyman husband painted the walls, installed shelving in the closet, moved furniture, and got me comfortably settled. We made use of what remained of my mother's living room furniture. The two Queen Anne wingback chairs from my childhood fit the ambience of the old house. Mama's large, carved wooden Chinese wall hanging took a place of honor on my office wall. What would have looked out of place in Russ's and my home looked welcoming in my office. I loved having my own space, a "room of my own," to work out of. At the winery, my former office was dismantled, installed with a conference table, and christened "The Founder's Room." After a few years, with increased staff and every space needing to be used for offices, Alison took it over as her office.

At our first meeting, in February 2011, the YES board members I'd recruited crowded around the conference table in the new office, discussing what "building our community through innovation and collaboration" could look like. The energy in the air was palpable.

I proposed a number of projects that interested me. Some captured their attention, others not so much. The ones I could persuade them to get behind, we took on. One board member, with young children of her own, told us about a childhood literacy project she'd dreamed about starting. She convinced us to take that on too.

Our enthusiasm coalesced around six diverse projects to pursue our first year. Books for Babies would provide every newborn at the Willamette Valley Medical Center with a new book for parents to read, including a message on why it was so important to read to babies. Koncert for Kids would bring music enrichment to McMinnville elementary students. Women's leadership luncheons would bring Yamhill County women of different generations and professions together. Living History would focus on community history, starting with McMinnville a hundred years ago, using old photographs and a tour of historic homes. Agriculture would take two tacks: first, a food collaborative to help build a robust local food economy; second, a celebration of Yamhill County's unique trifecta of talented chefs, small, diversified family farms, and famous wines.

When Russ left in the morning to walk up the hill to work at the winery, I got in the car and drove to my McMinnville office. I conducted YES business from my laptop computer, sitting at my mother's tall secretary desk, listening to classical music, loving my freedom and my own space. Our board met over lunch, which I enjoyed preparing. We made our important decisions while we ate family style, passing around a large stainless steel bowl with one of my favorite lunch salads, along with warm bread just out of the oven from the bakery down the street.

By the end of our first year, YES had received a 501(c)(3) classification and accomplished its initial goals. By 2016, YES's childhood literacy program had expanded and served almost 40 percent of the county's children five and under. It's Enriching Lives through Music program (ELM), worked with another nonprofit to fund a Youth

Nik and me at a Bounty of Yamhill County dinner, 2012. (Photo credit: Andrèa Johnson.)

Mariachi Project and was poised for expansion, and the Bounty of Yamhill County (BOYC), a weekend of culinary adventures in Oregon wine country, had become a nationally acclaimed event; and YES had the beginnings of an endowment fund.

With YES, I had discovered the entrepreneurship of the elder. What put YES in this new category was that this time my climb was not about ascending the ladder of career success, not about accumulation. Rather, it was about giving away, using what I had gained to add to the quality of life in my community—what I have come to see as the role of the elder.

As president of the Yamhill Enrichment Society (YES), which put on the Bounty of Yamhill County (BOYC), I wanted to address the attendees, thank them, and tell them about our YES projects. We had no stage or podium to lift me above the several hundred guests, so Russ got a ladder from the winery and held it while I climbed up to welcome people. It added a rustic touch. 2014.

Held at the peak of harvest season, the BOYC was designed to showcase the area's splendid chefs, family farms, and famous wines. What could be better than a farm-to-table meal in a vineyard setting, accompanied by great wine and conversation. 2014. (Photo credits this page: Andréa Johnson.)

A YEAR OR TWO after I passed the baton, I went back to the winery to look up something. I couldn't find my files. I had left Bill's and my presidential papers in file cabinets. Together, our papers traced the ups and downs of the business, with harvest and production records, sales and marketing plans, financial projections and actuals, legal issues, vineyard records. Everything that the winery did for the thirty-seven years that Bill and I ran the business resided in those papers. Alex and Alison had found themselves short of space, and decided to clean house. All the old papers had been removed. They'd put them in storage but really wanted to throw out as much as they could.

I couldn't let them do that; the history of the early wine industry in Oregon would be lost to future generations. It was already looking different than it had only ten years earlier. As founders of the Oregon wine industry, our records might someday help historians reconstruct its origins.

From my stint in the 1970s as an archivist at the Southern Historical Collection at the University of North Carolina, Chapel Hill, I knew how valuable primary sources could be in understanding the past, which I believed both relevant and important. The papers of the early vintners needed to be preserved.

McMinnville's Linfield College, with its new Center for the Northwest, its historic hosting of the annual International Pinot Noir Celebration, and its wine aficionado president, could be the perfect place to house the history of the Oregon wine industry. When I proposed the opportunity to start a repository of Oregon wine history to Tom Hellie, Linfield's president, his face lit up with interest. He wasted no time finding a donor, outfitting a climate-controlled space, hiring an archivist, and establishing the Oregon Wine History Archive.

Linfield's wine industry archival project began in 2011 with the donation of records from Sokol Blosser's first thirty-five years. I personally packed up boxes of early correspondence, old vineyard records, marketing plans, photographs, and financial particulars, which got carted off to be archived for posterity on temperature controlled shelves in twenty-eight linear feet of boxes. Linfield's original goal was to get the papers of six of the early couples: the Ponzis, Letts, Adelsheims, Redfords, Eraths, and Sokol Blossers. Records from our era would be the last ones on actual paper. Future records would be electronic.

Encouraged by the response to their project, Linfield solicited grants to expand their scope. They procured early editions of the *Oregon Wine Press,* and papers from industry events like the International Pinot Noir Celebration (IPNC) and the Oregon Wine Board. Rachael Woody, the curator, engaged students and faculty to procure oral histories from the Latino workers who were critical to building the industry. Two people important to Sokol Blosser became part of the oral archives: Ofelia Galaviz, who worked with me in the vineyard in the 1980s, and our vineyard manager for many years, Manuel "Luis" Hernandez. The Wine Archive digitalized their material and put on a large exhibit in 2013 during the IPNC with video interviews and photographs detailing the early history of Oregon wine. Linfield College succeeded in establishing itself as the major source of Oregon wine history. When the Oregon Historical Society put on a special traveling exhibit of Oregon wine history in 2015, Linfield's Wine Archive was their resource.

Helping preserve the early history of the Oregon wine industry took me back forty years to when I studied history, with dreams of being a historian and making the past understandable to the present. I had no idea I myself would do something that would have archival significance. Launching the Oregon Wine History Archive gave me the chance to play at the two ends of the history continuum: both making history and preserving it.

Removing my presidential papers from Sokol Blosser was one more step in erasing my presence at the winery. Although the staff welcomed me when I appeared, so much had changed; there were so many new faces.

As the founder, I was invited to meet with new hires to tell them how the winery started and about its early days. I represented the past. The present and future of the winery belonged to Nik, Alex, and Alison. I wouldn't have had it otherwise, yet it felt bittersweet. I didn't want to go back, but I did think fondly of the days when I had been the winery's Grand Poobah.

....

Cider-Braised Pork Tacos
with Peaches, Fennel Slaw,
and Cider Reduction

The grand finale of the weekend of culinary adventures that comprises Bounty of Yamhill County (BOYC) event has always been held at Sokol Blosser Winery. It is a major fundraiser for my organization, the Yamhill Enrichment Society (YES), and is also a celebration of what is special about Yamhill County. Called "Big Night," local chefs partnered with nearby farms to create small bites. Guests visit the chef's tents to load up their plates, then return to their tables to feast. Sommeliers come around to serve wines from over two dozen of the local wineries. Red Hills Market is always one of the favorite booths and the market's chef, Jody Kropf, shared his delicious recipe for cider-braised pork tacos. He is always paired with his farmer friend, Trevor Baird, whose peaches are famous throughout the county and at their peak of ripeness when the event is held in late August. My favorite wine with this is a nicely chilled bottle of Sokol Blosser White Riesling.

Makes 6 to 8 servings

For the braised pork
   2 to 3 pounds pork shoulder or pork butt
   1 tablespoon kosher salt

½ gallon fresh apple cider (if you're in Oregon, look for
   Baird Family Orchards apple cider)
12 ounces IPA beer

For the reduction
   2 cups fresh apple cider
   Kosher salt and freshly ground black pepper

For the fennel slaw
   ½ fennel bulb, trimmed
   ½ red onion
   ½ jalapeño chile, stemmed
   1 green onion, finely chopped
   ¼ cup prepared garlicky aioli, or ¼ cup mayonnaise mixed with
      1 clove garlic, minced
   ½ teaspoon kosher salt
   2 tablespoons olive oil
   Finely grated zest of ½ lime
   1 tablespoon fresh lime juice
   ¼ cup chopped fresh cilantro

For the grilled peaches
   2 firm but ripe peaches, halved, and pitted
   Olive oil
   Kosher salt

For serving
   18 to 24 four-inch corn tortillas
   Fresh cilantro leaves, for garnish (optional)

To make the pork, preheat the oven to 275°F. Season pork all over with the
1 tablespoon salt, then place in large Dutch oven or other ovenproof pot with a

lid and add the cider and beer. Cover the pot, place in the oven, and cook until the pork is fork-tender, about 3 hours.

To make the reduction, pour the 2 cups cider into a small saucepan. Place over low heat and cook until the cider is reduced to about ½ cup, 30 to 45 minutes. Season to taste with salt and pepper. Set aside until serving time.

To make the slaw, using a mandoline, carefully shave the fennel, onion, and jalapeño thinly. Alternatively, using a very sharp knife, slice the vegetables as thinly as possible. Place the shaved fennel, onion, and jalapeño in a bowl along with the green onion. In a small bowl, whisk together the aioli, salt, oil, lime zest and juice, and chopped cilantro. Add the aioli mixture to the bowl with the fennel mixture and stir to coat evenly. Cover and refrigerate for 30 minutes or longer to allow flavors to blend.

For the peaches, preheat a grill or stovetop grill pan over high heat. In a bowl, lightly coat the peach halves with olive oil and season lightly with salt. Grill the peaches until lightly browned, turning to cook all sides, 2 to 3 minutes. Transfer the grilled peaches to a cutting board, let cool, and then chop into small chunks. Set aside.

When the pork is ready, remove it from the oven and let it cool slightly. Using two forks, pull the meat into shreds and keep warm.

When you're ready to serve, have all the ingredients ready on the counter top. Warm a skillet or stovetop grill pan over high heat. Add the tortillas to the skillet and cook until warm and soft, about 1 minute per side; wrap the tortillas in foil as you go to keep them warm.

Divide the tortillas among 6 or 8 plates. Top each tortilla with a spoonful of shredded pork, slaw, and peaches, then drizzle with the cider reduction. Garnish with cilantro leaves, if desired, and serve right away.

CHAPTER NINE

Family Ties

W hen Bill and I launched the introductory vintage of our new winery in 1978, we did so in the first dedicated tasting room in Oregon. Sokol Blosser's building set a new benchmark of Oregon wine hospitality since, to that point, the few existing wineries greeted the public in converted garages, barns, and sheds. Designed by John Storrs, one of Oregon's most renowned late twentieth-century architects, the first Oregon tasting room was a modest 1,200 square feet, with one public tasting space. The low profile and gray stucco building sat on a rocky knoll, tucked in among old oaks, firs, and maples. A large window at one end centered on a view of Mount Hood where, on clear days, the view was spectacular.

Fast-forward thirty years. Oregon Pinot Noir's international reputation, with the Dundee Hills as its center, meant visitor counts to Sokol Blosser had risen to more than thirty thousand a year. That was the good news. The bad news was that our twentieth-century state-of-the art tasting room had become woefully inadequate.

We'd known for years that the tiny kitchen and the office, each with barely enough room for one person, were too small for our needs. Our talented hospitality team managed to work around our limitations, setting up an auxiliary tasting area in the outdoor courtyard during the busy summer months, and making sure caterers knew to prepare everything off-site.

But by 2010, even our temporary measures were insufficient. Success had created a troubling predicament. The shortcomings of our facility meant we were unable to give the increased number of visitors the attention and the wine experience that we and they wanted. A new building would stretch us to the limit financially, but not acting was negatively affecting our business.

After lengthy board discussions of the pros and cons, we decided it was time to undertake the largest capital project in our history. That this became a defining moment in the life of our family, as well as the winery, became apparent with time.

Once the hard decision was made, the family rallied around the project. Bill and our hospitality manager, Michael Brown, took the lead in interviewing potential architects, looking for someone who, like John Storrs in the 1970s, would appreciate our sense of place and tie the new tasting room to the land. They visited tasting rooms in Oregon and California for ideas.

Nik recommended we talk to Brad Cloepfil, a Portland architect whose innovative designs for museums in Seattle, St. Louis, Denver, New York, and Quebec had received international recognition. Was it possible he might like to design something on a much smaller scale, like a winery tasting room? No harm in asking.

I think we were fated to work together; Brad told us he had grown up spending summers at his uncle's farm in Yamhill County, not far from us, had been watching the growth of the wine industry, and had been waiting for the right winery to work with. The more we

Bill and I checking the plans during the construction of what became known as the John Storrs Tasting Room. Four-year-old Alex, wearing his favorite Big Bird shirt, and faithful dog, Muffin, supervised us.

Thirty-five years later, Alison and Alex re-created the scene as they checked plans for the new hospitality center, with Alison's dog, Twix, standing by. (Photo credit: Carolyn Wells Kramer.)

interviewed other architects, the more excited we got about Brad. Scared we might be biting off more than we should, but excited by the potential, we hired Brad and his group at Allied Works.

When the Sokol Blosser family engaged me to design their new tasting room I was captivated by the possibilities. I have known and loved the landscape of Yamhill County my entire life; my parents were raised in nearby Newberg, Oregon, and my family has farmed in the county for over fifty years. To build in this landscape was a reverie, a site I had already filled with aspirations.

I wanted the building to be part of the terroir, a natural outgrowth of the vineyards, as well as capture the soul of the countryside, to be a place of repose and reflection. The Sokol Blosser family welcomed these explorations and was extraordinary to work with—a visionary group with a passion for their work, product, and home. The resulting building was more than we had hoped for, the emblem of a fruitful collaboration. It holds a very special place in my heart, and remains one of the most fulfilling projects that I have the pleasure of returning to as often as I can get away.

Brad Cloepfil
Principal, Allied Works Architecture,
Portland, Oregon, and New York City

For the next year, the family met with Brad and his team, usually in his Portland office, surrounded by sketches of possibilities. We watched him think with his pencil, sketching different ideas on sheet after sheet of transparent paper. Construction started in 2012, and the new Sokol Blosser tasting room opened in July 2013.

Seeming to rise out of the land among our vineyards and

Designed by Brad Cloepfil and opened July 1, 2013, the wood and glass building seemed to rise out of the landscape. With spaces for different activities, like a catering kitchen that doubled as a space for wine and food pairing, a library for special tastings, a lounge for Cellar Club members, and a large deck, the building gave us the ability to accommodate multiple small groups at the same time. (Photo credit: Andréa Johnson.)

majestic native Oregon oaks, the low-profile building with its living roof of multiple sedum varieties paid homage to the vineyard's terroir. At 3,600 square feet, it was triple the size of the old one, but instead of one public area, the new tasting room provided a variety of distinct spaces. Unlike most large, open tasting rooms, ours had a number of areas designed to give customers options.

With acclaim from both the architectural and wine media, our tasting room set a new benchmark for wine tasting hospitality in Oregon. What Brad created embodied the spirit of the Sokol Blosser family. It was more than just a building. Renowned curator and architecture critic Aaron Betsky captured Brad's genius when he commented on another of Brad's creations, "This is not a display of architecture, but a marker to the presence of art, a container for light and image, and a moment of art in . . . America."

Michael Brown, whose background in fine dining had supplied much of the vision for how we would utilize our new building, dreamed aloud that one day Sokol Blosser would have its own chef who would cater private events as well as winery ones. His suggestion articulated one of my wishes, unspoken because I thought it was unreachable; hearing Michael say it, as if it were a possibility, activated my hopes.

In anticipation of one day hiring a chef, we built a large kitchen in our new tasting room and placed a long wooden table down the middle that could be used for groups sampling food and wine pairings, cooking demonstrations, or just preparation space. Our new kitchen allowed us to feature the culinary element, which we had always advocated, more prominently alongside our wines. It was a major contrast to our old tasting room, which had only a minuscule kitchen. In addition, we created an eating space on a secluded area of the deck that opened right off the kitchen. Called the Farm Table, it accommodated a party of up to ten for a private event. It became my favorite space to entertain. Sitting at the table with friends, engaged in lively conversation while looking out over the vineyards and the valley, eating fresh, local, sustainable food and sipping wines to go with them, was a perk of the wine business.

Two and one-half years after the new tasting room opened, Michael got the go-ahead to hire a winery chef. It felt like we had achieved another milestone when Chef Henry Kibit joined the Sokol Blosser team. We had finally been able to bring food and wine together the way we had always wanted.

For his final interview, I had sent Chef Henry four of our wines (Chardonnay, Pinot Gris, Pinot Noir, and Evolution Big Time Red), with instructions to create a dish to accompany each. Working out of the kitchen in our new hospitality center, Henry wowed us. All his wine and food pairings were spot on and one was transcendent.

The boldest and most memorable pairing was a farro and treviso salad paired with Evolution Red. This combination elevated the dish and the wine beyond what either could achieve on their own. The combination was unusual for several reasons. Chef served the salad at the end of the meal, which I loved as a light note to finish on. Pairing a salad with a red wine is daring and conceptually hard to understand. Indeed, when it appeared, I was suspicious. After eating the bitter greens and getting the pop from the dressing, a sip of the light and fruity Evolution Red neutralized the bitterness of the greens and completely changed the experience. Tart and bitter became soft and almost sweet. It enhanced the fruity quality of the wine and softened the harder edges of the salad. Exquisite.

Michael Kelly Brown,
Vice President, Sokol Blosser Winery

While Brad's building rolled out a new paradigm for winery visitors, the old tasting room held many memories and years of our history. Over its thirty-five years, in addition to its many day-to-day visitors and the many public events the winery hosted, the old tasting room had held diverse private events: an intimate fundraising dinner with Congressman Les AuCoin for high-end donors; a lunch for Madame Lalou Bize-Leroy, owner at the time of Domaine de la Romanée-Conti; small wedding, birthday, and anniversary celebrations; a bar mitzvah; and annual winery staff Christmas celebrations, which started as potluck dinners and white elephant gift exchanges and evolved to catered affairs.

We christened our memory-filled stucco landmark the John Storrs Tasting Room and continued to use it for selected private events. Perhaps someday, as Oregon's first tasting room, it will be declared a historic building.

OUR FAMILY HAD STARTED drifting apart when Bill and I bought out our partners in 1996 and our five family members—Bill, myself, Nik, Alex, and Alison—became the sole board of directors. Bill was busy managing the Portland office of a large firm and the kids were busy with their own lives. The result was that the family gave me so much freedom that I ran the business as if I were the sole owner, calling board meetings infrequently and mainly for updates. The other four family members didn't feel involved but, as long as the winery was doing well, they left me alone. There was never any apparent conflict, we just seemed to go our own ways. Bill's and my divorce furthered family separation since we met as a family only at winery board meetings.

When Alex and Alison came on as employees and I decided to transition control of the winery to Nik, Alex, and Alison, the family board suddenly became a vital piece, taking on responsibility for policy and oversight. We still got together only for the business, but the dynamics slowly changed as it took all of us working in concert to navigate the transition, mentor Alex and Alison in their new roles, face the recession, expand the Evolution line, resolve our sales challenges, and build a new structure to welcome the public.

If the winery is somehow what split us up, in that running it gave me the courage to leave Bill, I also see it as bringing us back together by presenting us with challenges we had to band together to face. As board chair, Nik brought his experience in expanding his own company with investors, building national sales, and reporting to a nonfamily board. He took the lead in holding Alex's and Alison's feet to the fire, asking for clearer spreadsheets, more sales accountability, better packets of information for board meetings, and an overall level of reporting from the copresidents that required financial rigor and strategic vision. His demands were never hostile, but always succinct and to the point. When he finally complimented Alison on an excellent board packet, she knew she had cleared a high hurdle.

The process of creating a new hospitality facility was the final piece that cemented in place a revitalized, stronger family relationship. Taking out a new loan that put us deeper in debt, deciding on an architect, and arguing over a builder required each of us supplying ideas and perspective. Alex and Alison contributed as seasoned leaders, Nik as the head of a mature business of his own, Bill and I with our backgrounds of experience. As we wrangled to consensus, gratitude, love, and respect for each other healed old wounds. Individually, except for Nik, whose marriage to Deborah stayed solid, we each found new partners and entered second marriages—mine to Russ in 2007, then Bill and Dorinda's in 2011, Alison and Javier's in 2012, and Alex and Ginny's in 2014. Holidays and birthdays became family occasions once again.

For several years after Alex and Alison had taken over, going to the winery had felt awkward and I stayed away. After the new hospitality building was finished, I found myself trekking up the hill from my home more often. It was not just that we had created a beautiful space and I loved being there, or that Russ and I had a puppy we needed to walk or had bluebird boxes along the winery road we were monitoring. The new space we created symbolized a victory for family relations as well as a home run for the business.

———

SOKOL BLOSSER WINERY TRULY became a family business when the reins passed to the second generation, although that was never our goal. Bill and I didn't start out to build a family business. We were just doing our thing. When my father suggested our winery would be the next family business (his tannery being the first), I nodded in agreement but what that could mean didn't sink in. It wasn't until Bill and I and our children wholly owned the winery, and I then faced ceding control to our kids, that I began to understand the special challenges and rewards of family business.

What I appreciate most as a family business has been the ability to be ourselves, to carry over the reality of who we are in private into our business. We also have what I consider a luxury, as a private company, to look beyond short-term profitability, a drawback of investor-held companies. Profitability is the vehicle to take us toward our vision; it's not the destination.

We care about the well-being of our employees, our community, and the earth. We live the triple bottom line of people, planet, profit in our private lives. Owning Sokol Blosser Winery as a family allows us to exercise those values in running our company. We were proud to apply for and receive B Corp certification, one of only three Oregon wineries to meet their exacting standards. Our challenge now comes in keeping those values alive through future generations.

Bill and I devoted our lives to creating and developing Sokol Blosser Winery. Our success was the result of hard work, perseverance, and ingenuity in the face of obstacles. Luck played only a small part. But I believe luck blessed us in one very important way—with exceptionally competent and talented kids. Their wisdom and compassion cannot be explained simply by good parenting.

When Mom was president of the winery, she basically ran things as she saw fit. Fortunately, this was almost always a good idea and from a business perspective she made solid decisions, built strong relationships, and managed with heart. However, there were a few times when having a few more checks and balances would've been helpful. As a family, we didn't know how to function as a board. At the time, I was just learning what it meant to have a board, as I had assembled one at my own company. I know now that recruiting a talented board and using them in an optimal way takes a long time. Like a decade.

A few years later, when I became the chair of the family board, basically overseeing my brother and sister, I did my best to try to instill the importance of my new governance knowledge. This was a huge challenge, and for the first several years was very frustrating. We would flip back and forth between trying to discuss high-level strategy and complaining about where a new bush had been planted. Mom and Dad had amazing historical perspective and experience, but also didn't want to be the ones to question Alex and Alison on their decisions. So I tried to hold it together, and several times I almost quit. But thankfully we all worked together and communicated well enough to make it through to the board we have today.

Nik Blosser
Chairman of the Board, Sokol Blosser Winery

Nik, Alex, and Alison spent their childhood at the vineyard, accompanying Bill and me, playing and later working in the vines. Because Bill and I were involved with every aspect, our kids experienced the rhythm of the seasons and the sights, smells, and sounds of a working vineyard. The vineyard and winery became part of their DNA, drawing them back when they pursued other paths.

Despite starting his own business and living in Portland, Nik kept his love for the vineyard front and center. He lobbied for years for us to build an extra house on winery property so he and his family could spend time at the vineyard. His oldest son, Alexander, started at age fourteen working at least two weeks every summer in the vineyard, staying with his Uncle Alex, for whom he was named.

Young Alexander worked as his father had, doing whatever was needed and came away with increased respect for our vineyard workers and a feel for the land. In 2016, Nik brought his second son, Jacob, with Alexander. They all stayed in the newly erected "third-generation house" that had finally come to pass.

Alex's sons, Nikolas and Avery, liked to hang around the winery

Nik, myself, and Bill, all Stanford University graduates, spoke at a Sokol Blosser Winery dinner at the Stanford Faculty Club in 2016. The Club had been built while Bill and I were still undergrads and here we were, fifty years later, coming back to celebrate.

Three third-generation boys worked in the vineyard in 2016. From left to right: Alex's son, Niko-las (named for his Uncle Nik), Nik's sons Jacob and Alexander (named for his Uncle Alex), the oldest of the third generation. Alex is in the background.

with their father and started working during the summer when they turned fourteen. Harvest saw them at the winery as much as possible, washing totes, sampling grapes, and joining in the crew's table tennis competition.

Alison's oldest child, Dario, wanted to participate and one day during harvest she found him crushing grapes in a bowl. "I'm making wine," he told her. The legacy was being passed on; he was eight years old.

Thinking about future generations, Alison arranged for a family video so Bill and I could talk about how we started, and Nik, Alex, and Alison could talk about growing up with the winery. The video filming ended with a dinner with all three generations, and the youngest were given the chance to talk about what they liked best about the vineyard and winery. I was struck by how much their comments related to being with their cousins and enjoying the good food that always seems to accompany family get-togethers.

The four youngest of the third generation, each wearing their new Sokol Blosser logo jackets. Nik's ten-year-old daughter, Anna, is in the middle. Alison's children are the youngest, three-year-old Luca on the left and Dario, eight, holding eight-month-old Isabella.

All three generations, from founders down, spouses included, came to the first full Family Retreat, one day of winery-related events. (Photo credits this page: Carolyn Wells Kramer.)

We held our first three-generation family dinner at the winery in 2015, with spouses and all of the third generation, ages two to fifteen, attending. (Photo credit: Carolyn Wells Kramer.)

Since each generation gets farther away from the founders' passion and commitment, our dedication will live on in the video when the original generation is long gone, inspiring our heirs with a legacy of pride and stewardship of the business. Nik, Alex, and Alison are well aware that family business survival declines sharply with each generation. The American Family Business Institute estimates that 30 percent of family businesses survive into the second generation, 12 percent to the third, and only 3 percent to the fourth. Time will tell where the Sokol Blosser family will land. It would be grand to be in the 3 percent.

....

Farro, Roasted Fennel, Feta &
Treviso Radicchio Salad

Our winery chef, Henry Kibit, wanted to create something unusual to go with one of our casual red wines. The obvious choice for the wine would have been a juicy hamburger or something similarly rich and meaty, but he decided to try something vegetarian instead—just to prove it could be done. He made this dish for his final job interview and it was a big hit. The vinaigrette makes more than you need—save the rest for salads or vegetables. The dish was made to pair with our mellow, easy drinking Evolution Big Time Red.

Makes 6 servings

1 cup pearled farro

Coarse sea salt

1 bay leaf

1 fennel bulb

2 tablespoons fresh lemon juice

2 tablespoons extra-virgin olive oil

For the vinaigrette

1 tablespoon minced shallot

1½ teaspoons Dijon mustard

¼ cup red wine vinegar

½ cup grapeseed oil

¼ cup extra-virgin olive oil

½ head radicchio, preferably Treviso

3 tablespoons chopped fresh flat-leaf parsley

Freshly ground pepper

8 ounces feta cheese, crumbled

Preheat the oven to 400°F.

Put the farro in a saucepan and cover with 4 inches of cold water. Add a generous pinch of salt and the bay leaf and bring to a boil over high heat. Reduce heat to medium-low and simmer, uncovered, until the farro is tender, 20 to 40 minutes, depending on the type of farro.

While the farro is cooking, trim the fennel and then cut lengthwise into eighths. Put the fennel in a bowl, then add the lemon juice, olive oil, and a sprinkle of salt. Toss well. Transfer the fennel to a baking sheet, arranging the pieces in an even layer, and taking care that a cut side of each fennel piece is facing down. Roast until the fennel is tender and well caramelized on the side touching the pan, about 20 minutes. Remove the fennel from the oven and let cool to room temperature.

Drain the farro through a strainer, transfer to a large bowl, and remove the bay leaf. Allow the farro to cool to room temperature.

To make the vinaigrette, in a bowl, combine the shallot, mustard, and vinegar and whisk until blended. While whisking, slowly drizzle in the grapeseed and olive oils until well blended and slightly thickened. Add 2 tablespoons of the vinaigrette to the bowl with the cooled farro and toss well. Set the remaining vinaigrette aside.

Cut or tear the radicchio into 1-inch pieces, discarding any tough core pieces. Add the radicchio pieces to a small bowl of ice water and let stand for about 10 minutes (this helps crisp it and remove any overt bitterness). Drain the radicchio, dry well, and add it to the bowl with the farro.

Add the roasted fennel, parsley, and a little more vinaigrette to the bowl with the farro mixture and toss well. Season to taste, adding more salt, pepper, or vinaigrette if desired.

Divide the salad among serving plates. Sprinkle the feta cheese over the top and serve right away.

....

Blueberry Clafoutis

A favorite with my grandchildren, this is my variation on the traditional French custard-and-fruit dessert, using less sugar than the original and an alternative milk and flour. Using coconut or almond milk and oat or almond flour lend modern flavors and textures to the classic dish. I love to make this in the summer, using blueberries from our own bushes and eggs from our own hens. I change the fruit to honor the season and have used this basic recipe to make clafoutis from strawberries, blackberries, figs, rhubarb, apples, and pears. I vary the amount of sugar depending on the sweetness of the fruit, and I vary the liqueur accordingly—for example, orange liqueur is wonderful with rhubarb, and apple brandy is a natural with apples. The beautiful appearance and deep flavor of the clafoutis belie how easy it is to make. Ice cream or whipped cream makes it even more festive.

Makes 8 generous servings

    3 tablespoons unsalted butter,
        plus butter for greasing
    4 cups fresh, ripe blueberries
    1 cup unsweetened full-fat coconut milk
        or almond milk
    1 cup oat flour, or half oat flour and half almond meal
    ½ cup granulated sugar, or to taste
    Small pinch of coarse sea salt
    4 large eggs
    2 tablespoons kirsch

Preheat the oven to 350°F.

Butter a 9-inch glass pie dish and spread out the blueberries evenly in it. Set aside.

Measure the coconut milk into a 4-cup glass measuring cup. Add the 3 tablespoons butter and cook in the microwave on high heat in 30-second bursts, until melted. Set aside to cool slightly.

Put the flour, sugar, and salt in a bowl. Use a fork to stir the ingredients and smooth out any flour lumps.

Add the eggs to the coconut milk mixture and whisk until well blended. Add the kirsch and stir well.

Add the dry ingredients to the coconut milk-egg-kirsch mixture and whisk until well blended. Slowly pour the mixture into the pie plate over the blueberries, giving the mixture time to settle into the crevices between the berries. Carefully put the pie dish in the oven; the dish will be very full. Bake until the middle is set and the surface is a little puffy, about 40 minutes.

Transfer the dish to a cooling rack and let cool to room temperature; it will lose its puffy appearance as it cools. Cut into wedges to serve.

CHAPTER TEN

Oregon Pinot Noir
Comes of Age

In August 2013, Alison and I were asked to be keynote speakers and share our experiences as women in the wine industry when the national organization of Women for WineSense held its biannual gathering in Newberg, Oregon. We arrived from different directions and met in the parking lot. Almost seven months pregnant with her second child, I could see the fatigue around Alison's eyes as she eased herself out of her car. I had an urge to wipe the tired lines away, like I did tears when she was little. But I could only smile, try to cheer her up, and hope that she would rise to the occasion when we got inside.

I had been a member of Women for WineSense since it began in Napa in 1990. I wanted to convey to the current membership the important role Women for WineSense had played in the 1990s, a critical time as the American wine industry expanded. In my talk, I recounted its founding when anti-alcohol forces were gaining momentum and had lumped wine into the catch-all category of "drugs and alcohol."

I had seen prohibition forces at work in elementary school when Alison participated in the DARE (Drug Abuse Resistance Education) program, a scare approach aimed at fourth grade students. She came home horrified that Bill and I imbibed alcohol. We had to convince her that her parents weren't villains because they made wine. We had encouraged our kids to take a sip of our wine at dinner and try to describe what they tasted, but after taking the class, Alison refused to let her lips even touch the glass, afraid she would become addicted. I had grown up with wine as part of a family meal; I wanted our children to look at it similarly.

Women for WineSense became the antidote to the prohibition forces, affirming wine in moderation as part of a healthy, balanced lifestyle; that most wineries were family farms; that wine accompanied a good meal. That was our view at Sokol Blosser too. We were thrilled when, in the early 1990s, wine and health were married in the "French paradox." Scientific proof that red wine bolstered heart health probably did more than anything to disentangle wine from the "drugs and alcohol" category and give it the special place it now holds. Many healthy diet recommendations, such as the University of Michigan Integrative Health's Healing Foods Pyramid, now include wine in moderation. Dr. Curtis Ellison, a former Chief of the Department of Preventive Medicine and Epidemiology at the Boston University School of Medicine and one of the researchers for the French paradox study, helped give wine its unique niche when he proclaimed: "A glass of wine each day could be more effective at preventing heart attacks than lowering your cholesterol."

Susan Sokol Blosser is the rare person with the will to use her very good mind, big heart, and unflagging energy for the common good. Her long involvement with Women for WineSense (WWS) is one example. Two years after WWS was founded in 1990 by a group of riled-up women in

Napa and Sonoma bent on saving wine from a groundswell of anti-alcohol sentiment, Susan was launching the first WWS chapter outside California. That Oregon chapter was the first step toward what quickly grew into a national organization.

A few years later, as she was preparing to hand over the successful Sokol Blosser winery to the next generation—not an easy task for an engaged founder—Susan was recognized by WWS with a Lifetime Achievement award for her leadership in developing the wine industry in Oregon. That 2008 award would not be her last. In 2015, the national board of directors selected Susan Sokol Blosser to be the first non-Californian inducted into the Women for WineSense Hall of Fame, joining Margrit Biever Mondavi, Ramona Nicholson, me, and WWS cofounder Julie Johnson.

Women for WineSense, in its vibrant twenty-sixth year in 2016 and grateful for Susan's contributions, may have to come up with more ways to honor her ongoing achievements. She hasn't stopped.

Michaela Rodeno
CEO of St. Supéry, Napa, 1988–2009
Cofounder, Women for WineSense
Cofounder, Villa Ragazzi, Napa
Author

After I spoke, I stepped back to let Alison talk about growing up in the wine business. Our remarks showed the different perspectives of our two generations. This was the first time I had seen her talk before a group since she introduced me in Toronto in 2007, six years earlier. She stepped up to the microphone, her pregnant belly prominent through her fitted outfit, her demeanor composed and confident. None of her fatigue or preoccupation with issues back at the office showed. An inveterate teacher, my comments had been a historic look at the wine industry, serious and educational. Alison's became a cheerful counterpoint.

I looked at her in wonder as I found myself laughing along with the rest of the women. Alison had the audience's enthusiastic attention as she described growing up in a family so business-oriented that their idea of vacation was working a wine festival, never playing at Disneyland. She talked about what made her want to come back to the family business. "When I went to college," she said, "I became determined to work in the real world. I wanted a job where I could make real money." She stopped here and looked around. With a dramatic pause, she added her confession, "Well, folks, I learned the real world is not all it's cracked up to be. It didn't take long for me to realize that working for my family in our family business was a dream job." Was this poised, funny person the same unsure young woman who overcame timidity to stand in for me at a winery dinner when I broke my ankle?

She explained how we spent three years transitioning from me, a single president, to her and her brother as copresidents. "The copresidency is a unique model and one everyone told us was fraught with challenges," she said. "However, as you may have figured out by now, my family never takes the easy route." Someone asked what it was like working with her brother. "It's honestly great fun," she said. "Yes, there are times I want to strangle him. And," she added, continuing her sisterly frankness, "we're very different people. But we have a deep love and loyalty not just to each other but also to our shared vision and common goal to be amazing stewards of our business so that we can hand it off to the next generation in even better shape and with even more opportunities than we received it." I tried not to puff up like the proverbial Jewish mother, but I had an urge to gesture and exclaim, "My daughter the president!"

Alison left the gathering right after dinner. I walked her to her car, wishing again I could smooth away the worry lines on her face.

"I couldn't believe how funny you were tonight," I told her.

"Especially since I know how worn out you are." Alison stopped and looked at me.

"Mom," she said. "I'm a serious person. That was the professional me talking. I was performing." Then she grinned. "I learned it from you," she finished.

"I love you, babe," I said, as I gave her a hug. "I love you too, Mom," she said, and she opened the door to get in her car.

As president of Bouchaine Vineyards in Napa during the 1990s, I was constantly in the marketplace meeting and greeting the many people, distributors, retailers, restaurateurs, cooks, and kids (or so the fresh-faced twentysomethings seemed to me) who sold my wines. Wine events were a special draw. I cannot explain why this industry has evolved this way. Perhaps it is the convivial nature of the product we make.

So it is within that context that I found myself in Telluride, Colorado, in 1993 at the Telluride Wine Festival. These gatherings are common in our business and, quite frankly, a lot of fun. This is an excellent way to network and see old friends.

I ended up not in a hotel, but in a mountainside chalet with a winegrower from Oregon, Susan Sokol Blosser, and her young daughter, Alison. This was a lovely opportunity to make a new friend. First night into it, Susan and I eschewed the parties and ended up in a spirited game of Hearts with Alison. As she sloughed off the Queen to one of us, thirteen-year-old Alison revealed that she wanted to be an architect and spent much of her free time designing homes. Her "blueprints" (drawn by hand with pencil and ruler; I have some in my files to this day) were extremely detailed, yet her design demonstrated her broad sense of the world we live in. Susan and I became close friends, so I've had the pleasure of following Alison's path since that initial meeting.

After I moved to Oregon myself and became involved with the local wine industry, I started working with Alison, not just as a leader at Sokol

Blosser Winery, but in our community at large. She had learned a great deal shadowing her mother all those years: strength, determination, vision, compassion, clarity. But I watched Alison evolve into her own grown-up self: mother, wife, business leader, good friend, sister, daughter.

Eugenia Keegan
Oregon General Manager, Jackson Family Wines

THE OREGON PINOT NOIR wine industry has been considered officially launched when David and Diana Lett planted the first Pinot Noir vines in the Willamette Valley of Oregon in 1965. Slow to start, there wasn't much to celebrate in 1990, the twenty-fifth anniversary of that event. Oregon Pinot Noir was virtually unknown outside of Oregon. Of the seventy bonded wineries at that time, only a handful sold beyond the state's borders. The occasion went by without notice.

It took determined effort by a small group of wineries and another twenty-five years for Oregon Pinot Noir to become a demand item at the best restaurants across the country. But when success came, it was stunning. The *Wine Spectator*, the nation's largest and most read wine publication, acknowledged Oregon as the equal of French Burgundy in 2012—a wonderful validation and a great boost for wine sales. A few years later the publication revealed that in 2015, while Oregon accounted for 1 percent of US wine sold nationwide, the state produced a whopping 20 percent of the 5,436 American wines the publication had awarded ninety points or higher. Little Oregon, the Cinderella sister to California's giant wine industry, with only 1 percent market share of the US wine produced, represented 20 percent of the country's highest rated wines.

The Willamette Valley Wineries Association decided that surviving for fifty years was worthy of celebration. The event planners wanted to celebrate the success of Oregon wine, to recognize those who had been critical to that success, and to reconnect many who had not

When the Willamette Valley was named Wine Region of the Year, 2016, by one of the wine media giants, Alison and Eugenia Keegan both represented Oregon at The Wine Enthusiast's Wine Star Awards Gala in Miami, Florida. January 2017.

seen each other in years. That's how three hundred folks active in the Oregon wine industry since the early days came to fill a large ballroom in Portland on a cold, showery February evening in 2015.

An invitation-only event, invites went out to those who had been important to the early Oregon wine industry—bankers who took a chance and loaned to wineries at a time it was considered excessively risky; accountants who had advised us business-ignorant winegrowers; politicians who supported the industry with favorable legislation;

The Willamette Valley Wineries Association celebrated the fiftieth anniversary of the first Pinot Noir planting in the Willamette Valley with a giant party. It was a reunion of sorts, reuniting many who hadn't seen each other for years. For us it was a chance to see old friends. Here we are surrounding one of our favorites, Dave Adelsheim, who founded Adelsheim Vineyard shortly after we started. From left to right: me, Dorinda Parker (Bill's wife), Bill, Dave Adelsheim, Alison, and Nik. 2015. (Photo credit: Carolyn Wells Kramer, courtesy of the Willamette Valley Wineries Association.)

distributors who took on our early wines and helped build the industry; restaurateurs who supported the budding industry by prominently featuring Oregon wines on their wine lists; and winery and vineyard owners from all fifty years, many no longer in the industry. Not all of us who started were still active in the industry. Dick Erath, Bill Fuller, and Myron Redford had sold and moved on. Chuck Coury and David Lett had died.

As I greeted and hugged my compatriots, many of whom I hadn't seen in years, it struck me how old we'd become. I remembered us as fresh-faced and smooth skinned, straight-backed and athletic. We had become elders, with brows permanently creased, the lines around our eyes deeply etched, and our joints stiff. It had been over forty years for some of us, working together to build an industry, while competing to sell our wine.

We were the ones who knew what Oregon was like before wine

came on the scene; who knew how hard it was to learn to grow wine grapes in the Willamette Valley—to learn to farm at all. We remembered how many years our wine was scoffed at before it was taken seriously. We knew the struggles of building a market for Oregon wine.

We also knew the thrill of being first, of doing something people told us was impossible, of watching the face of a wine buyer taste our wine for the first time and witnessing the reaction of pleasure and surprise at its quality. Those of us still involved felt the bond, stunned to realize that Oregon could boast over seven hundred wineries, with five hundred just in the Willamette Valley. Look what we had started. The old days may be gone, but the memories live within us.

When I was twenty-six and Susan and I had just bought our first eighteen acres of land, it was not even a fleeting thought in our minds that fifty years hence we might be celebrating a half-century of wine industry success in Oregon. Or that many of the original group that took the crazy risk to plant grapes would now be proudly watching their kids carry on the business: the Campbells, the Letts, the Ponzis, the Casteels, the Vuylstekes. Or that we would have reached that inevitable time when we would begin remembering those who had passed on: Dave Lett, Chuck Coury, Richard Sommer, Sylvia Henry, Vic Kreimeyer, Bill Welch, Cal Knudsen. But, it happened. There we were, some three hundred of us, warmly slapping one another on the back, tasting the marvelous wines we had created, and reminiscing about days past. Even former Governor Neil Goldschmidt was there—it was largely his enthusiasm for what we were doing that extended our vision from merely Oregon to the world. I was heartened by how good the old-timers looked and that the gleam of optimism and good cheer was still in their eyes.

Bill Blosser
Cofounder, Sokol Blosser Winery

ONE SPRING, I TOOK a seat at the back of a huge ballroom and watched the wine industry women stream in to the opening session of the 2016 Women of the Vine Global Symposium. Alison, holding her third child, two-month-old daughter, Isabella, sat next to me. Together, we surveyed the scene before us: fashionistas in spiky high heels; women in skirts of all lengths, leggings, or drapey dresses; jazzy scarves and wraps. This was a celebration of individual taste.

Twenty years ago, wanting to fit into the male business world, my cohorts and I tried to match the standard male dress code with a blazer or suit, usually black. At the Women of the Vine Symposium, there wasn't a pantsuit in sight. Firmly ensconced and confident of their place in the business world, these women felt free to express themselves in appearance and, as the conference unfolded, in their opinions.

This was the conference's second year, held at a resort in Napa, California. I had attended the first year, amazed at an assemblage of women from the upper echelons of the wine industry. It was jaw-dropping for us few old-timers who knew the extent to which the wine industry had always been a man's world. I said a silent "Wow" and tried not to look as surprised as I felt. We joked with each other. "We could have done this twenty years ago," one said. "Except there would have been only five of us."

The handful of men in the audience was barely noticeable in the buzz of 650 women finding their seats while chatting, juggling coffee, notebooks, and cell phones. These high-powered women, decision makers across the United States in different arenas of the wine industry, had descended on Napa to meet other women in the industry, make business connections, and share their experiences. The ballroom vibrated with their energy. Deborah Brenner, the diminutive dynamo who founded the Women of the Vine organization and organized the gathering, had the vision of bringing women in the wine industry together. In an almost unimaginable feat, she had convinced a number of the large competing wholesalers in the country to jointly underwrite the event, a tribute both to her talent and to the rise of women in key roles.

I was especially eager to hear the keynote speech by Maggie Henríquez, CEO of the House of Krug, probably the most prominent and powerful position of any woman in the industry. She came to the stage in a simple dress, her long straight hair parted in the middle, definitely not my image of someone who ran an international business which included Moët Hennessy, Veuve Cliquot, Moët & Chandon, and Ruinart, as well as Krug champagnes. She spoke to us without notes for forty-five minutes and it was clear her message came from the heart. Trained as a systems engineer who navigated her way through the male business world, what guided her through her thirty-seven-year career, she told us, were three core values: respect, gratitude, and generosity. She gave us examples of her experience where serendipity had arisen at the alignment of those three. There was a hush when she finished— then an explosion of applause and a long standing ovation. I'm sure her wines got a lot of new fans that day.

My role at the conference was to moderate a panel on family business, for which I enlisted four women to illustrate different aspects of this special business niche. My success in turning my presidency over to Alex and Alison had given me unexpected status as an elder stateswoman.

———

ON THE MORNING OF April 18, 2016, the news of a major Oregon winery sale broke in a special e-mail blast from *Wine Business Daily*. The Oregon wine industry folks who, like me, scan the headlines while nodding over morning coffee, were undoubtedly jolted awake by the surprising news. Jackson Family Wines, the huge California winery conglomerate with international properties, had just bought a small but very prestigious Willamette Valley winery, Penner-Ash Wine Cellars. This was not the first sale of an Oregon winery to an out-of-state buyer, but this one elicited an unusual amount of emotion.

I didn't start taking Alison with me to winery events until she was a teenager, but Alison's daughter, Isabella came to her first wine event at two months. Here we are in Napa, at the largest gathering of wine industry women I'd ever seen, the Women of the Vine Symposium. 2016.

Lynn Penner-Ash had made history in 1988 when she came up from California to be the winemaker at Rex Hill. One of the few trained professional women winemakers at the time, she was also the first female winemaker hired in the Willamette Valley. She not only raised the quality of Rex Hill's wine, she inspired other women to follow her lead. When she left Rex Hill to start her own winery a decade later, Penner-Ash Wine Cellars became one of Oregon's favorite wineries, and Lynn one of Oregon's superstars. News that she had sold stunned the industry.

Reactions to the sale varied. On one hand, people said how exciting it was for Lynn and her husband, Ron, to have built a business valuable enough to attract a high bidder; Oregon wine's credibility rose with a well-known California operation buying in, and Lynn and Ron could retire in style. On the other hand, it was another signal that the local wine industry, which had been a tight-knit, collaborative group, was breaking up. When local wineries reported to out-of-state headquarters, there was not the same loyalty and commitment to the local community. After Dick Erath sold his winery to Washington State's Chateau St. Michelle, the winery's sales might have increased nationally, but the winery almost disappeared from the local wine community. Whatever it meant, the sale of Penner-Ash represented the evolution of Oregon wine. Industry dynamics would certainly change as more large, out-of-state players became involved.

I wanted Alex's opinion, since he was more connected to the current wine community than I. "Did you see this coming? Did you know it was for sale?" I asked. "No, Mom, but with a few exceptions, everyone's for sale. When a generous offer appears and there's no other exit plan, it's hard to say no," he replied. "The only ones not for sale are family wineries that are committed to the next generation, like us. Without kids who are willing or able to run the business, one exit for the founder is to sell." I guess he was right, as I heard that after the Penner-Ash sale was announced, Jackson Family Wines was flooded with calls from other Oregon wineries wanting to be considered for a place in the Jackson Family portfolio.

I'm often asked my opinion on the future of the Oregon wine industry. It's a hard question to answer. My own life has been a series of unexpected twists and turns. Who could have predicted that after a conventional childhood in the Midwest, I would have moved to the West Coast and pioneered a new industry there? That I would have three children, leave my marriage after thirty-two years, run for office, write three books, or start a nonprofit? With that in mind, how could I possibly predict the future?

I've watched the landscape around me evolve from wheat fields, prune orchards, and turkey farms to vineyards; and the towns of Yamhill County wake up to a new life as wine country destinations.

I have no insight into what lies ahead. The only certainty is change and the wisest path is to greet it, open to its possibilities.

Of course I have concerns. Our climate, so ideal for Pinot Noir, could transform irreparably with warmer and more violent weather. Harvests of Pinot Noir in the twenty-first century routinely begin more than a month earlier than did harvests in the 1970s and '80s. The collaborative culture of the Oregon industry could erode as more aggressive players buy up land and dominate the industry. I fear the loss of farmland as wineries build restaurants and event venues instead of planting grapes. We try to plan for the future, knowing that unforeseen twists and turns are inevitable.

....

Russ's Grilled Wild Salmon

Grilled wild salmon is one of my favorite meals. It's simple and elegant and needs no special sauce, which would only mask its superb flavor. These are Russ's notes and his recipe. He is the salmon chef. Salmon is the iconic fish of the Pacific Northwest, a symbol of our wild, roaring, free-flowing rivers, and one of the original sources of sustenance for the Northwest's Native peoples and many of its animals. They are an anadromous fish, which means that they are born in small streams, swim down the rivers out to the ocean to spend their lives eating and growing, then return to their exact place of birth to spawn and die. Their young then restart the cycle.

Populations of wild salmon have dwindled, but as dams are removed and overfishing is controlled, there is hope they will rebound. Until then, my advice is to eat only wild salmon, not farmed salmon, which can use questionable environmental practices, but do so sparingly and mindfully, and always with an appreciation of how special this fish is. If you are a salmon lover like we are, you'll want to have on hand an implement to pull out the fish's pin bones. You can use special fish tweezers that are sold for that purpose; many chefs use a surgical hemostat. Even clean, needle-nose pliers will do if you have nothing else.

Makes 4 servings

About 1½ pounds Chinook (King), sockeye (red), or
    coho (silver) salmon fillet, in one piece
Salt and freshly ground pepper
Finely grated lemon zest or granulated
    lemon peel
Chopped fresh dill or dried dill
Good quality extra-virgin olive oil

If the salmon fillet is from the front half of the fish, there will be small, needle-like pin bones, which should be removed before cooking. Lay the fillet flat on a plate or cutting board. Run your fingers lightly along the length of the fillet, feeling for the tips of the bones. When you find one, use tweezers or pliers to grasp the tip of the bone and pull it out at an angle. Look at the fillet and you'll notice the rest of the tiny bone tips protruding from the flesh in a straight line from the first bone down the length of the fillet. Continue to probe with your fingers down that line, feeling for the bones and then using the tweezers to pull out each bone, one at a time.

In order to cook evenly, you want the salmon pieces to be approximately the same size and shape. Using a sharp, thin knife, cut the fillet into even pieces, which will be about 5 to 6 ounces each. For a large, thick fish, like Chinook, the pieces may be only about an inch wide. For smaller, thinner salmon, like sockeye or coho, the pieces may be 2 to 4 inches wide.

Pat dry each salmon piece with paper towels and arrange the pieces skin side down on a plate. Season the flesh side with salt, pepper, lemon zest, and dill to taste, then brush each piece with a thin coating of olive oil.

Preheat a gas grill so the grate is very hot (if you have a grill thermometer, it should be at least 500°F). You need a very hot grill to keep the salmon from sticking and to form a nice crust.

Lay each salmon piece on the hot grill grate flesh side down, then adjust the heat so the temperature is maintained at around 400°F. Grill, turning once about halfway through, until the fish is cooked to your liking. The cooking time will depend on the thickness of the pieces and how rare or well-done you want them. For rare salmon, cook thin pieces for 2 to 3 minutes per side and thick pieces for around 4 minutes per side. For fish that's more well done, add a minute or two per side, adjusting the timing to your preference. If the salmon pieces stick when you try to turn them, it's because the grate wasn't hot enough or they're not quite ready to be turned. Transfer the salmon pieces to a platter and serve right away with your favorite side dishes.

Here's a final little secret—if you cut into a salmon piece and it isn't quite done enough for you, 10 to 20 seconds in the microwave will fix it right up.

CHAPTER ELEVEN

Reflections

Twenty-seven years after my father, Gustave Sokol, died, I went to my first Sokol family reunion. I met relatives I never knew I had, reconnected with cousins I had met as a child, and discovered surprising information about my family. I learned that my father, whom I never heard speak anything but English, had grown up speaking Yiddish. He apparently never stopped, as I was told that he and his business partner regularly conversed in Yiddish. Since I never heard him speak a word of Yiddish at home, I was shocked to realize how little I really knew about this pivotal person in my life. This new knowledge made me think about the part of his life I did share.

The daddy I knew devoted his life to the leather business he had started in Milwaukee in 1955. I picture him in his well-cut suit, white shirt with fancy cuff links, Sulka tie, Allen Edmonds shoes, and fedora. He went to his office six days a week. Business consumed 98 percent of his time, energy, and thought.

But the remaining 2 percent included a passion for fine wine and food. His business took him to France once a year for La Semaine du Cuir, (Leather Week) where he came under the spell of French cuisine. *Between Meals,* A. J. Liebling's memoir of his gustatory adventures in France, became Daddy's food bible. Daddy found a wine merchant in Milwaukee to recommend wines for the wine cellar he created in our basement. In time it was filled with the best vintages from Bordeaux, Burgundy, and the Mosel. Because vodka, gin, and bourbon were customary in his social set before meals and at parties, my father made a statement serving his premier cru wines.

My older brothers and I were the beneficiaries of this enthusiasm. Daddy always had a glass of wine before dinner. Choosing the right one became a ritual, worthy of discussion. He would tell us why he chose what he did and something about the wine estate. We grew up drinking wines that are considered legendary today. As the youngest child living at home during the peak of his wine collecting, I benefited the most. I had no idea at the time that I was training my palate for a life where wine and food would be my livelihood.

Wine accompanied dinner, and eating well was a core family value. My mother kept sides of beef, lamb, and pork in the freezer, and even as processed foods came into vogue, we still ate fresh fruit and vegetables. Daddy would come home after his Thursday afternoon golf game every August with a big bag of fresh picked corn he'd bought from a farm stand. Mother had a giant kettle ready to go. Every ear would be consumed.

Our family went out to eat often. It was always a special occasion for which we dressed up. We would have been horrified to see someone in jeans come into the restaurant. Karl Ratzsch's, the height of fine dining in downtown Milwaukee in the 1950s, holds the place of honor in my childhood memories. I remember the sense of anticipation as Daddy pulled up in front of the boldly Bavarian building with its colorful Germanic tile façade. Inside, waitresses in dirndls maneuvered around strolling musicians in lederhosen. Dark wood, red leather chairs, white tablecloths, and large beer steins and platters covered the walls, creating an Old World feel. The hearty food fit the ambience.

No self-respecting family restaurant in the 1950s would have dared start a meal without presenting a relish tray as soon as we were seated. A combination of fresh and pickled vegetables, a relish tray might include zigzag-cut carrots, celery sticks, whole radishes, sweet and dill pickles, green and black olives, green onions, pickled baby corn and sweet miniature peppers, all artfully arranged on a platter with compartments for each item. The relish tray whetted the appetite, easing us into the dining experience.

From there, we went to the first course, liver dumpling soup, a clear tasty broth with a large fuzzy-looking meatball. When those were cleared, plates mounded with Old World entrees appeared: lamb shank with potato pancakes and red cabbage, Wiener schnitzel topped with fried egg or, my mother's favorite, sauerbraten with spaetzle.

Gastronome Liebling would have approved of these robust epicurean dishes. Portions were not huge, but these were hearty meals. I smile to think how far eating trends have veered from this cuisine. Restaurants featuring epicurean vegetarian foods lay far in the future. But the meat course was just the beginning. We never skipped dessert and always ordered strawberry schaum torte.

The Cadillac of meringues, perfect schaum torte is stiff on top and chewy inside. Topped with a scoop of vanilla ice cream, crushed strawberries, and whipped cream, every bite was divine. The menu also offered a schaum torte with chocolate sauce but we always stuck with strawberry. One time the family went to Karl Ratzsch's for dessert after attending a wedding and my brothers and I oohed and ahed so much over the schaum torte that my father ordered another round for us.

———

My father and Karl Ratzsch's were on my mind in the spring of 2016 as I flew across the country, from my home at Sokol Blosser

Winery to my hometown of Milwaukee, Wisconsin, for one full day of eating events. Even though my children had taken over the business, they sometimes asked me, as the matriarch and founder, to represent our winery at special events. Eating and drinking facilitate business transactions in every industry but, in the wine trade, wine and food is the business. Pairing them well is the holy grail; showing how great Sokol Blosser wines paired with food would be was this trip's mission.

I was looking forward to coming back to the scene of my childhood and seeing the changes in the ten years since my last visit. Viewing the city from the spiderweb of new freeways, the majestic old stone buildings I remembered were barely visible among the metal and glass skyscrapers dominating the skyline. The sturdy brown War Memorial Art Museum, so avant-garde when built in the 1950s on a point overlooking Lake Michigan, now seemed matronly next to the soaring white architectural wonder that was the new addition. But the changes couldn't hold back the memories. I wondered if the schaum torte at Karl Ratzsch's was as wonderful as I remembered it; I didn't have time to find out.

The first meal on my agenda was to host a lunch for twenty wine buyers from local restaurants. If they could see how well Sokol Blosser wines paired with food, they would order the wines for their restaurants. The menu at Harbor House restaurant was carefully crafted to match the wines with the current culinary trends toward lighter foods, with creative combinations, an emphasis on fresh fruit and vegetables, and colorful presentation.

After starting with freshly shucked oysters on the half shell and Evolution Sparkling while the guests gathered, we all sat down. The three-course meal began with citrus fennel salad paired with Pinot Gris; succotash with sautéed Gulf shrimp, grilled corn, and butterbeans, with a roasted tomato vinaigrette paired with Rosé of Pinot Noir. Roasted halibut with fingerling potatoes, asparagus, wild mushroom, and black garlic vinaigrette showed off how well Pinot

Noir paired with fish, even a delicate one like halibut. A light dessert of fig preserves, cheese, walnuts, and baguette finished the meal. Judging from the cleaned plates and number of wine orders, the luncheon was a success on all fronts.

Dinner that night, the second meal I had flown in for, was for the public, not the wine trade. The Milwaukee Art Museum periodically offered special winery dinners for its members, held in its spectacular new addition, designed by Santiago Calatrava. When Sokol Blosser was invited to do such a dinner, we jumped at the chance. Neither Alex nor Alison could attend. Though I was filling in for my kids, it seemed fitting for me to travel back to my hometown to be the host.

Chef Jason Gorman had chosen to celebrate spring with a morel mushroom theme. He had flown these prized mushrooms in from Oregon and featured them in every course, along with a different Sokol Blosser wine. Seventy museum members and their guests filled the airy space of the Café Calatrava, named in honor of the Spanish architect. My brother, Henry, and his wife, Susan, who still lived in Milwaukee, came to join me.

The printed menus on the table listed the courses to come and the wines paired with them. The first course, a smoked sea scallop with morels, brown butter vinaigrette, rhubarb, and frisée, caused a stir. Smoked scallops were unusual, and who would think of serving rhubarb with them? When they appeared, paired with a Rosé of Pinot Noir, guests tasted it and broke out with exclamations of amazement at the combination of flavors. It went on from there through four more courses, with the guests rhapsodizing over the food and wine. What a treat to dine like this. When the chef came out to take a bow with me, we both got a standing ovation. It was the second meal that day that made me glad to be in the wine business.

The guests, relaxed and happy, thanked us for an extraordinary evening of food and wine. I beamed. Not only had our successful event added to the quality of life of our guests, but Sokol Blosser and Oregon

The Sokol Blosser/Morel Mushroom dinner at the Café Calatrava in Milwaukee was my second event with Chef Jason Gorman. Almost ten years earlier, when he was chef at Dream Dance in Milwaukee, he and I had collaborated on a dinner at which I read from my just released memoir of the early days of Oregon wine, At Home in the Vineyard. *At our joint dinner in 2016, we were two seasoned pros, reunited for a triumphant return. His food had evolved from excellent to fabulous and I like to think our wine did the same.*

Pinot Noir had prestige that we could not have imagined when we planted our first vines. Tonight's success captured the heart, the vision, the social purpose of wine—to contribute to the enjoyment of life in the accompaniment of fine food. I said a silent prayer of gratitude that Bill Blosser and I had decided so long ago to start our great adventure.

....

Schaum Torte

Schaum tortes are another name for pavlovas or meringues, but seemingly they're only called Schaum tortes in my home state of Wisconsin. This recipe is adapted from Milwaukee's *The Settlement Cookbook*, first published in 1901 by local women to raise money to help the flood of European immigrants. Money from the sale of the cookbooks funded a new site for the Settlement House, Milwaukee's first nursery school, and numerous other projects. I have the thirty-first edition, given to me by my mother shortly after it was published in 1954. Egg whites can be tricky to work with, but there are a few tricks that will ensure success. First, have the eggs at room temperature, which will make them easier to beat. Take the eggs out of the refrigerator about 30 minutes before you plan to start the dish. Next, be careful when separating the egg whites from the yolks—even a little bit of yolk in the bowl can hinder the beating process. Finally, a little vinegar helps prevent overbeating. These delicious little tortes can be served with a variety of toppings.

Makes 6 servings

6 egg whites, at room temperature
2 cups granulated sugar
1 teaspoon vanilla extract
1 teaspoon cider vinegar or distilled white vinegar
Toppings of your choice (see Note)

Preheat the oven to 275°F. Line a large baking sheet with parchment paper.

To make the torte bases, put the egg whites in a clean bowl (any debris or grease in the bowl will hinder the beating process). Using a mixer with very clean beaters, beat on medium-high speed until the whites look opaque but moist, 2 to 3 minutes. Reduce the speed to low and gradually add the sugar, a few tablespoons at a time. Add the vanilla and vinegar with the last few batches of sugar. Increase the mixer speed to medium-high and beat until the egg whites are firm, glossy, and hold stiff peaks, 1 to 2 more minutes.

Using a large metal spoon, portion 6 even mounds of the egg white mixture onto the prepared baking sheet, spacing them 1 to 2 inches apart. Use the back of the spoon to create an indentation in the center of each mound to hold the toppings later.

Bake the torte bases until dry to the touch (they should have no sign of browning), about 45 minutes. Remove the torte bases from the oven and let cool on a metal rack until room temperature. These are best when served the same day they are baked.

When ready to serve, divide the torte bases among individual plates and layer with your favorite toppings. Serve right away.

Note: I grew up enjoying them served with vanilla ice cream and sliced strawberries. You could also use other berries or fruit in season, chocolate sauce, or coffee ice cream and whipped cream.

CHAPTER TWELVE

One Final Word

Sokol Blosser had such an improbable start. Bill and I were unlikely candidates for success: two liberal-arts graduates with no farm or business experience, planting a grape variety with a poor track record in the United States, and deciding to locate in a state with no wine industry. I am always asked what made us plant a vineyard, in Oregon, and at a time when a wine industry barely existed. It's the obvious question, the first one. But I don't think it's the most interesting one.

The intriguing question is: How did we survive? People start wild, weird things every day. They usually don't last. We started a wild, weird thing that did. How can I explain that? Was it fate? Maybe some of it was. Our decisions were backed up by research but clearly we were willing to take risks. Continual learning, especially from our mistakes, also contributed to our survival.

Life was different when we started in the 1970s. Not simpler, really, but different. Words and phrases now part of everyday vocabulary didn't exist then. When we started farming, we talked about the environment but not about biodiversity, the soil food web, or sustainability. We didn't think to call ourselves entrepreneurs. E-mail, the Internet, cell phones, and laptop computers were not part of our vernacular or our arsenal of business tools. Now we use computer software for accounting, sales and marketing, wine production, and communication in ways that we couldn't have imagined thirty years ago. In every part of our operation, we embraced change and continued to learn.

I sometimes view my years of running Sokol Blosser as making a series of choices that, once made, simply created new messes to deal with. Conditions changed, new information surfaced. Whatever I did, whatever I decided, I always knew there would be mopping up somewhere. We always had to be willing and able to move quickly, to shift gears, grab new opportunities, and redo things that weren't working. Nik, Alex, and Alison found they've had to navigate the same way.

Public perception is that the winegrower leads the good life at a leisurely pace. In truth, wine is a fast moving, competitive business, made even more so by the flood of new wineries, both domestic and foreign. Enter any wine store, and you are confronted with hundreds of different wines from which to choose. Restaurant wine lists contain so many wines that they can be read like books and measured in inches. Most people buy only one bottle at a time, so much of the wine just sits, waiting for customers.

Meanwhile, behind the scenes, wineries are vying to get their bottles onto the shelves and onto the lists. For every wine in a shop or on a restaurant list, there are dozens of others that don't make it. As the market for Oregon wine increases, so does the competition. Placing Sokol Blosser wine in the best wine shops and restaurants, and then keeping it there, will always require constant attention and effort.

Continual learning, adaptability, and willingness to compete have helped Sokol Blosser survive. But there is more to the story. I can reduce our survival and success to one word: grit. The challenge, the excitement, and the satisfaction have been in clearing the hurdles, maneuvering past the obstacles, and finding the best route.

———

As much as the effort of starting and running a business energized me, the vineyard has been much more than simply my livelihood. Being among the vines has fed my spirit through good times and bad. I find solace walking in the vineyard when I feel gloomy and joy when I am upbeat. Being among the vines transports me into a different world. I can feel myself start to unwind.

I know that, while to me the vineyard may seem peaceful and serene, it is actually full of diverse, fragile, multileveled, and action packed life. High above the vines a pair of red-tailed hawks ride the wind currents. Lower down swallows swoop and swirl, snatching insects from the air. A red-winged blackbird whistles its mournful cry from a nearby pond. In the vine canopy, bluebirds and finches flutter, poking for food. Beneath the vines the soil quivers with the bustle of small creature activity. Trails of pushed-up earth between telltale mounds reveal subterranean comings and goings as moles and gophers till the soil in their search for food. From high in the sky to deep underground, the vineyard hums with life, predators and prey.

I love the flow of seasons, like a multi-textured tapestry, woven in earth tones, that is our family vineyard. They could be a metaphor for my life. Spring in the vineyard, when the buds unfold into light green, rosy-tipped baby leaves, full of promise with their miniature clusters and tiny tendrils, always fills me with hope. The bright new growth appears cheerful, ready to meet whatever comes. The vines never know what the year will bring and, of course, neither do we. But spring radiates optimism.

The vineyard seems to get down to work during the summer as the green leafy canopy expands vigorously to cover the wire trellis, and its grape clusters start to grow to maturity. In summer, I breathe in a potpourri for the senses—the early morning dew, intense midday heat, birds chirping, multicolor fragrant flowers, the vines in bloom, shadows cast by the setting sun, starlit skies at night.

Harvest represents the successful culmination of all the hard work. The vines, having weathered the seasonal ups and downs and brought the plump purple clusters to final fruition, willingly yield their bounty. There is gratitude for having made it this far and relief at surrendering the fruit.

In the months after harvest, the vines slowly turn translucent and golden. They lose their leaves in the waning days of the year as they pare back and go dormant, echoing the aging process that I feel more keenly with each passing year.

During dormancy, the vines regroup beneath the reddish-brown earth. For months, they appear to just be brown, rough-sided sticks stuck vertically in the ground. Then, when they're ready, they begin again their leafy, colorful, and productive cycle. They're still the same vines but they reinvent themselves every year.

The vineyard inspires and mirrors us. Sokol Blosser Winery and the Sokol Blosser family have remained the same business and the same individuals over the years, but like the vineyard, each has had its own seasons of hope, development, ripening, and renewal. We are stronger for it. Indeed, we, like the vines, have found it's the only way to grow.

CPSIA information can be obtained
at www.ICGtesting.com
Printed in the USA
BVOW06*1449251017
498622BV00010B/238/P